SLANTED

How an Asian American Troublemaker
Took on the Supreme Court

Simon Tam

Troublemaker Press

NASHVILLE, TENNESSEE

2019 Troublemaker Press

Publisher's Note: *Slanted: How an Asian American Troublemaker Took on the Supreme Court* is a work of nonfiction. Nonetheless, some of the names and personal characteristics of individuals involved have been changed in order to protect the privacy of individuals. Any resulting resemblance to persons living or dead is entirely coincidental and unintentional.

Slanted: How an Asian American Troublemaker Took on the Supreme Court/ Simon Tam. -- 1st ed.

Author Photo: Sarah Giffrow, Upswept Creative
Cover Illustration: Ibrahim Moustafa - Art Director, Color Cubic
Cover Layout and Design: Michael John - Founder + Creative Director, Colorcubic
Library of Congress Cataloging-in-Publication Data has been applied for.
ISBN 978-1-7336291-1-9

You do what you think is right and let the law catch up.

—THURGOOD MARSHALL

TABLE OF CONTENTS

FOREWORD

If you are reading this, thank you for giving this book a chance! In this age of peak content and smart phones designed to hack our attention with never ending scrolling and pretty colors, I can imagine a book ostensibly about an Asian American band fighting a trademark dispute might find it hard to push through the noise.

But this book is about so much more than that. Part touring indie band road stories, part commentary on the contemporary Asian American experience and part legal drama, I assure you that you would be hard pressed to find a better written, more earnest and entertaining personal story of gut wrenching heartbreak and triumph than the one you're about to read.

I first met Simon Tam and his band The Slants (at the time made up of Ken Shima, Joe Jiang, and Yuya Matsuda) in January 2017 in Portland, Oregon. I was interviewing them as the focus of a field piece segment for *The Daily Show with Trevor Noah* regarding their infamous Supreme Court fight to trademark their band name.

I was excited to meet them, firstly because of how crazy their story was and secondly as a stand up comedian myself, I was sure that we would be kindred spirits as fellow live performers. And finally, yes, because they were also Asians in America.

I was right because we all hit it off right away. I interviewed them, we joked around, they showed me around their creative lives in Portland, and we all went for Dim Sum afterwards. It felt like hanging out with old friends at home, even though Dim Sum is a

Cantonese Chinese cuisine and two of the Slants are of Japanese heritage. Because sometimes to be Asian in America is to take the closest thing to cultural familiarity that we can find in a Portland suburb. Nothing unites Asians more than lack of food options.

We all got it. We understood what the struggle was like, and we knew the sacrifices we already made. The long hours practicing, and the even longer nights on the road. The drive and energy required to make sure the financial and logistical side of a creative career works, all while trying not to lose the joy of why you started doing it in the first place.

We also understood it from the additional shared perspective of trying to do all that as Asians in America and the family and community pressures that that entails. There was a lot of unspoken mutual respect and understanding in our initial meeting and all our subsequent interactions. We literally didn't even need to talk about it, or even explain what "it" was. We just knew.

This book is the exploration of what that unspoken "it" is. What is it like to try to make a living from your art? What is the Asian American experience? How do those two already heady challenges intersect and how should you face them? And what drives someone to fight a Supreme Court case with no money for the right to call yourself an obscure slur?

The story of The Slants is the perfect vehicle to discuss the realities of being an Asian artist in America. Instead of being able to let our art speak for itself we are often forced into a political battle for our own identities. We are often asked by society to pick a side - which community is our art supposed to speak to? Asians? Or everyone else?

Mirroring the infighting of the Slants' musicians over the years, the Asian American community is not a monolith. And the differences in our approach to these challenges can and has divided us. Are we being "too Asian"? Or "not Asian enough"? You're not going to please everyone, so you might as well do what you think is right.

That is exactly what Simon choose to do. His story is the story of perseverance. The stubbornness to do what you think is right, and to do what you love, despite everything seemingly going against you.

I say choice but as you read his story it becomes clear that it was no choice at all. He did what he did because that's who he is. This soft spoken, hard working, measured, fiercely intelligent man was a professional touring musician, while completing his MBA, being a social advocate and fighting a Supreme Court case. Whenever I check in with him he's always creating something. Writing musicals, giving talks, podcasts and writing books such as this one. Any one thing that Simon does would be considered a full time job. The fact that he managed to do all of it simultaneously is mind boggling.

To Simon, Ken, Joe, Yuya and the others, thank you for letting me be a small part of your amazing story. To the reader, I hope this book inspires you to follow your passions and be a good trouble-maker. Long live the music. Long live The Slants.

Ronnie Chieng

PROLOGUE

Oyez! Oyez! Oyez!

It's a blistering cold winter morning. Even inside this concrete mammoth, I can hear the wind howling outside.

I'm with my band, using a private side entrance to go through security for the Supreme Court of the United States. It's like TSA PreCheck at the airport: we get to keep our shoes and coats on while walking through the metal detectors, and everything else is placed on a dirty conveyor belt to be examined by security officers staring at CRT monitors. More importantly, we get to skip the line.

The queue outside is several thousand long. It's filled with people who have waited on the sidewalk all night, including professional line-standers who have been hired to hold a place like they would for a new iPhone release or U2 concert tickets, hoping to be one of 250 who will be able to sit inside the courtroom. That was almost me. For the weeks leading up to this day, I wasn't guaranteed a place inside the Supreme Court even though the case being argued, *Lee v. Tam*, literally has my name on it.

For the past eight years, I've been locked in a battle with the U.S. government over my band's name. That's right: nearly a decade of slugging it out with the authorities because we wanted to call ourselves the Slants, an identifier that represented self-empowerment while providing a bold portrayal of Asian American culture. That portrayal made bureaucrats uncomfortable; they sent over three dozen attorneys working for the Department of Justice and United States Patent and Trademark Office to silence me, fueled false rumors about my work, and put me through perpetual legal drudgery, in hopes that I would give up. But I didn't. I believe that the Slants is a name worth fighting for.

We make our way up the stairs and through another set of security gates until we finally walk into the Supreme Court. In my life, I've only experienced this level of surveillance measures while working with the government: playing inside a maximum-security prison and performing on active military bases.

White marble columns adorn all sides of the room. It's the same Greco-Roman style as the entrance and hallways leading up to this point, almost teasing the Gladiator-like combat to come. Behind the columns is a plush red velvet curtain, and a large gold clock hangs above the raised dais where the justices will sit. A gold rail cuts through the middle of the room, dividing reserved seats for members of the court (with padded chairs) and attendees who are simply observing (hard wooden pews).

Everything about the place screams tradition, a sense of the old. In a less cynical world, *EQUAL JUSTICE UNDER LAW,* the words inscribed on the front of the building, would mean something in this environment. They would be a proclamation of truth and the values being represented by the government. But it's January 2017, and we're in a new world now, one where Donald J. Trump will be sworn in as president in a few days. We're now living in a country where First Amendment rights, free speech and the freedom of the press, are in danger.

"It's smaller than I thought," I tell my bandmates, "At least the Federal Circuit had balcony seating."

The Court Marshal guides us to the second row of pews, leaving the first row completely empty. As people begin taking their seats around us, they start making the connections in their head: a group of four Asians who look fairly young sitting together. It must be the band! I can hear whispering and feel the fingers being pointed in our direction behind me. A group of law students nearby finally asks, "Are you in the Slants?"

The question brings a smile to my singer's face—he loves attention and being recognized—the spotlight is something that nearly all lead singers enjoy. As a member of the band, Ken is here in solidarity. But this really isn't his fight—he walked into the ongoing case two years ago, after I had already been carrying the torch for almost six years. If it weren't for my constant preaching about the right to claim our identity, I'm not sure how much the issue would even matter to him. That much is evident when the students begin asking him about our case, and he starts diverting to me.

I provide the same answers, anecdotes, and stories to them without much thought because they are the same questions that I have been answering for years. At this point, I'm like an ATM of rehearsed answers on the name of the band, Section 2(a) of the Lanham Act, the nuances of trademark registration, and perhaps more importantly, how our struggle was different from the Washington Redskins. I could answer those questions in my sleep. Most of these answers could be found online with a simple search, including my own Op-Ed pieces, but they want to hear it straight from the source. In the eyes of this introvert, it's a withdrawal of my energy and attention.

The people in attendance are genuinely interested in what happens today—certainly enough to wait all night through sub-freezing temperatures to be here. But they were here for entirely different reasons. They were here for a spectacle, to witness history in the making. I could hear the people behind me saying, "The Supreme Court justices are like mythological creatures. We hear about them all the time but it's so rare to actually see one in person."

Then, someone signals the Court Marshal. It's Colleen Connell, the wife of the attorney arguing on my behalf this morning. She's pointing at me as she asks, "This is Simon Tam, the litigant in this case. Shouldn't he be sitting closer? At least in this first bench?" He looks a little annoyed but politely explains that he'll ask. A few moments later, he comes back and says, "I'm sorry, but we're reserving these seats in case someone important shows up."

I chuckle. It is a spectacle indeed. I'm nervous even though I know that oral arguments are just a charade. People like to pretend that the sixty minutes spent before the justices of the court determine the outcome of a case that has been winding through the legal system for years. They don't. Arguments are an old tradition that provide a more exciting public show for what is really happening underneath: thousands of pages of legal briefs being summarized by court clerks, hoping to provide legal analysis of what is being argued. Most of the justices walk into the room already knowing which way they're leaning on a case. Oral arguments are just a way to tease out the extremes of the law, and sometimes, to mess with attorneys as a cat would batter a toy. Our government loves hanging on to old traditions, whether they are effective or not.

We are here because of the law I helped take down just a year earlier, the disparagement provision of a rather obscure bit of trademark law. The original clause was written in 1939 and became part of the Lanham Act passed by Congress in 1946, deep in the era of Jim Crow laws. It was never intended to protect racial and ethnic groups—segregation was still alive and well. The Trademark Office was giving out registrations to offensive marks for candy, sweets marketed with names like "Black Sambo," "Golliwog," and "Wampum Injun." And of course, the government approved over a dozen registrations for "Redskin." But in the last few decades, when communities of color and LGBTQ groups started filing applications for terms that were being reappropriated, the government used the disparagement clause of the Lanham Act to prevent some trademarks from being registered (like DykeDolls for lesbian dolls). The Lanham Act was used to deny representation for marginalized identities. They created a narrative that trademark registration was intended to protect the sensibilities of the public. They argued that this law was the line of defense, even though they were discreetly using it to silence attempts to shift the discourse on language.

I argued that this violated our First Amendment rights. Isn't choosing our own identity the very basis of all free expression? A federal court enthusiastically agreed with me and struck down this outdated law. But the Department of Justice filed suit and dragged me here, to the Supreme Court: the final boss stage of the legal system.

I lean back against the cold, hard bench, as I think back on the journey of the band that got me here. It isn't the typical story of sex, drugs, and rock n' roll. From our inception, the Slants have been about challenging stereotypes, including those for a touring band. The years were far more complex, fun, and weird than anything that would be discussed before the court today. From crashing anime conventions to facing white supremacists, standing up to childhood bullies as well as the government, that journey was fueled by my deep belief that apathy is not compatible with love. But I didn't begin there. I originally just wanted to create the representation I found lacking for Asian Americans, and in doing so, stumbled my way through challenges designed to keep people from disrupting the status quo. It's ironic: I would have never found myself here if it weren't for the government trying so hard to suppress that desire for representation. I found my identity through this struggle. Only a handful of cases have been brought by Asian Americans before the U.S. Supreme Court, yet each one shaped our nation in significant ways. Like it or not, my name would soon be added to the list.

I direct my gaze to my right and see my band, all dressed in our black suits: Joe, Ken, and Yuya. It's an entirely different lineup than when I first started this band. Back then, we were eager to share our brand of 80s synth-pop with the distinct swagger of late-70s punk rock. Getting started as the world's "first and only all-Asian American dance rock band" revealed aspirations larger than life. But frustrations over our legal troubles, drunken fisticuffs, and an aging lineup caused the band to slowly shed members until the Slants became something entirely new. No one ever tells you that part of the cost of fighting a Supreme Court case might include losing some of your closest friends. That isn't in any of the fine print. But I'm still here, wearing my suit and my lucky dinosaur socks, hoping that once this all ends, we can finally just be a band again . . . or whatever a band actually becomes after they've resolved a major legal case in the high court.

Only one act has ever been to the Supreme Court before: in 1994, 2 Live Crew received a unanimous ruling in their favor, which paved the way for hip hop artists to freely use parody in their music and ensured lyrics like "Big hairy woman all that hair it ain't legit; 'cause you look like Cousin it" would adorn the shelves of every law school library in the country. Maybe one day, textbooks will contain a refrain from our song dedicated to the Trademark Office, "From the Heart," which we had sung on the steps of the Supreme Court just a few days earlier.

I shake my head while I daydream of that idea. Probably no other band subjects its lineup to workshops around social justice, diversity, and inclusion like I have. That work brought us to soaring heights, like being asked by the Department of Defense to spend our holidays performing for troops serving overseas. Most recently, we were invited to join President Barack Obama's Act to Change Initiative to fight bullying in schools. These officials were all in D.C., but none of them showed up for us on our day in court. The government was keen on calling our band when they wanted to reach Asian Americans, proclaiming us champions of the community. The same government was just as quick to toss us aside, calling us racist against our own community, when they wanted to highlight the dangers of free speech.

Racist. Hero. Stubborn. Fighter. Chink.

I've been called many things on the way to this moment, but ironically, I've never been called "a slant." Really, I just prefer the term "troublemaker." It was the term given to me by our country's government, one that I proudly reappropriated into my own identity. I stare resolute at the lecterns before me, wishing that the justices could hear the deeper story behind this band, the one that couldn't be expressed in our legal briefs and the one that was relatively ignored by the media. Instead, all they wanted to talk about was football—the racist name of one team in particular. Even though I am arguing for freedom speech, I can't argue on my own behalf—I can't even sit anywhere near my attorneys.

I look at the row in front of me and think back at the Court Marshal's words, *we're reserving these seats in case someone important shows up*. The row is empty. Apparently, no one is more important today than me. But my scale is different: no one is more important and I'm no more important than anyone. *Equal Justice Under Law*. This case is much bigger than me or my band; the law that I've been fighting is one that has been suppressing the rights of marginalized communities for years.

It's also been touted by the government as proof that they indeed do care about racism. *Look! We're fighting hate speech by not allowing offensive trademarks to be registered! We're protecting you from yourselves!* By focusing on offensive words, they were hoping to distract us from harmful policies.

The clock strikes 10:00 a.m. precisely. The Court Marshal is now standing before us and invokes us to stand. He proclaims loudly,

"The Honorable, the Chief Justice and the Associate Justices of the Supreme Court of the United States. Oyez! Oyez! Oyez! All persons having business before the Honorable, the Supreme Court of the United States, are admonished to draw near and give their attention, for the Court is now sitting. God save the United States and this Honorable Court."

The shaman-like incantation swirls in my head as I hear the ceremonial mallet smack against hardwood, the sound reverberating through the courtroom like a snare drum. I look around the room, my eyes landing on many familiar faces. There are several law professors whose classes I've guest lectured in as well as legal counsel from the ACLU, Pro Football, the CATO Institute, and the U.S. Chamber of Commerce. I even see an attorney that I went on a date with once—I met "LovelyLawyer84" online—but she decided to pursue a more interesting prospect. Funny these things come back around. I look back at the Court Marshal.

Oyez! Oyez! Oyez!

Each time he says this, it sounds like oh-yay as in, "Oh, yay! We're finally starting!" The gavel hammers down a few more times and the room uniformly and unceremoniously begins to sit down. I look at the justices in front of me and try to get control of my wandering mind, but only one thing comes resurfacing each time: What the fuck is an oyez?

CHAPTER 1
SOME GREAT REWARD

POP!

"What was that?!" I yelled at Aron, the lead singer of my new band.

He was behind the wheel of the van I had just bought. It's fall 2007. We had the Murder City Devils' *Empty Bottles, Broken Hearts* cranked, and we could barely hear each other. It's one of my favorite albums to listen to while on the road, and with this being our first tour, it only seemed appropriate.

POP! POP!

"There it is again! Pull over!"

The sound increased in volume and frequency. It reminded me of the final stages of microwaving popcorn, except the kernels were aluminum and exploding underneath the hood. Our engine was bursting, the rattling gradually slowing as we pulled over and shut it off. Our excitement about getting to Los Angeles through this overnight drive was only slightly shaken, however, and I left a message for the guy who sold me this lemon, hoping to get answers. It was so new (at least for us), we could still smell the spray paint on the side of our trailer: a bright red rising sun with large letters proclaimed that this tour machine belonged to THE SLANTS.

The lights of a highway patrol car illuminated the interior of our van. I tensed up slightly. We were 164 miles outside of Portland, just out of the protective liberal bubble for a van filled with rock n' rollers of color. While most people think of cities like Portland and Salem when they think of Oregon, when the town names start to end in *lin* or *burg* or *ville*, the political hue goes from deep blue, straight past purple, to a fire engine red. It's one of the parts of the Pacific Northwest where Oregonians curiously speak with a Midwestern drawl.

I watched as the silhouetted highway patrolman walked up, the brim of his wide cowboy hat casting a large shadow over our back windows. We traded pleasantries and explained that the van was making loud noises, so we pulled over to investigate.

"Well, y'all can't stay here. You gotta' move on," he said in a friendly, but firm voice. He looked over the van and trailer, squinting his eyes at the design emblazoned on the side, then pointed his flashlight at each of us. "So what's the Slants?"

"We're a Vietnamese polka band," Aron said. The other musicians in the back struggled to hold back their laughter.

The officer gave us a look of consternation and ordered us to drive up to the next exit, where we could wait for the repair shop to open. Looked like we were going to sleep in the van tonight. It was freezing, and I packed for California weather, so I rummaged through the merch in our trailer and layered up in Slants' hoodies. I've always believed that a requirement of being able to tour is re-sourcefulness—might as well put that to use.

I let out a heavy sigh as I locked the trailer back up. I thought I was done with touring in old, busted vans. This was supposed to be a new start on my terms: chasing my music dreams with an all-Asian American band.

* * *

My first awareness of "race" came when I entered kinder-garten. Before that, I didn't really think about racial identity or what it meant. It didn't even cross my mind that my brother, John, was different, even though he had medium dark hair while I had jet black hair. But then it was San Diego in the 1980s. When John's biological dad would visit, I just thought he was a family friend. My parents didn't tell me that my mom had been married previously until I was a teenager because they thought the notion of a family half-siblings would confuse us. Ironically, the idea of being a mixed-race family never once crossed their mind as being weird: We were a family and that was that.

My parents immigrated to the United States from Asia: my father, from the Canton area in China; my mother from Taipei, Tai-wan. They met while they were both working at a restaurant in San Diego. They both worked really hard to provide for our family. And because they didn't want to see me or my siblings struggle as much they had, they stressed the importance of a formal education. Their dream was to have a family of doctors, lawyers, and computer engineers. My father didn't want me to have his hands—the calloused hands of a kitchen worker, with hardened skin that could grip a hot wok without flinching.

My dad would tell me parables instead of bedtime stories. One lesson was about strength: He had me break a single pencil, which I easily snapped in half. Then, he took a small handful of pencils and asked me to repeat the task with a dozen. No matter how much I struggled, however, I couldn't break that many at once.

"This is why family and community is so important," he said. "With one, it can be easily broken. But together, you cannot break them."

My dad's favorite refrain might as well have been a tattoo on his forehead: "Work with your brains, not with your back."

To emphasize this point, my parents would frequently buy activity books and games for math, writing, and reading comprehension. The lessons began as soon as I could talk. My parents even sent me to pre-school a year early so that I could get a head start.

When we first walked onto the grounds of my elementary school, I felt very much at home. The school was in my backyard—literally. Only a chain link fence divided the property between our home and the school's field. It was so close that sometimes *agong*, my grandpa, would watch me playing soccer during recess. I remember looking at the field from my window, excited to go to my first day of school and see what the fuss was all about.

When I first enrolled, the administrators had me take some placement tests. The many years of working through activity books allowed me to test several grade levels ahead of kindergarten. While I was proud of my achievement, the school guidance counselor took my parents aside and had a separate conversation that I wouldn't learn about until almost three decades later.

My parents told me that the exchange they had with the school went something like this:

"We're really impressed by Simon, he has a lot of potential. We think he'll do very well but we would like to put him in special classes so he can do even better."

"Special classes?" my parents asked. "Like to skip grades?"

"Well, we will test him for that later. But these classes aren't about that. He seems to be doing just fine. We're not worried him now that he's here, to be honest, we're more worried about you."

"What do you mean?"

"Your English. You speak with a deep accent and we're worried that it may affect how your children speak. So these classes will help him speak like an American . . ."

"Our son is an American!" my father said. "He was born here in San Diego."

"Well, an American citizen, yes, but he doesn't look or sound American. We'll put him in ESL classes so he can speak like one. We also need you to stop speaking oriental languages in the house whenever possible. Whenever you speak to him, only use English, if you can."

Whether we realized it or not, our family was being asked to assimilate to American culture by erasing portions of our own. There was no room to hold both identities—I had to choose one culture or the other. The school recommended against me going to Chinese school: an after school program for ABC (American Born Chinese) children to learn how to read, write, and speak Mandarin formally. I was to only learn English while my cousins and the few friends I made at the Taiwanese Sunday school went to Chinese school. To this day, I am illiterate in Mandarin, Taiwanese, and Cantonese, my first three languages.

These days, many schools are desperate to have integrated language programs, especially for Mandarin, since dual-fluency is tied to success. It's assumed that people who are bilingual are more intelligent and expand possibilities for companies. I've tried to make up the lack of that experience with Rosetta Stone and podcasts I listen to during commutes, but this has yielded only limited success. When I visit family in Taiwan, I'm filled with shame that I can't properly communicate with them. I'm bluntly wielding the tools of language, but can't do much more than order food or find a bathroom. Contrasted with my near-fluent Spanish, it makes me wish I could do more. When my extended family looks at me, I imagine they just wonder, "How did he learn English so well? And where did the Spanish come from?" Or perhaps, "What can't he converse with his own family?"

* * *

My parents used to play family home videos on the television. At two, I was already grabbing an acoustic guitar and jumping on the coffee table to play a concert for the family. The grainy footage and cacophony showed that I loved putting on a show.

I really fell head-over-heels in love with music once I got better acquainted with my dad's hi-fidelity stereo. When I was six, I used to lie in front of the speakers for hours, watching vinyl records spin, and learning how to use the tuner to pick up FM stations. We had our own small collection of records and cassettes—mostly goofy songs sung by children. Those annoyed me. What I really wanted were the large LP discs in my father's collection: the Rolling Stones, the Beatles, and Elvis Presley. With the radio, I would be entranced with pulsating, arpeggiated keyboards and electronic disco beats, the early sounds of synthpop music.

I loved pop music.

For my seventh Christmas, John gave me *Some Great Reward* by Depeche Mode on cassette—which featured hits like "People are People" and "Master and Servant"—probably because he was tired of my blasting *Music for the Masses* nonstop. I brought that tape to school for show-and-tell. We listened to "Master and Servant," my favorite cut from that album. I still find it hilarious that in my innocence, I subjected a class of second graders to a song about sadomasochism:

> *Domination's the name of the game in bed or in life*
> *They're both just the same*
> *Except in one you're fulfilled at the end of the day*

In any case, the teacher didn't even notice.

Around this time, my cousins Wynne and Nelson started taking piano lessons. My siblings and I were insanely jealous. After some begging, my sister, Ro, and I were able to join them at the same music store. Though, it was really my aunt Lin who helped make this happen. She was my mom's youngest sister, and she was always looking out for us. When my parents were busy at work, we'd spend our summer with her. She'd take us swimming, to the video arcade, and to the beach to make sure that we could have some proper childhood experiences.

Like our cousins, my sister also started on piano. But I wanted something sexy—the electric guitar, the devil's axe, the tool of the six-stringed samurai. My parents gave me a ukulele instead. I couldn't tell the difference, so it didn't matter to me. I just knew that plucked strings were an important part of rock stardom. I had already taken that first step, I was on my way. The quantity of strings and the sound that they made could be figured out later.

Time spent with our cousins started changing. Instead of running around in the backyard playing hide-and-seek or pretending to be Teenage Mutant Ninja Turtles, we'd play "band." It was an intricate process of spreading copies of the *Pennysaver*, back issues of the *San Diego Union Tribune*, and magazines across the living room floor so there wasn't a square inch of carpet visible. This was our stage. After creating the foundation, we'd gather whatever made the most noise to use as instruments: toy pianos, pots and pans for drums, and my trusty ukulele. We would pound away at everything and scream at the top of our lungs, because that's what rock stars did.

I looked at the television and thought, *I'm going to be on MTV one day.* My parents viewed the same TV as a device that would help my English so that maybe one day I could earn that coveted PhD.

My dad had a fairly successful restaurant business when he moved to the U.S., but my mom convinced him to sell it when I was born as the work was so demanding. But once the kids were in school, and mom's parents moved into the house, it seemed like the right moment to finally have something of their own again. The restaurant, House of Canton, would become a second home for us. We'd help run the restaurant, do homework there, and even sleep in the office until the customers who stayed past closing would leave.

Before I started fourth grade, we moved from San Diego to Spring Valley to be closer to House of Canton. It was the fourth home we lived in as a family. Music was something we hung onto. Ro started taking trumpet lessons at Garrett Band Instruments, a music store near our restaurant. Meanwhile, I begged and begged for something other than the ukulele—especially when I learned that it wasn't actually a guitar. I could never make it sound like what I heard from rock n' roll records I spun on the stereo. I remember counting all four strings on my humble ukulele and realizing that this was the main reason why it didn't look or sound like any of the guitars displayed at the store. If my sister got a new instrument, why couldn't I?

Walking into a music store for the first time can be like a young wizard's first experience at Ollivanders Wand Shop in Harry Potter: the instrument chooses you. All around the world, some version of Diagon Alley exists, whether in band class at school or at the Guitar Center. New musicians often choose instruments because they are drawn to certain sounds: brass rather than woodwind, strings instead of rhythm, etc. But just like in the world of Hogwarts, while wizards can definitely use other wands, they don't just feel *right* when they aren't the one.

Many people ask why I play bass instead of guitar. The reality is that I play both, though neither particularly well. I've picked up a couple of instruments throughout my life, and what I've played really has depended on the role. In high school, I played the marching baritone—which sounds like a trombone and looks like an inflated trumpet—for my class while I was also the lead singer/guitarist for my band, the Rockaway Teens.

Of course, people also pick up the guitar to impress girls and the drums to annoy their parents, or choose to sing to shine in the limelight. Ultimately, I chose the bass guitar because it felt underappreciated and overlooked. Maybe, as the middle kid, I felt like I could relate to it. It was a mightier version of the ukulele; at least it had the same number of strings. That fact that I was a huge fan of Guns n' Roses and really loved Duff McKagan's chorus-fueled bass powering the band didn't hurt either.

At this point, I didn't know what I wanted to do with my life—I was only ten. But I knew that I felt so connected to the expression of music, that to tear it away would be to tear apart a piece of my soul itself. Music was the only thing that made sense, especially when the world around me made very little.

On the basketball courts at school, students tormented me on regular basis. It didn't help that I was new to the neighborhood and that I spent most of my time outside of school helping at my parents' restaurant. It especially didn't help that I was one of the few Asian students there. Being different made me a prime target.

They'd throw balls, punches, rocks and insults. Despite making a few friends—tough for a kid that moved around as much as we did—I couldn't shake the feeling that I was an outsider. It enveloped me like the oversized hand-me-down t-shirts I wore from my brother John (six years older and three sizes larger than me).

Transitioning to middle school meant being thrown into a larger pool of students, many of whom I didn't know or share any classes with. That also meant that most of the students were older and bigger than me. Seventh and eighth graders seemed much more intimidating.

One day, I stayed back to clean up the schoolyard after P.E. It was a regular responsibility that would rotate with different students. Four older kids waited for me, hiding behind a wall nearby so I wouldn't see them. The teacher had already gone inside the locker room, yelling at the guys to hit the showers. Everything was quiet on the field and on the courts except for the sounds of my sneakers shuffling along the blacktop, until my ears started ringing and my vision blurred. I'd been hit in the back of my head by a basketball. As I stumbled towards the edge of the court, I cried hot tears.

Before I could turn around, I was pushed. Hard. My hands stung as they met the loose gravel, pebbles scraping my skin and leaving tiny cuts that would later turn to blisters.

I tried to scramble away as these boys laughed and hurled insults. The thing that scared me the most wasn't the fact that there were four of them, but rather that they were smiling, grinning. They weren't angry. They were enjoying this moment.

One of them ran up and threw sand into my face, which stuck to my sweat and tears and hardened. As I wiped at my eyes, another kicked me in the stomach, and I doubled over.

"Look at this Jap!" I heard one of them yell. "I can't believe sand can even fit in those slits!"

"This gook isn't going to do anything," said another. "What a little chicken shit."

They laughed some more.

Finally, I stood up and threw back: "I'm a chink! Get it right!" They were stunned. "You guys are so stupid, you can't even be racist right."

Confused, they stopped. And they walked away.

* * *

Kyle and I were one of the few people at our high school that listened to punk rock. Hot Topic hadn't hit the malls yet, so the idea of wearing all-black, having dyed or spikey hair, or using a novel wallet chain made from linking safety pins together was especially not cool. But we wore them anyway.

Kyle and I had met freshman year of high school, and we found ourselves in a band together, playing songs I wrote along with the standard punk rock covers of the Angry Samoans ("My Old Man's a Fatso" was a favorite) and Operation Ivy. The music was a mix of mid-90s pop punk, inspired by groups like Mr. T Experience, the Queers, and Screeching Weasel. We tempered it with terrible songs I wrote to sound like the Exploited, Crass, and the Sub-Humans. While most of our jam sessions were in our bedrooms and garages, we did end up playing a single house party. The attendees were too drunk and high to care, but still, I loved it.

I would scour encyclopedias and albums for inspiration for our songs. Sometimes an idea would come from maps: I thought "Katmandu" was such an interesting sounding place, it deserved to be written about. Other times, it would be my own personal struggles with being extremely shy, yet crushing on girls. Our "hit" was a song called "Anti-Social Boy," written after waking up from a dream about the capitalist state in the middle of the night. Kyle and I would spend hours on the phone talking about anarchy and social-ism—concepts introduced to us through punk. I'm not quite sure we really got any of it (or if any of the artists did either), but we could definitely connect to the emotion behind it, and the frustra-tion that democracies were failing to uphold their own intended values.

To make a statement about how much he believed in the lifestyle we were desperate to emulate, Kyle showed up to school with bright pink hair sculpted into eight-inch liberty spikes all over his head. I thought it was amazing. I even told him, "You look so punk!" No one else at school shared my awe of this look. Teachers frowned, giving Kyle dirty looks as he walked into the classroom. Students would snicker and point. Almost no one at school had dyed hair at the time, so this was a giant pink target on his head. Throughout the day, his cheeks would flare up red as he nervously smiled in response to people's jokes.

As per usual, I was supposed to meet Kyle out in front of school. There was an area at the top of the stairs with a short railing, flagpole, and the administrative offices that overlooked the parking lot and waiting area for cars. It was always bustling with activity. You could hear rap music being blasted from the cars of older students, honking horns from impatient parents, and the idling of diesel engines from the school busses.

As I was walking up to our spot, I noticed a group of half a dozen students had circled around Kyle, taunting him.

"Are you some kind of fag or something? Why do you have pink hair?" one of them asked.

His face just burned as sweat started to trickle out from his spikes. He nervously laughed with them.

"Look at this faggot! He can't even say nothing."

"His face just looks like he has bright berries. Maybe he's a clown!"

"Yo clown, why do you look like that? How come your mom lets you out the door looking like that?"

One of them gave him a light push. A security guard who was watching the scene play out nearby turned away. I couldn't take it any longer. I was squeezing the railing with one hand because I was so nervous. I didn't want them to notice my shaking. I mustered the little courage I had and finally yelled, "Maybe it's because his mom isn't stupid and ignorant like you are. Maybe she doesn't judge people by how they look!"

The laughing immediately stopped. The silence that followed seem to last an eternity. They turned to look at me instead. While I didn't have bright pink hair, I looked a bit clownish myself: wearing an oversized t-shirt with a band logo drawn with permanent markers underneath a camouflage army jacket covered with home-made patches safety-pinned on. The gel I used to spike my hair with was ineffective against my thick Asian hair, leaving a shiny and wet-looking flop of black on my head.

"Yo, what did you say, Jackie?"

I looked around. I was confused. I didn't see anyone else near me who could have said anything. They were staring at me, their glares cutting me down to size.

"He's talking to you, Jackie." One of the boys flashed a smile. "Is this faggot your *boyfriend*? Are you trying to start something?"

The other guys started laughing, one of them exaggerating it by doubling over and pretending to wipe a tear.

I suddenly got the joke. They were calling me Jackie . . . for Jackie Chan. The logical part of my mind went into overdrive: *I'm nothing like Jackie Chan. He's much older than me. He has a big, flat nose (mostly from it being broken so many times). He has that weird bowl-cut mullet. Most importantly, he knows something that I don't: martial arts.* I had taken one week of karate with my cousins when I was in fifth grade. But in no way did that prepare me for taking on a group of older, larger, meaner students in a one-on-six melee.

I could see the fear in Kyle's eyes growing, like he was saying, "We're going to get our asses beat. Again."

So, I did the only thing I could think of: I struck the single martial arts pose I could remember from karate camp and gave them the meanest look I had in me. It was a look fueled by the countless other bullies who had pushed me to the ground, mixed with a healthy dose of embarrassment and nervousness.

"Don't call me Jackie!" I wailed. "You're either stupid or racist if you can't tell the difference."

To my surprise, it worked. A couple of them took a step back.

"Hey, now. We were just messin'. We don't want any of your chop-socky shit. We were just playing!"

That was the second time owning up to a stereotype worked. And it wouldn't be the last.

I wish I could say that all of my encounters as a kid were victorious or brave, that I didn't let the countless remarks get to me. But when you're an adolescent trying so hard to be cool, to be accepted by your peers only to be rejected at every turn, it wears you out. I still remember the embarrassment I felt in elementary school when a teacher asked me to share the origin and meaning of the fortune cookie in class during Chinese New Year. Our family didn't ever share fortune cookies beyond handing then out at the restaurant, so why the hell would I know? Years later, I learned that fortune cookies were actually developed in California, a clever twist on some a Japanese confectionary.

Then there were all the teachers over the years that would call on me in math, fully expecting me to illuminate the class with a brilliant answer even though I could barely follow along. I couldn't hang in Calculus! And even though I excelled in English Lit, I was seldom asked to share my interpretations (It was a Christ-type, it's always a Christ-type). I always felt helpless, wishing I could retreat into some corner, secretly praying that I could be a normal white kid like everyone else.

In a moment of teenage fury during my sophomore year, I told my dad that I was ashamed of being Chinese.

"How could you say that?" He said. "Your mom and I work so hard for you, your brother, and sister! You should be proud of who you are!"

"Dad, I'm tired of getting killed out there."

That day, my father, who rarely expressed any kind of emotion, displayed heartbreaking sadness in the middle of our restaurant. I felt guilty, but not enough to stop me from continuing to disassociate myself from everything I considered Asian—

Chinese, Japanese, or otherwise. It's not like people could tell the difference or cared enough anyway, so why should I?

* * *

Perhaps it's no wonder that I eventually found myself moving to Portland, OR, known as "America's Whitest Major City." How I found myself on tour with a punk rock band that I admired, even though it meant dropping out of college and giving up on a full scholarship. It allowed me to get some space away from my family, my roots, Southern California. It let me get away from the heartbreak of losing Perla, my high school sweetheart. And it led me to sleeping in a broken down van with an obscure racial epithet spray painted on the side, waiting for a tow truck on the side of the highway.

I thought that was all in the past. With my previous band, we crammed into a minivan that was almost forty years old. On tour, we spent more time waiting for a repair than we did driving. With the Slants, I thought things had changed. I believed in this idea so much that I took a second mortgage out against the house I lived in to fund our first album. I'd gotten this van and trailer from another touring band because I thought it'd be dependable.

But there I was, spending the night in Oakland, Oregon, trying to get to back to California, to prove that the path for this band was unlike anything anyone had ever seen. At this point in my life, I identified more with what I did (play music) rather than who I was (an Asian American), even though this band combined both—and maybe the former would help with the latter. Our first tour was booked around an anime convention, which felt like a good idea at the time.

"Start it up again," Aron said. "The windows are starting to ice over."

As soon as the ignition engaged, the sound of slapping returned. This time, it sounded like a tiny helicopter firing up. I left it running just long enough for the heat to melt the frost.

While the rest of us curled up and waited for morning, Aron drank everything we had left—which was a lot. This was only the first night of tour. Eventually he got out of the van and peed on our new trailer. When he saw the closed door upon his return, he just assumed that we had locked him out. Aron repeatedly drop-kicked the sliding passenger door, leaving a dent the size of his boot and breaking the handle off.

"What's wrong with you?" I asked, reaching over and opening the door. "It was already open!"

After a moment, he said, "Oh," realizing it was unlocked the entire time. "Well you shouldn't have closed the door and let me think it was locked."

My innovative all-Asian band with all of our high-minded ambition wasn't any more immune to lead singer syndrome than any other group.

"Sorry I can't do nothin' 'bout that door of yours, though," the mechanic said to me in the morning, after he'd replaced our misfiring piston. It didn't matter; we didn't have time to waste. We had a show to get to. I put the charge onto my credit card, and we got back in our dented van and drove straight down I-5 toward Los Angeles.

CHAPTER 2
WHAT ABOUT COLLEGE?

EVEN THOUGH I GREW UP IN SOUTHERN CALI-
FORNIA, it had never really felt like home. The experience had
been wholly isolating. It wasn't that I needed a new start, I felt like
I never started at all. The idea of telling my parents about my alien-
ation, loneliness, and otherness used to torment me. All families
have their quirks, but the influence of familial devotion in a Chinese
family can't be emphasized enough. Filial piety—loyalty to one's
parents, and bringing honor to the family by taking care of them—
is one of the core values of Chinese culture. And when you pair that
with the Fifth Commandment,[1] *honor thy father and thy mother* any kind
of heartbreak or shame being brought to parents is simply devastat-
ing.

---

[1] Exodus 20:12. Interesting note: It's the fifth commandment for Protestants
but the fourth for Catholics

I knew that my parents had even more challenging experiences than I did. My mom grew up in extreme poverty in Taiwan. Her family had to sell all of their children except their youngest, including my mother, as indentured servants in order to survive. She moved away from it all when she could. I remember watching *The Joy Luck Club* film with her. She cried because the stories of their struggles getting to America all reminded her of her own. She would sometimes tell me stories about her host families. The worst ones barely fed her and made her sleep on the floor in cold corners of overcrowded bedrooms. The wealthy, generous hosts would treat her like another child in the home, except with more chores, and they would give her a place to eat at the table with the family and a warm bed for her own. Once, when we visited Taiwan as kids, I thought we were visiting blood relatives. We addressed everyone in the giant house as *ayi* and *jiùjiu*, aunt and uncle; but they were actually a host family who stayed in touch well into her adult years.

My dad didn't have a typical childhood either. At thirteen, I was working on my music in San Diego, but at that age, my dad was making wontons on the streets of Hong Kong. Several decades before my dad was born, his grandfather (my tài yé, great grandfather) came to the United States to work. Eventually, he became a citizen and was able to go back to China to retrieve his wife, my dad's grandmother, and bring her to the U.S. Their plan was to bring my dad back with them. To do this, they would have to bribe the Chinese government and lie about his age, claiming he was only eleven. They journeyed from Hoi Ping to Hong Kong, a trip that took nearly two days by boat and train. But when they finally got to the

U.S. embassy to prepare for their trip across, they were told that the small quota set for Chinese immigrants was filled. The only option they had was to leave my dad. They went to the U.S. to find a solution while my dad survived making wontons in restaurants, getting a job at a local factory, and attending junior high in Hong Kong. Five years later, my dad got a notification from the U.S. embassy to pack his things and get ready to move. His grandfather had befriended a U.S. senator, who was able to get my dad into the country as a political refugee.

Of course, when he got here, things weren't much easier. The U.S. forced my dad to enter high school again, even though he had already graduated in China. After school, he worked at an Asian grocery store and served as a line cook at a restaurant. He sent any extra money he had back to family in China. But because the U.S. still had many anti-Chinese policies, the only way to do that was by traveling to Mexico and wiring the money across. He worked tirelessly to help support the family, who suffered immensely during the aftermath of the Communist Revolution. Eventually, he sent enough money to bring the entire family over.

This was filial piety.

My parents viewed everything through the lens of opportunity and hard work. Education in America, once obtained, could never be taken away. A college education meant I could avoid the back-breaking work they had had to endure their entire lives. I remember helping my father fill out job applications whenever an opening for a supervisor position at Albertsons opened up. I never thought how, despite being fluent in spoken English and enjoying seniority, needing to rely on your child to help you be considered equal at work could affect your own morale. He always blamed his lack of education for being denied advancement, not any possible prejudice. For my parents, an education also meant a guarantee that I would be financially secure, so I could take care of them in retirement and pay them back for their sacrifices. It meant fulfilling my filial duty as their son.

But music never fit into that equation. The luxury of pursuing a passion was something that my parents never had. Responsibility to the family always came first. When I told them about my new band and the promise of finding myself in Portland, they listened with shock:

"But what about college?" my father said.

We were sitting in the living room in the house in Spring Valley.

"I want to move before I graduate," I said. "And since I won't have residency in Oregon, I'll have to wait at least a year before finishing so I don't have to pay out-of-state rates."

"But you have a scholarship, you don't have to pay."

"Those scholarships get cancelled if I stop."

They winced.

The silence that followed felt like an eternity. My father frowned, the wrinkles in his forehead suddenly appearing, and his greying moustache folding over his lips. He sighed deeply. My mother's furrowed brows quickly looked back and forth between us.

"Simon, we just want you to be happy," she said.

Here it comes, I thought: another lecture about how happiness was tied to financial stability. Another story about their sacrifices and hard work that I took for granted. More guilt to pile onto my doubt about being able to take care of them properly one day.

But that lecture never happened. My mom looked at my father while she spoke to me, almost like she was telling him how to respond.

She said, "You've been so sad for the last few months. If moving will make you happy again, you should move."

"And finish school," my dad interjected. "Promise you'll graduate. Promise me that my son will be the first in our family to do what I never could and get a college degree."

"Yes, of course. I promise I'll make you proud one day."

We sat together and cried.

* * *

Nobody told me that the city I was moving to was WHITE. With the exception of Chinatown, I rarely saw any people of color. Coming from Southern California, this was a totally bizarre development. I wasn't aware of things like redlining or the Chinese Exclusion Act yet, so I didn't know that this monochromatic place was created deliberately. I learned that Portland had a nickname:

"America's Whitest Major City" and obviously seemed to live up to the name.

I never really reflected on our country's culture of whiteness and how it affected me despite growing up in it. It just was all around—nobody defined it, it was the default culture, as if the country wasn't actually built predominantly by immigrants and enslaved people. There's no *White History Month* because every month seems to be a celebration of whiteness—literature, history, government, and most of the arts as well. The irony is that whites never wanted to recognize how they participate in and benefit from this culture of whiteness; they wanted to celebrate their own diverse heritages instead (French, Irish, Swedish, and so on).

In our country, whiteness is equated with power—at the very least, it means not being treated worse than the folks at the bottom. It was and is our very own caste system. A system that changed the rules to benefit the people at the top when convenient: at one point, the definition of "white person" rejected groups like Jews, Italians, and the Polish. In the late 1800s, immigration from southern and eastern Europe increased dramatically, so those ethnic groups were considered "not quite white." They would often find themselves working side-by-side with African, Mexican, and Chinese laborers.[2] But less than two decades later, the racial categories for immigrants changed at a time when race riots were happening

---

[2] "Race: The Power of Illusion." PBS. 2003. https://www.pbs.org/race/000_About/002_03_c-godeeper.htm.

all over the country; white mobs were viciously attacking blacks and ethnic immigrant groups due to ethnic tensions. The Irish were extremely defensive of labor and housing markets against the growing population of ethnic minorities. Oppressed blacks were outraged that police officers were not bringing known murderers of black children to justice. In 1919, Irish gangs in blackface began attacking Polish neighborhoods in Chicago in an attempt to convince Poles, and other Eastern European groups, that they were "white" and should join the daily violent attacks against blacks.

The whites in power positioned whiteness as anti-blackness and found it politically advantageous to divide people by skin color: The formerly non-white Poles, Italians, Jews, Russians, and other immigrant communities from Europe were now considered white. Immigration laws favored those from the newly formed "white" block and harshly limited those outside of it. This sentiment also fueled the creation of white enclave communities across the country. The definition of white wasn't the only racial group classification to change: the definition for who was considered black changed numerous times leading up to Virginia's Racial Purity Act of 1924, which declared that any person with "one drop" of African blood would be considered black (though other states had different standards so the racial status for many people would change if they crossed state lines). Mexicans were classified as white and allowed to naturalize for most of U.S. history, especially when demand for labor intensified, until the 1970s when they were reclassified as

"Hispanics." The Census didn't even recognize multiracial populations until 2000.[3]

Asians and Asian Americans have had an equally convoluted path for racial categorization, unintentionally bringing some of the most influential court cases to shape U.S. history. In 1922, the case *Takao Ozawa v. United States* was argued before the United States Supreme Court. Ozawa was a Japanese American who was born in Japan but lived in the United States for twenty years. In 1915, he applied for citizenship under the Naturalization Act of 1906, which only allowed "free white persons" to naturalize. At the time, all of the benefits of citizenship, home ownership, and access to education were determined by race: only whites were guaranteed access to these privileges. Ozawa argued that Japanese people should be classified as "white." However, the Court unanimously rejected his argument, writing that "the words "white person" were meant to indicate only a person of what is popularly known as the Caucasian race."

---

[3] The history of the census demonstrates how the government really didn't know how to handle Asian Americans. Asians didn't even start getting counted until 1860 (and then, only as "Chinese"). Between 1910-1940, you could be counted as "Hindu" or "Korean," but both options were dropped by 1950 (the option to identify as Korean reappeared in 1970). South Asians weren't recognized until 1980. It appears the census threw their hands up in 2000 when they added "other Asian."

Three months after *Ozawa*, the Supreme Court issued a similar ruling in *United States v. Bhagat Singh Thind*. Thind was an Indian Sikh who identified himself as a "high caste aryan, of full Indian blood." Despite being fully Caucasian according to all anthropological definitions, the Court argued that he did not meet the definition for Caucasian in the "common understanding." As a result, many Indian Americans had their citizenship revoked and landowners had their property stripped from them.

Thind inadvertently demonstrated that race is a social construct. Even though many people equate race with skin color or other physical features, it is not biological. DNA sequencing shows that all human populations are one species that originated in Africa: variations in eye color and skin color have developed through natural selection and adaptation to UV light.[4] In fact, there is more biological diversity within racial groups than between racial groups.[56] But none of these ideas were taught in school even though that history is crucial in explaining how and where families live today. Most of what I learned about the law and racial justice came from my own research efforts, which were prompted by my own experiences.

---

[4] McChesney, 2015 The Science You Need to Know to Explain Why Race Is Not Biological

[5] Cosmides, L., Tooby, J., & Kurzban, R. (2003). Perceptions of Race. TRENDS in Cognitive Science, 4 (7), 173-179.

[6] Duster, T. (2009). Debating Reality and Relevance. *Science, 324 (5931)*, 1144-145.

With strong anti-immigration and segregation laws in place and the unanimous Court decisions in *Ozawa* and *Thind*, which further defined "free white persons," the Federal Housing Administration developed the practice of redlining: the denial of services (such as banking, insurance, and health care) to communities of color. This shaped where people could live. It was called redlining because maps would have certain neighborhoods, mostly those that were predominantly black, outlined in red; residents in these neighborhoods were prevented from obtaining home loans and developing businesses.

Even though *Brown v. Board of Education* and the Civil Rights Act of 1965 ended public segregation *de jure,* racial segregation continues to exist *de facto,*[7] because of public policies, lending practices, and how redlining shaped communities. These attitudes and policies extended into other communities of color as well.

The first Chinatowns formed in the mid-1800s, resembling many of the other ethnic settlements formed by Europeans. As anti-Chinese sentiments grew, violent massacres drove Asians into Chinatowns looking for safety in numbers. However, this fueled stereotypes that Chinese immigrants were unable to assimilate and

---

[7] *De jure* connotes "as a matter of law," whereas *de facto* is Latin for "in reality." Legally speaking, racist practices continue to exist *de facto.*

provided grounds for the Chinese Exclusion Act of 1882.[8] This sentiment made it nearly impossible for our communities to live anywhere outside of a Chinatown. Whenever Chinatown neighborhoods became desirable, outside forces would drive residents out: sometimes through arson and violence, other times through shrewd real estate practices since many state laws prevented Chinese from being able to legally own the land they lived on. Florida's state constitution still bars Asians from being able to own land—even though it is unenforceable, every attempt to repeal those provisions have been defeated at the ballot box because voters are afraid it would allow undocumented immigrants to buy land. In recent decades, gentrification has displaced Chinese families from many Chinatowns, turning vibrant cultural hubs of resilience into shallow, symbolic nods to a dark past.

One of the most troubling stories is that of Vanport, which was Oregon's second largest city at one time. Created adjacent to Portland during World War II, it was the nation's largest wartime housing development and one of the areas where blacks and post-incarceration camp Japanese Americans could settle. When a flood destroyed the city in one day in 1948, it left thousands of Japanese and black families homeless, but they were denied access to housing in the vast majority of Portland due to redlining.

---

[8] When the Chinese Exclusion Act was renewed in 1892, Congress added a requirement for Chinese Americans (including U.S. born citizens) to carry photo ID at all times or risk deportation.

Even though redlining was officially outlawed in 1968, many of the practices are still continued today: a 2011 audit found that Portland landlords and leasing agents discriminated against black and Latinx residents 64% of the time. It's no wonder why Portland developed a reputation for whiteness: it was deliberate.

* * *

When I moved to Portland in 2004, I kept up with a habit that I developed while living in California: importing movies from Asia. My collection continued to grow, especially with action films from Hong Kong Cinema. I loved movies about the *Yakuza* and *Triads*, the Asian mafia of Southeast Asia. They presented a different version of glorified mob movies like *Goodfellas* and *The Godfather*, one with elements of the Chinese culture that I grew up with. While Jackie Chan was my favorite, I also bought everything that Chow Yun Fat, Tony Leung Ka-fai, and other Hong Kong film stars produced.

In the first few weeks of moving to Oregon, I quickly missed hearing my first languages and seeing anything related to my culture, so the films that I was importing from Hong Kong were the easiest way to feel like I was still connected with something other than "white culture," whatever that meant. In Portland, that seemed to mean microbreweries, ugly sweater parties, and coffee. I didn't care much about any of those things, so I connected through the silver screen.

I didn't go to the movie theatres. Since I didn't have cable, I never interacted with movie trailers. I was almost always playing shows at night, so I didn't have the chance to catch most movies while they were playing. Still, I kept hearing about the film *Kill Bill*. My friends suggested it since they knew I loved anything with Triads or Yakuza in it. As a fan of Quentin Tarantino's other films, I thought I'd give it a chance.

I bought *Kill Bill* the day it was released. I can still remember watching the bright yellow disc with three black lines slide into the DVD player.

The film has a very distinct, iconic scene in its final act: a mixed-race woman named O-Ren Ishii (played by Lucy Liu) walks into a Japanese restaurant with the Crazy 88's, the Yakuza gang that she led. Tomoyasu Hotei's song, "Battle Without Honor or Humanity," plays in the background, signaling a new kind of badass intro music that has since been used in films like *The Transformers*, *Shrek the Third*, and *Team America: World Police* for a similar effect.

For most people, this was just another trademark scene from Tarantino: a classic walking-to-develop-character shot also appears in *Reservoir Dogs* and *Jackie Brown*. But for me, it was something much different. In fact, I remember pausing the movie because I couldn't quite figure out why it was having such a profound effect on me.

I realized this was the first time that I had ever seen an American-produced film that depicted Asians as cool, confident, and sexy. For my entire life, I could only get that kind of representation by importing movies from Hong Kong. The only people who looked like me in the movies were emasculated, exoticized, or ridiculed. People would quote Papillon Soo Soo's cringe-worthy line ("Me so horny! Me love you long time!") in *Full Metal Jacket* so often, most forgot where it even came from. Characters like Long Duck Dong in *Sixteen Candles* gave people license to repeat his ridiculous, racist lines to my face as a kid ("Ohh, no more yanky my wanky!"). Imagine growing up your entire life and never having anything in mainstream pop culture except this type of representation. It got to the point where I'd wince every time an Asian face would pop up in a film because I wouldn't know when their racist stereotype would come back to haunt me. To be clear: I never blamed the actors— they need to pay the bills and I understand accepting the few roles that are available—but I do believe that the lack of diversity in pop culture is a reflection of social power structures.

Kill Bill was different. Sure, it was about a white woman (played by Uma Thurman) who would mow down powerless Asians with a sword made by one of their own, but that one scene showed me that there could be something different in American cinema. It was empowering. I started thinking about my own art, and how the void existed there as well.

I thought: If Hollywood was bad, the music industry was much worse.

The gatekeepers for art that I had lived and breathed since my very first memories did not allow people who looked like me in. Despite having almost eighteen million Asian Americans in this country, we had no representation on the Billboard charts, in music magazines, or on MTV (this was 2004—Asian Americans would not see a top ten Billboard hit until October 2010, when the Far East

Movement finally reached that status). The only way to explain this phenomenon was to believe that either Asians were not biologically and culturally predisposed to be playing good music, or, like the city of Portland, the system was designed that way through institutionalized and sometimes unsaid policies.

I knew: something needed to change.

That night, in the middle of the film, an idea for an Asian American band was born. Of all people, it was Quentin Tarantino that provided this initial spark. But the last thing I wanted to do was to start a political project: I just wanted to celebrate our cultural identity in a bold way, through music. My punk rock upbringing dictated challenging the old, false stereotypes that plagued me and prevented people who looked like me from entering the mainstream music industry. And this kind of punk rock statement always begins with the name.

I started asking friends, "What's something you believe all Asians have in common?" The resounding answer was always an immediate, "Slanted eyes."

Slanted eyes. It was the source of ridicule when I was younger, the target of nearly any insult. Kids thought it was hilarious to pull their eyes back, in a "chink eye" manner, to make excessive caricatures of my natural features. It was something I always associated with pain, not pride. But even with a lifetime of these experiences, my initial reaction to this answer was never one of insult, horror, or offense. I didn't wince. Instead, I was always filled with sincere curiosity.

The idea that all Asians have slanted eyes is a misconception: Not all Asians have slanted eyes, and Asians are not the only people to have this feature. But the band-name-generator part of my brain spit out "the Slants." It could be a badass reference to our own perspective, or slant on life, as well as our journey to unpack these false stereotypes as people of color. It was a way to pay homage to the work of activists who reappropriate words and imagery for self-empowerment and join a larger movement.

The bullying I'd experienced as a kid hadn't really gone away, I'd realized. It had just become something subtler and more passive. It invaded the spaces of social interaction, business, and dating.

A few years ago, I met a woman at one of our shows who perfectly demonstrated this. I was trying to get water for my band members and she was blocking the station, so I asked if I could get by. She assumed that I was using it as an excuse to hit on her, and she told me that she wasn't attracted to Asians.

"No worries," I said. "I'm not attracted to racists."

"I'm not a racist!" she shot back. She was shocked that I'd even say such a thing. "I'm not a racist. I just don't find Asians attractive, so I could never date one."

What fascinates me is how many people having dating preferences similar to this woman. When I've told friends about the encounter, they respond that it isn't racist to have a dating preference because you can't control the "spark" of making a connection.

For most of my life, I have heard the refrain "I don't date Asians" or some variation on that.

Dating problems can get accentuated with gender as well. For example, Asian women are the most sought after group in online dating because they are seen as exotic and submissive.[9] This leads many Asian women to be objectified and treated as a fetish.[10] On the other hand, Asian American men rank lower than any other group in terms of desirability. Stereotypes about anatomy and our effeminate nature perpetuate the emasculation of Asian American males, making emotional connections difficult.[11]

With the Slants, I wanted to defy expectations, not only to drain the denigrating venom from this outdated term but also to turn other stereotypes upside down. Asians and Asian Americans have been perpetually seen as foreign, quiet, and demure, unable to

---

[9] OkCupid. "Race and Attraction, 2009–2014 – The OkCupid Blog." The OkCupid Blog. September 10, 2014. https://theblog.okcupid.com/race-andattraction-2009-2014-107dcbb4f060.

[10] Mukkamala, S., & Suyemoto, K. L. (2018). Racialized sexism/sexualized racism: A multimethod study of intersectional experiences of discrimination for Asian American women. Asian American Journal of Psychology, 9(1), 32-46. http://dx.doi.org/10.1037/aap0000104

[11] The largest study ever conducted on penis size found that there was no correlation between race and anatomy. The British Journal of Urology also discovered no correlation to height, weight, hand size, or any other urban stereotype to be true either. https://www.ncbi.nlm.nih.gov/pubmed/8709382

drive or speak English well, and all looking the same. Those stereotypes have been hammered into me since birth both through direct
and indirect messaging from school, the movies, books, and the music industry. In order to fight that using the Slants, I needed to dig
into my rock n' roll roots.

* * *

By 2006, I had already spent nearly two years trying to recruit for the Slants, but I had only spoken with about a dozen Asian
American musicians. I had moved to Portland to join a horror punk
band called "The Stivs," and I knew plenty of white musicians. But
recruiting Asian American musicians in America's Whitest Major
City proved tougher than I anticipated: most of them weren't a good
fit for one reason or another—they didn't have the availability
needed for the band, they weren't interested in my creative vision,
or they simply didn't have the musical chops.

That spring, I met a talented half-Chinese drummer who
was taking his craft seriously. After watching his band Redshift play
at a local club, I thought he could be a potential fit. We met up a
few times, and I showed him some rough demos of songs I was
writing for the Slants. Eventually, he decided to join a different band
instead, Silversafe, since they actually had other members to play
with. But since we got along well, we decided to stay in touch. His
name was Tyler Chen. Years later, he would join the Slants as our
longest-serving drummer and became one of the groomsmen in my
wedding. But for the time being, he was content to watch our story
unfold as a bystander.

I was invited to a local anime convention at the end of the summer. I was excited because I assumed there would be a ton of Asian kids there, maybe some who could play music. I'd never been to an anime convention before; I didn't know what to expect.

The convention, Kumoricon, was taking place in the ballrooms of a small Red Lion Inn in North Portland. I loaded up with business cards and flyers in hopes of spreading the word about the band. At this point, I was the only member, so it was more like trying to recruit people for my longtime solo project that had yet to take off.

It was a Friday afternoon. I pulled up to a mostly-filled parking lot and began walking towards the hotel's front doors. As I climbed the steps, I could see hundreds of people dressed in costumes of their favorite anime, video game, and manga characters. It was a rich, colorful display, as if I were seeing a film come to life right before my eyes. What a contrast: the Red Lion Inn was typically used for business conferences. The rich, dark wood of the walls and neutral carpet was a jarring backdrop for such a whimsical display. I followed my white friends, who were walking in the direction of the registration table.

Out of nowhere, I heard a young girl scream "ASIAN!"

I quipped, "Where? I'm looking for some!"

Within a few seconds, a short, teenage girl, dressed in what looked a sheepherding outfit with multiple layers of doilies tackled me to the ground. Before I could say anything, she got up and skipped away without explanation.

"Yo, what just happened?" I asked my friends as I stood up.

"You just got glomped by a Lolita."

"Glomped? Lolita? I don't know what's going on. Why did she scream 'Asian' like that?"

"It's just a thing. Lolita is a kind of fashion. And she probably glomped you because you're Asian, and there aren't very many here, so it's a big deal if they see one. You're like extra cool here."

Immediately, I felt a sense of regret.

I paced through the hallways of the convention, trying to recognize what I was seeing. It wasn't like San Diego Comic-Con—a huge comic book and pop entertainment convention I attended as a kid—at all. Most of the anime being screened had titles I'd never heard of before. Many of the attendees acted like they were fueled entirely by energy drinks. Anime theme songs were blasting from portable speakers everywhere I went. I felt like an outsider in a place that was supposed to be celebrating Asian culture. This wasn't Asian culture. It was just a caricature of it.

The exhibitor's hall was a large room filled with toys, props, and souvenirs. Perhaps here I could finally find something I understood, like a transformable Robotech Veritech fighter. *Robotech* was a popular anime series in the 1980s that featured mecha that could be transformed into planes by their human pilots. My brother had an original toy from the show, but I had broken its arm off when I was younger. Later, I found out that it was worth hundreds of dollars and had been trying to replace it ever since.

No *Robotech*, but thousands of white kids obsessed with a small part of Asian culture. The same *Dragonball Z* comics that I'd borrow from my cousin were now being sold by entire sets, except these were published in English, not in Kanji—one of the written forms of Japanese comprised almost entirely of Chinese characters. There were robots and recognizable, but overpriced snacks from the Asian markets that I loved growing up. The same snacks that provoked other students to mock me in elementary school were suddenly highly coveted! There were large wall posters of Visual Kei, flamboyant and androgynous glam rock stars, the Japanese equivalent of the Cure and Motley Crue having a stylish rock and goth baby. Under the posters were bins filled with CDs.

Since I was a teenager, I'd had a magnetic attraction to album bins. I could easily spend hours in a record shop looking for rare titles. Whenever I was on tour with my other bands, any precious moment of free time we had was usually spent in record shops. Unconsciously, I started walking straight to this booth and flipping through discs in shiny jewel boxes. But I was shocked: the asking prices for these import CDs ranged from $40-$60! I couldn't ever imagine paying that much for a disc, especially for unknown artists.

Two young women walked up right on cue. They wore large headphones and cat ears.

"Have you ever heard of this band?"

"No, but the cover art is really cool!"

"And it's only $55! I'm going to get it."

As they ran up to pay for the album, it dawned on me: I needed to book anime conventions. The opportunity was too good to pass up: huge events where kids were willing to give Asian culture a shot—even though some of them took things way too far. If they were used to paying four or five times the price of a retail CD, what would happen if I brought in something much more reasonable? I may not have found any Asian American musicians at this convention, but a new market opened up to me that was otherwise invisible.

A few days later, I got ready to send a message to the general email at the convention. I just had a small problem: I didn't have a band yet. I didn't even have any songs up. The only thing I did have going for me was a Myspace profile and theslants.com domain reserved for a future website. So I did the only thing I could do: I faked it.

I started filling the Myspace page with photos of actors from my favorite Hong Kong films about triads and included close-up pictures of me performing with other bands. I even used Photoshop to edit photos of billboards in Hong Kong with "The Slants" and those same actors—as if we were already had a presence overseas. I created biographies with backstories for each of the five people in my "band" and filled in the details of my previous acts to establish credibility. Then, I emailed the convention with a link to the Myspace page.

They wrote back immediately, wanting us to perform as an honored guest for the following year!

Despite having no proof of a real band or any music on our website, I somehow managed to get the attention of an event that would have thousands of people attending, people who were obsessed with Asian culture—enough to tackle complete strangers in public.

This plan eventually paid off, which is what brought us back down to Los Angeles the following year for our very first tour, a series of shows planned around a small anime convention in the fall of 2007.

CHAPTER 3
RAW POWER

IT'S AMAZING TO THINK HOW MUCH CAN CHANGE IN JUST ONE YEAR. In 2006, the idea for the Slants was just an idealistic dream. By 2007, I was already on the road with my newly assembled band in support of our first release, *Slanted Eyes, Slanted Hearts*, which was hastily recorded in my garage (dubbed "House of the Rising Sun" in the liner notes since the window pattern on the door resembled the bursting solar rays of the morning). Most of the songs were birthed as punk rock bass riffs (written while I was in the Stivs) but reimagined with a synthpop twist. Aron wrote almost all of the lyrics, preferring to sing words of his own composition rather than anyone else's. They were inspired in part by personal experiences of being bullied or being in love, though numerous references to film were scattered throughout as well.

Our anthem to Asian American identity, "Sakura, Sakura," reclaimed an old schoolyard rhyme that several of us had to endure. Instead of "Chinese, Japanese, dirty knees, look at these" (combined with the tormentor pulling their eyes back), we proclaimed,

We sing for the Japanese
and the Chinese
and all of the dirty knees
do you see me?
We sing in harmony!

Somehow, these songs about feeling like an outsider resonated with geeky white kids at anime conventions and dive bars around the country.

Now we were on our first tour: as I looked up at the marquee hanging over the Whisky a Go Go, I could see our name in lights. It was our first tour and our first show in Southern California—I couldn't believe they had our name on top! A documentary about Charles Manson was being filmed that day, so THE SLANTS is actually emblazoned in the background of *The Six Degrees of Helter Skelter* during the story's climax. A large bronze sign by the front door proudly boasts other bands who've rocked the walls of this club: the Doors, Janis Joplin, James Brown, Led Zeppelin, and Guns n' Roses. But I didn't think about how we were actually part of music history now. All I could think about was seeing Perla again.

* * *

Perla was my first love. When I met her in high school, she was a tall, skinny Latina with braces who loved playing field hockey. She was active in her church and curious about new music. Something about us just clicked. We would spend hours on the phone every night, talking about our favorite bands and our respective dreams. Each week, we would meet up for youth group, eat Mexican food (her mom made the best tacos!), and go record shopping. She had a crush on one of my friends, Sammy, so I intended on setting them up until I realized how quickly I was falling for her.

One Tuesday night, I wrote a song about how I felt, how special she was to me. Even though I had been nervous about sharing this for weeks, I felt surprisingly calm as I read the words over the phone like a poem and asked, "Will you go out with me?"

Silence.

I didn't know how to respond. I could hear whispering in the background—her friend Violetta was there. Finally, she said, "Of course, you silly. That was really sweet." I felt elated, but I didn't really understand what changed about our relationship other than knowing we shared mutual feelings about each other. It was probably the most innocent high school relationship start that I'd ever heard of. A week later, I gave her a single red rose when I picked her up to go out—a ritual that I repeated every Tuesday for the next seven years.

After graduating, Perla and I decided to go to the same college. Rather than go straight to a four-year university, we opted to attend community college so that we could be close to our family and still have plenty of time to work with the nonprofit that we were involved with. Working with that organization, we built homes, orphanages, and community centers in some of Mexico's most impoverished areas. To do so, we'd often use subversive ways of to address issues of systemic poverty, like smuggling supplies across the border and letting communities with the greatest need dictate allocation of resources instead of paternalistic leadership from abroad. It's where I truly learned to understand horizontal leadership structures. In fact, I learned more about life, business, and communication working directly with communities in Mexico than any university program about those same subjects.

All of our classes were together. Because we didn't have declared majors, we had quite a bit of freedom to figure out what we wanted to do. Every day I'd pack a meal for us, pick her up, and eat a little brunch before going to classes. After community college, we both moved out of San Diego to take jobs at the nonprofit when it relocated to Murrieta, CA.

In Murrieta, Perla and I opened up the Populuxe, a vintage clothing shop in Old Town Temecula, the county just south of us. With only a $2,000 loan to kick things off, we did all of the remodeling ourselves. When we couldn't find a counter, I built one from scratch using plywood sheets and rented tools at the hardware store. It always sat crooked on our uneven floors, so we'd use back issues of *Maximum Rock n' Roll* to keep it stable.

While we weren't making a ton of money, it was enough to pay the rent and treat us to the occasional lunch, too. One of my favorite things about having the store was treating it like a gigantic walk-in closet: I'd go into the store wearing one thing and leave in something entirely different (while pricing and displaying my original outfit). We worked when we wanted to, and we closed when we had better things to do, like leaving town for a show. It was very low-pressure, allowing us to live in a whimsical, fantastic world of music and fashion.

The Populuxe was our own version of The Room of Requirement in Hogwarts: it became whatever we needed it to be. It was more than a vintage clothing shop or place to meet bands though. It was living proof that whenever we were together, we were an unstoppable force.

But living in Murrieta could be isolating for people used to spending all their time around music—either going to shows or playing them. So Perla and I used to drive to shows in LA, Hemet, or anywhere we could find some music. With the store, we now also had a place to hold our own shows, mostly helping touring bands that we had met. One infamous show was with the Stivs, a punk outfit that included a founding member of the Huntingtons, a band we worked with over the years.

The Stivs was the band that eventually convinced me to leave California when they asked me to drop out of college, move to Portland, and join them as their next bassist.

This show in Los Angeles at the Whiskey a Go Go would be the first time Perla would see the Slants. It finally happened. After years of talking about this idea with her, I finally put together enough of a lineup and got us on the road. For me, that first tour wasn't just about making new fans at an anime convention or the clubs we were playing nearby. It was about showing Perla the man I'd become since she left me.

I loved Perla, deeply and unequivocally. We grew up together, our identities were tied together: several bands that we worked with even thanked us in the liner notes of their albums, calling us "the fabulous duo." But that was part of the problem: as we entered our early twenties, we started making new friendships and our identity as a couple was beginning to fragment. She started going to parties and hanging out with her new friends while I was at work.

In 2003, Marky Ramone came through town with the Speed Kings, his band at the time. It was a mix of rockabilly, punk, and Ramones covers. We ended up going to all of his shows in Southern CA, four of them in a row, befriending the band and their crew, and hanging out after every show. At the end of their night in San Diego, I needed to drive back for an early morning shift at work, but Perla stayed since her friends would give her a ride back.

The next afternoon, I met her at the Populuxe to get lunch, and she was bursting with excitement.

"Guess what?!" she exclaimed. "Marky kissed me!"

". . . What?"

"Yes! Marky Ramone kissed me! I kissed a Ramone."

"Well, he's technically not an original Ramone . . . and . . . but . . . wait. How did this even happen? I don't know how to feel about that."

"We were saying goodbye, he held me and then just kissed me. Oh, don't be upset. I think it's cool."

Of course, I was upset. My girlfriend of almost seven years kissed someone else the moment I left. I felt betrayed. But it wasn't just that one incident. She had been going out more, hanging out with different people, and getting attention from guys. It all felt so uncomfortable. She loved the attention, she loved getting dressed up and going out, and I felt like there was nothing I could do about it. Her new friends thought I was boring and ruined the mood since I didn't drink. They thought I dragged her down and she could do better. Of course, kissing a "rock star" definitely confirmed that.

I became silent and stared out the window. Neither of us said much. We kept working, she kept going out, and we started talking less—but I kept giving her a long-stemmed rose every Tuesday.

A few weeks later, she broke up with me. The news tore my world to pieces.

I later found out that she hooked up with some guy named "Scotty" at a party and was just excited about the prospect of something new.

It's hard when you grow up with someone. We change so much in our lifetimes, especially as teenagers and young adults. It's really hard to know ourselves, especially when we feel defined by a relationship with someone else. I lost that definition. I felt untethered, drifting, and alone. Her mom would call me on a regular basis to check on me, telling me that she was praying for us to get back together. I barely ate or slept for several weeks and talked the ears off of everyone around me.

Six months after breaking up, we met up for a late night dinner at Denny's. Back when we were younger, we loved Denny's. It was one of the few places open late, after a show, so we'd go almost every week. The vinyl booth put me right back in those memories.

Predictably, we started with uncomfortable small talk. The kind of conversation that didn't matter and could be easily forgotten. The kind that avoided any real thought or feeling. She was obviously happy whereas I was miserable. Then, I opened up.

"I'm moving to Portland."

"Wow, why would you do that? Your whole life is here," she smiled as she asked, like she was excited for the prospect.

"Well, the Stivs finally asked me to join the band."

I said finally because I had been pestering them for quite some time. I had known Cliffy for years, ever since he was in the Huntingtons and left it to start his horror punk band, the Stivs. Perla and I continued to work with them, I even shot press photos that ended up as album covers. I got along great with the band and longed for life on the road. I dropped hints about joining all the time. But they didn't really think I'd fit in—I didn't have the right "look." I wasn't sure if this was just coded language for being Asian American or because they'd usually seen me wearing attire from the Populuxe. I never asked.

Things started to change when they were in the middle of a full U.S. tour. Cliffy found out that their drummer was sleeping with his fiancé. So they dropped him in Kansas City. At first, they asked me if I could play drums. I had only started learning and didn't think I would be tour-ready quick enough to finish out their tour. But the thought stuck in their mind, and Cliffy eventually called me one night at 2 a.m., asking if I'd join as the bassist. I didn't hesitate, I said yes right away. I'd figure out the details later.

Perla asked what I'd do about school. I was only a few months away from graduating with a double degree on a full-ride scholarship and grant program. I didn't care. My life was still deeply entangled with hers: after community college, Perla and I had both enrolled in UC Riverside with the same philosophy major, we were running the Populuxe together, and we still had jobs at the same nonprofit with our desks next to each other. How could I explain that I wanted a new life? That every waking moment was suffering as long as I was reminded of what I'd lost?

"I just need a new start. I can finish school later," I explained.

"You should totally do it." She took my hands into hers and then said, "I miss us."

I melted immediately. My heart was racing, a smile started to creep up.

"I miss us too . . ."

"But honestly, I can't ever see us being together again."

I grimaced.

She continued, saying, "You're my best friend in the world. We know each other better than anyone else, we've been through so much together. I don't want to lose that."

"I know. I feel the same. I want to always be connected with you, even if we don't have the same kind of relationship that we had before."

We both knew in our hearts that we weren't the same people we were when we first met. There was certainly loss in not only our romantic relationship, but the shedding of innocence as we started becoming adults, watching childhood friendships slowly disintegrate over the passage of time, and experiencing the death of loved ones. But there was also a profound gain as well: timeless memories that we created together, the badassery of opening our own vintage shop, meeting our music heroes.

I even taught Perla how to play the guitar. Since we were always going to shows, her mom finally gave her one for her nineteenth birthday, a sparkling blue Danelectro that screamed Populuxe style. To complement that gift, I bought her a little amp and provided the lessons. We began with power chords so she could pick up punk rock songs rather quickly. Of course, that first song was "Blitzkrieg Bop" by the Ramones. She used to complain about how I insisted that she play with all down strokes, just like Johnny Ramone. With consistent practice, she finally got it—and a few years later, she ended up playing it on stage with Marky Ramone when he was on tour with the Misfits. That's how she met her future husband, Dez. I can still remember the excitement in her voice when she called me from backstage: "They were impressed that I even played with all down strokes, just like Johnny!" Friends who were in the audience sent me photos later.

I used to believe in this idea that every cell in our body is replaced over the course of seven years. I even thought it'd make a great song because it could articulate moving on, that our grief need not haunt us because our existence represents continuous healing and change. But it turns out that some cells never get replaced. Most notably: cells in the heart. But they can change: they can get stronger, they can work with other, newer cells, and life can go on.

In that moment in Denny's, I didn't know if we'd ever end up together again. I didn't care about any other area in my life—my career, school, family, my other friends. All I cared about was her. Nothing and no one meant more to me. But I also knew that hanging on to some evaporated dream wasn't going to add anything to her life. It certainly wasn't doing any favors for mine.

I looked into her eyes and just said, "Promise you'll visit me in Portland."

And she did. She was there, one year later loudly cheering me on for my first show with the Stivs. She provided a place to crash whenever I was passing through on tour and our friendship grew deeper. We spoke almost everyday about music, our dating lives, our families. A few years later, I flew down to Los Angeles for her wedding.

I was in a rush. My flight was late, which made picking up the rental car late, which meant I was going to arrive over an hour late. As I sped my way to the park where the ceremony was taking place, I saw her hiding out behind a building. It turned out that she held up the entire wedding until I got there, telling people, "I'm not getting married unless Simon is here!"

After the wedding, she moved to Newark with her new husband Dez, a punk rock legend in his own right (he fronted Black Flag and was the guitarist for the Misfits at the time). They were often traveling, so we'd meet in the most random of places, which is how they ended up at the Whisky A Go Go in Los Angeles during the Slants' first tour. Here I was, playing at one of the most iconic rock clubs in the country. The legacy of the musicians who were launched on this stage, including my hero Iggy Pop, cast a large shadow, subtly reminding me: *you don't belong here.* I was an imposter, and I would soon be found out, by the one person who I deeply admired no less. I nervously held my bass and wireless pack stageside while our introduction music blasted overhead.

Then I stepped onto the stage.

A funny thing happens when I walk onto any raised platform with a bass in hand and trusted musicians at my side: all nerves disappear along with any semblance of my everyday, offstage personality. I'm energetic and overconfident, as if years of playing pretend in my family's living room could adequately prepare me for a life of performing. Stage lights are lycanthropy for me: a mysterious transformation forms and I start becoming something else. I have no problem swinging my bass or yelling into faces, I feel a sense of complete freedom. One time, I even punched an old friend of mine in the face.[12] Most people who know me well are shocked at the contrast between my two different sides.

At the Whisky, our bombastic songs loosened stiff and jaded bodies: heads lightly bobbing turned into enthusiastic nods, foot tapping became stomping and jumping. Aron jumped out in full force, mic stand raised high overhead while Johnny and I flanked his sides. Johnny—or Jonathan—was a lifelong friend from San Diego. We formed the Rockaway Teens in high school with his older brother Tony. As he was of Mexican and Filipino descent, it never crossed my mind that my high school band was also all-Asian American until many years later. Jonathan was the only person tonight who also knew Perla when we were all just kids. The two keyboardists and drummer (Michael, Jen, and AC) that we had on stage with us would be out of the band in the following year, but that night, we were a force to be reckoned with. Perhaps we were all embodying a bit of The Stooges that night:

Raw power, honey, just won't quit
Raw power, I can feel it
Raw power, honey, can't be beat
Get down, baby and a kiss my feet

---

[12] To be clear, this was a total accident. He was standing way too close to the front and I didn't have my glasses on . . . so when I held the bass up, I just clocked him. He was a good sport about it! He had a giant smile on his face, yelled "YEAH!" and antagonized me through the show.

Playing the show and winning Perla's approval for the new band felt like justifying the risk and efforts I put into the Slants. Thankfully, she loved what we were doing and even wrote an encouraging note on our new trailer in permanent marker. For the next several years, this tour rig would be my home away from home, giving me a life on the road like a sailor, a long haul trucker, and Mormon missionary—but instead of delivering goods or the Good News, I was sharing Chinatown Dance Rock.

CHAPTER 4
YO HO

～

LIFE AS A TOURING MUSICIAN, I imagine, is a lot like being on the crew of a pirate ship.

Casual observers might see us as rogues who are trying to accrue fortune and fame in every town where we dock, but the reality is that most of the hours are spent drifting in transit, hanging on while we fight off scurvy (seriously, punk rockers need to eat some more fruit).

Like any other kind of organization, leading a band means that you are held responsible for the failures, but not necessarily lauded for the successes. The default assumption is that the manager needs to do their job: they get things done, that's the job. There shouldn't be any surprises, the manager just keep things going (even if you aren't getting paid extra for the work). In that sense, the true reward for doing good work is the ability to do more work. In another, being the ship's captain means you're no different than the garbage man. People don't thank the garbage man, they don't tip them when there's more rubbish to pick up than usual. No one thinks about the person who picks up the garbage—unless there's a problem with the garbage.

Most of the time, this is perfectly fine for me. I actually enjoy solving problems. This is probably why I've always been drawn to nonprofits: one is always engaged in working on problems, especially with the larger problems with the world. With a touring band, this means I'm responsible for keeping the ship afloat: the vehicle is running, the shows are happening, the conflicting needs of the members are being addressed. The challenge is that when you're also a band member, the lines get blurred when you're also seen as a friend, a boss, and an "equal" partner to the organization that you started to begin with. People don't want to listen to someone simply because they have the title (but they are more than happy to blame you when things aren't going well).

Don't get me wrong though, being on tour is fun. It isn't all work, broken down vehicles, and disagreements. There have been some unimaginable moments of levity as well. We'd have prank wars on Slants' tours (my team had the biggest victory when we froze our opponents' socks and underwear to the balcony during one of the coldest winters in Boston), we'd eat the best regional foods from each tour destination (you can't beat a New York slice or barbecue in Texas), and we'd meet some wonderful people. If it weren't for the musician lifestyle, I probably would have never seen most of North America, Europe, or Asia.

Touring in a band also teaches you a diverse set of skills that you need to survive, like learning how to change out tires without the proper tools or figuring out just how many meals you can create using the hot water tab at truck station stops. With the Slants, I was developing a new kind of street wisdom to make sure everything would run smoothly. For example, when we played punk rock dives in questionable neighborhoods, I would affix a mannequin head with a hat to a stuffed sleeping bag in the passenger seat of our van so people would think someone was on guard duty. It was the scarecrow of tour vehicles, creating a deterrent, like learning how to park a bus or van and trailer against a wall so vulnerabilities would be minimized. I also started memorizing the country by drive times. *Vegas? That's about four hours from L.A. unless you're hauling a trailer, then it's closer to six. Austin? That's about thirty-four hours from Portland.* I learned more about geography from punk rock than public school.

I never took shop or automobile classes in school but touring gave me a crash course in dealing with all kinds of mechanical problems. These problems were so frequent, it was like a strange bond developed with our tour vehicles that needed constant attention. One time, the suspension on our bus was so loose and the roads in Louisiana so shoddy, that it felt less like we were driving and more like we were sailing an old fishing boat down the highway. I remember looking out our large windows like they were portholes and watching alligators warm their scaly bodies on the banks of a swamp. I always had my fingers crossed, hoping we wouldn't be breaking down beside them.

Frequent travel by air develops a similar aptitude for resourcefulness, like learning how to hop on a plane with additional bags for free (you bring an extra carry on to the gate, then volunteer when they begin asking people to gate check their bags). Most of the time, airline staff are not happy to see us. You see their bodies stiffen when they see a pack of us walking up to the gate with music equipment in hand. *This flight is sold out, bitch. Good luck finding overhead space for that guitar.*

Before I had TSA PreCheck, I was almost always stopped at security. Large cases filled with wires always made them a bit anxious. At certain airports (like Tallahassee), I was always flagged for a "random security check" whether I was carrying music gear or not. One time, they justified it by saying it was because the banana in my bag looked suspicious. *Sure.* But a little kindness goes a long way. Like us, flight attendants travel for a living and they just want a little respect or appreciation.

On a flight to Taipei, I thanked the crew for being patient with us while dealing with all of our music equipment. The attendant learned I was in the Slants and that it was also my birthday, so they brought me a large bottle of champagne and a box of chocolates as a gift. "*Happy birthday from the crew,*" they said, as they also handed me their WeChat number. "*Be sure to send me details about your show in Taipei, I'd love to go.*" In retrospect, I wasn't sure if they were hitting on me or just being friendly, but either way, it was a really cool surprise.

One thing I never expected to pick up from touring was my social justice activism—and I really dove into that world, of all places, at an anime convention. In 2008, I was contacting every anime convention in the country trying to book the Slants. I started trading emails with someone named Solikha "Sonnie" Wright.

Eventually, we hopped on a call to talk about the Slants, and she strongly urged me to play the Middle Tennessee Anime Convention (MTAC in Nashville, TN) even though they were over budget, meaning we'd have to pay for our own expenses. The idea was that fans were so enthusiastic there that the merchandise sold would easily cover our flights. With some reluctance, I decided to take that chance.

When we landed in Nashville, we learned that there were six other music acts on the bill. Most anime conventions only had one or two. Sonnie loved music and stacked live bands night after night. Being in Music City, it seemed only appropriate. Sonnie was also an artist who ran a company called Stubby Chubby, and her booth was stationed next to us. She was a Cambodian-Japanese woman who had a natural, confident aura around her, possibly developed from her former life as a dominatrix. While she sold hand sewn sushi pillows, she also had an assortment of decorated paddles and collars that convention kids loved. There, we met her team, which included her husband Jeremy, and their friends Yad and Lizzie. Since they were also our liaisons for the event, we spent about sixteen hours a day with them.

On our first day, Sonnie asked a couple of us to join a panel she was running. She told me that we should get as much face time as possible so that we could get more attendees familiar with us and excited about the show.

"It's called in Asians in America," she told us.

"Cool," I said. "What's it about?"

"Asians . . . in America."

"Ok . . ."

"Trust me, it'll get interesting."

I grabbed two of my band mates, Aron and Jen. We walked down the hallway and joined some of the other Asian American guests who were at the convention—most of them were visual artists who illustrated, we were the only musicians. The room itself was very intimate: a small hotel conference room with about thirty chairs lined up in rows.

When the doors opened, every seat was quickly filled. Attendees started sitting on the floor in the aisles, standing up in the back, and watching from the doorway. Apparently, that can happen when you grab all of the Asian guests and put them in one room at an anime convention.

Sonnie stood and addressed the room. "Welcome to Asians in America. This is a free-form panel, so anything goes. Have you ever wondered something about Asians but were too afraid to ask or didn't know how to search for it? Now you can ask whatever you want. Food, penis size, whatever. Nothing is off the table."

I was a bit nervous. What did I get myself into this time?

The questions started trickling in . . . then it was like the dam broke loose, and we were flooded with all kinds of ridiculous questions:

"Do Asian women have a sideways vaginas?"

"Do Asians really drive that bad?"

"Do you eat food like hamburgers and pizza with chopsticks?

I couldn't believe it. Apparently, some of the people there had never met an Asian person before. They were plainly asking questions based on racial stereotypes. At first, we were mortified. But then we clapped back. Our answers got snarky, we didn't pull punches and weren't afraid to flip stereotypes to show the absurdity of the presumptions made about us. When the inevitable question about the Asian phallus came up, one of the other guests stood up and began unzipping his pants while saying, "How about I show you?"

A month after MTAC, we flew to Chicago for one of the largest conventions in the U.S.: Anime Central (ACEN). Sonnie was talking up the green room parties at ACEN, saying convention directors from across the country would be there. So with a box of CDs and my publicist, Alex, we made our way to the Windy City.

When we got there, the Stubby Chubby team was there to greet us: Sonnie, Jeremy, Lizzie, and Yad. Lizzie was even sporting a Slants' t-shirt and track jacket, which she picked up from our band when we were in Nashville. I didn't know it then, but I'd end up seeing her in Huntsville, AL the next month as well—and there, we'd make an unexpected and strong connection that would lead to a long-distance relationship.

Throughout the weekend, I gave away mediocre art that I drew on the back of flyers while trying to sell CDs from a shared space at Sonnie's booth. I also tried making the most of my time at the convention by leading several panels on Asian American identity and the music industry. Most of the time though, I was goofing off with Lizzie at the Stubby Chubby station, who was amused that my artwork could resemble the talent of an eleven year old with impressive accuracy. She had the grace of a ballet dancer and a sharp wit that would rival Oscar Wilde. We talked about our mutual love of books, Jackie Chan films, and delicious food.

On the second day of the event, I was looking through the program book to see what other events they had. I stared, almost not believing what I was looking at and passed the booklet over to Sonnie.

"How to Pick up an Asian Guy or Girl. It sounds like a workshop on picking the right breed of dog."

"I know!"

"This is really racist."

"Yeah, I know."

"We should totally go."

"I KNOW!"

A couple of hours later, we found ourselves in a huge convention center ballroom that easily had four hundred people seated inside. It was packed. We took seats near the front and waited. Soon, it was past the hour, but no one was up front or leading the panel. We asked the room moderator what was happening, and they said that the panelists didn't show up. So we walked to the front of the room, picked up the mic, and took over the panel.

"Welcome to How to Pick Up an Asian Guy or Girl! How many of you actually think the name of this panel is offensive?"

The only hands being raised were by Asian American attendees, many of whom showed up for the same reason we did: to find out who would put on such a workshop. Within a few minutes, we turned the panel into an Asians in America Q&A session, taking down stereotypes and fighting racism one answer at a time.

Despite the cirque-like atmosphere and the occasional eye rolling in these panels, I had a revelation: we were talking about important issues of racism and stereotypes about Asian Americans (at an anime convention of all places!). I couldn't remember having that honest of a conversation with white strangers, ever. People wanted to connect, they just didn't know how. By disarming them, using some light humor, and allowing brutal honesty, we were able to make progress by holding conversations they were afraid to have anywhere else. So I took the show on the road: I started offering the same panel, as well as spin-off versions of it, at nearly every event since then. All across the country, we started holding anti-racism workshops, but it all began in a small room in Nashville, TN.

* * *

I don't know how many people grow up thinking that they'd like to be an activist. We're not even taught that it's an option—perhaps it's because activism isn't necessarily a career, but rather a trait that can be embodied in any vocation. Yet, as children, we're told that we can become leaders. Leadership, like activism, is a trait that can be taught, developed, and be ingrained into any career choice

Even though I grew up with a deep desire to help struggling communities, I never identified myself as an activist. I saw issues such as poverty and hunger as things to be addressed through acts of compassion; I didn't understand them to be symptoms of systemic injustices. When I was a kid, my sister and I used to beg our parents for spare change so we could give them to the homeless who sat outside of the McDonald's. We loved watching their eyes light up as they'd hold their hamburgers with both hands and take that first satisfying bite to fill their empty bellies. When Perla and I got involved with building orphanages, homes, and schools in the poorest areas of Mexico, we didn't think of our work as acts of activism. Maybe I just didn't connect with the label—it often had a negative connotation, especially when tied to someone who worked in entertainment or the arts.

I remember the backlash that the Dixie Chicks faced for denouncing the war in Iraq in 2003: thousands of people burned their albums, and so many death threats were made that they had to use metal detectors for every show on tour. People kept asking *How dare they?* There was an implication that entertainers needed to just shut up and play. There were accusations that their unpatriotic comments were only done for publicity's sake even though it hurt their career for years.

So even though I started the Slants to make a statement, it was originally a subversive and understated one. I didn't think of challenging stereotypes or providing representation as activism, but rather, as a form of expression. But shortly after we started playing, Asian American newspapers started writing articles on us, saying we were kicking down the doors of clubs to turn stereotypes upside down. Then, we started receiving letters from kids thanking us for simply existing, for giving them an Asian American band they could point to and a reason to be proud of their heritage. Some of them identified with my stories of being bullied and were encouraged that life could indeed be better. Whether we liked it or not, I knew we would be judged as role models in some kind of capacity. It was like those first moments on the Whisky stage where I felt like an imposter . . . an imposter with a responsibility to answer the calling no matter how I felt.

The panels at anime conventions solidified this idea in my mind that we needed to step up in terms of our responsibility as Asian Americans. We couldn't remain silent while we saw injustices.

We started getting more involved. Reports showed that Asian Americans students received some of the highest rates of racial harassment in schools,[13] so we volunteered with anti-bullying organizations. Almost a fifth of Asian American junior high and high school students were violently attacked, which paralleled my own experiences. When we learned that Vietnamese women had

---

[13] A UCLA study found that 54% of Asian American students experienced bullying in the classroom compared to 31.3% for whites, 38.4% for black students, and 34.3% for Hispanic students. In 2011, 17% of Asian American students were violently victimized (e.g., had a knife or gun pulled on them, were stabbed, cut, or physically assaulted). Fearing retribution, bullying of Asian Americans is often underreported by students. Asian American Psy chological Association. *Bullying & Victimization and Asian American Students*. 2012.

higher rates of cervical cancer than any other racial or ethnic group, we pledged all of the profits from our second album to fund research into why the disparities existed. And, when I saw how brutally the North Korean regime treated its citizens, we raised money and awareness to help refugees escape. I would donate signed bass guitars that I bought at pawn shops, volunteer as a spokesperson, and even auctioned myself off as a date a couple of times in order to raise money for the things we cared about. How could I not do anything? We had a platform and if there was a chance to effect change in some small way, it seemed like we needed to say and do something. Be it the Dixie Chicks, or many years later, Colin Kaepernick, I could now see what artists and athletes who were also activists were feeling: they didn't have a choice. Their conviction wouldn't allow them to shut up and play.

For years, I felt like I was swinging back and forth between two extremes: was I an artist or an activist? But then I came to the realization that they are not opposing things. They're often the same thing.

At its most basic level, art involves intentionality and creativity from the artist. And while motives and mediums may differ, art is a reflection and statement of the artist on the world. Activism is no different. In fact, the most successful movements in activism have always incorporated art, and most major revolutions in art involved some kind of activism. Rather than seeing the world as it is, artists and activists see the world for what it can be. Whether it's the backbeat of drums or the marching of protesters, both art and activism create change in our world. But while I was integrating these

ideas of justice into all areas of the Slants' work, nothing would prepare me for what was to come: a challenge that would shake me to
my very core and force me to confront what it meant to be an artist
or an activist. I didn't know it then, but I would soon be fighting for
the dignity of self-identification. That larger battle was sparked by
the most mundane activity: filing to register my trademark.

CHAPTER 5
PAGEANTRY

~

IT'S FUNNY HOW LIFE CAN TAKE A TOTALLY UN-EXPECTED DIRECTION depending on the people you let into your life. If Perla wasn't in my life, there's no question that I would have made vastly different choices. If I never met the Stivs, I wouldn't have moved to Portland and probably wouldn't have started the Slants. In my 20s, everything changed when I became friends with a lawyer.

It was 2009 when I met Spencer Trowbridge. He was the epitome of the overly cautious attorney. Nearly everything he said had some kind of clause, clarifying statement, or qualifier, even on topics not necessarily related to legal matters. In fact, one of his most commonly used phrases was "not necessarily," which he would use to explain the multiple counter narratives to any kind of statement he made. He had an office with Swider Haver, a boutique law firm overlooking Pioneer Square in downtown Portland.

To say Spencer was detailed oriented was an understatement—he was the guy who literally spent hours every day for months practicing every single note in Van Halen's "Eruption" guitar solo so he could perform it at his birthday party. If the "Well, actually . . ." meme were a living attorney, that might be Spencer. That's definitely the kind of quality you want in someone working on your legal case. On top of that, he was one of the nicest, most genuine, and encouraging people I've ever met in the entertainment industry.

I started working with Spencer because I needed help that year. One of the anime conventions cancelled their payment as we were flying home, which resulted in numerous fees for the bounced check. I passionately wanted to fight and make sure that the organizers knew what they had done was wrong. Much to Spencer's chagrin, I would call and email them and their attorneys to point out their numerous infractions, while I was waiting for him to draft and snail mail the newest response. I was so impatient for justice! Eventually, we settled with the group for a few hundred dollars. As ridiculous as it sounds, it cost me as much money to fight for our original payment as what we ended up with. But for me, it was about the principle. It didn't matter if I went broke fighting to right a wrong.

While working with Spencer, I offhandedly told him about something that had happened to some of our fans in Arizona. Apparently, they saw "The Slants" advertised at a venue in town, so they bought tickets. It turned out to be a different (non-Asian) band who was using our name. When they asked for a refund, management told them, "You bought tickets for a band called the Slants and we have a band called the Slants. You don't get a refund." Sadly, there was nothing that I could do but mail them some signed posters for their trouble. I knew sometimes bands had similar—or even the exact same name—and it just confused fans, but I didn't really know how to fix it. I remember "Blink" having to change their name to "Blink 182" because of an Irish electronica artist using the name, "Snakepit," a super group of former members from Guns n' Roses becoming "Slash's Snakepit" because another group in Los Angeles was already using the name. Of course, there are also the countless examples of bands who break up and individual members trying to tour under the banner of their former group's name.

"Have you ever thought about applying to register your trademark?" Spencer asked. "That might help with any confusion over these kinds of things. Besides, you guys have been touring all over and in the headlines. It's an important next step for your career."

"Well, I registered some copyrights, doesn't that help?" I was a little concerned because this sounded expensive. I knew he meant well and he even gave us a break on his hourly rates when working on the cancelled payment issue, but I was barely able to pay the bills as it was.

"Not necessarily . . . copyrights are different. They protect your music but don't do anything for your name." He sensed my hesitation before explaining, "If you're worried about the cost— don't be. It's only a few hundred bucks and in a few months, the whole thing will be over."

I reluctantly agreed. Things turned out a bit differently than imagined. How could I possibly know that eight years later, this simple act would take me all the way to the Supreme Court? This little trademark application would soon put me through a crash course in intellectual property (IP) law that would last longer than my undergraduate and graduate studies combined. That education was really helpful, especially since I noticed that many of the people writing articles or jumping into debates about trademark law didn't really understand how it worked. In fact, many articles mix up trademark with other kinds of intellectual property rights.

The three branches of intellectual property law are copyrights, patents, and trademarks. The United States Patent and Trademark Office (USPTO), known more simply as the Trademark Office, handles exactly what their name states: patents and trademarks.[14] The U.S. Copyright Office oversees copyrights. Copyright is usually focused on literary and artistic works, like books and music, whereas a trademark is related to items that define a brand, like a logo or tagline. Patents are for inventors, like *Back to the Future*'s Dr. Emmett Brown—though if he actually sought patents on his inventions, he could have licensed out his work and not have had to live in the garage of the Brown mansion in Hill Valley.

---

[14] Don't worry if my explanation of trademarks seems a bit confusing because I've seen journalists, law professors, and even federal judges screw up even the most basic IP law concepts.

Contrary to general understanding, a trademark is not granted by the government—only a registration is. Trademark rights are developed as a result of use in the marketplace. A registration is not necessary for someone to use a name, but it does grant valuable benefits and can protect someone if there's any confusion as to who actually holds the rights. In fact, one of the major reasons why trademark registration exists is to protect consumers from inadvertently buying the wrong product—sort of like when our fans bought tickets to the wrong concert. Registration helps reduce confusion because it helps avoid duplicate trademarks.

Music artists deal primarily with trademarks and copyrights: copyrights for their songs and trademarks for their name, logo, and other brand properties. It is so important in the industry that many record labels will refuse to sign an act if they are unable to secure a registration for their name. I once met an attorney who represented Destiny's Child. They told me that the group was originally called Destiny, but they were forced by Columbia Records to change their name since there were too many acts with a similar name. It seemed to work out for them, especially Beyoncé. As an aspiring artist with some marginal success, the trademark was an important next step for my career. That's why Spencer rightfully recommended that I apply for registration.

A few months after we submitted our application, Spencer called to let me know that there was a problem with the application. He told me, "The Trademark Office rejected your application because they said that the Slants is disparaging."

At first, I thought it was a practical joke, but I realized that when it came to legal affairs, Spencer was more like one of *Arrested Development*'s most deadpan characters:

Michael Bluth: Are you serious?

Wayne Jarvis: Almost always. I was once voted the worst audience participant Cirque Du Soleil ever had.[15]

I started thinking, Does disparaging mean what I think it means? No, that can't possibly be right . . . they can't possibly be that ignorant of what we're doing.

"Are they saying we're racist to Asian people?!" I blurted out.

"Disparaging . . . but yes, they're saying something to that effect."

"I didn't even know there was a law about that. There's all kinds of offensive stuff out there—I mean, look at the Washington Redskins, don't they have trademarks?" I started thinking about the many potentially offensive music group names out there: NWA, the Revolting Cocks, Anal Cunt, and Dick Delicious and the Tasty Testicles. Of course, there were also pornographic companies and comedy groups. How did they all get away with it if there really was a strict, puritanical law on trademarks? And why would they make a

---

[15] Hopefully, this does not make me Michael Bluth—or any Bluth for that matter.

fuss over our band when there were so many worse things registered? I asked, "What does the rejection actually say?"

Spencer proceeded to read me the small bit of law that would soon be forever ingrained into my mind: Section 2(a) of the Lanham Act.[16] The law said that trademarks could not be registered if they were considered "scandalous, immoral, or disparaging." But it isn't just what the general population considers to be disparaging—the government has to find that it is considered disparaging "to a substantial composite of the referenced group."

"We've just spent the last few years touring and doing anti-racism work across the country," I told him. "We worked with dozens of social justice organizations around the country, and our biggest group of supporters are Asian Americans. Who did the Trademark Office say was actually offended by our name?"

"No one."

"What do you mean no one? You just told me that they have to find a substantial composite!"

"No one. Not a single person. But they did cite UrbanDictionary.com and there are photos of Miley Cyrus pulling her eyes back in a slant-eye gesture."

"You gotta be kidding me . . ."

---

[16] Aka "The Disparagement provision"

"Nope, I'm looking at Miley Cyrus right now. Her picture is pretty offensive!"

He didn't have to tell me. Asian Twitter was already all over the controversy stirred up by the widely circulated photo of the teenage pop star pulling her eyes back, apparently mocking Asian Americans with that pose. In a classic sorry-not-sorry maneuver, she said she was simply making a "goofy face" and that people took her intentions out of context.

It should have been obvious to anyone that our situation was different. I asked Spencer to forward me the documents so I could see the rejection for myself. There it was in plain sight: a clear reference to UrbanDictionary.com. I couldn't believe the absurdity of it all. The federal government was using the kind of sources that would be rejected in a junior high classroom to deny me rights! I asked Spencer what we could do.

"I think there's just some kind of misunderstanding. It's probably some kind of government bureaucrat who doesn't get what you're doing. I think we should appeal. Anyone can see that you have wide support from your community, though not necessarily the examining attorney at the Trademark Office. We just need to make him aware of it."

We couldn't find any examples of people who successfully appealed a 2(a) rejection, but we did find plenty of instances where someone was using a reappropriated term. Some of the more recognized trademarks included the television show Queer Eye for the Straight Guy and Technodyke, a popular queer-centric women's media channel. I also found hundreds of other registered trade-marks that included the term "slant" but weren't subjected to the accusation of being scandalous, immoral, or disparaging like we were. None of them were rejected under the same law even though they had similar names. I also thought it was kind of strange that it seemed everyone who registered some kind of variation for the trademark on "slant" didn't appear to be Asian.

The next step was to find other people who were also wrongfully rejected so we could learn from their experience: Dykes on Bikes, a pro-lesbian motorcycle club, and Heeb, a Jewish media company. With the former, the Trademark Office deemed "dyke" to be disparaging to lesbians, claiming that the term wasn't em-braced or used in a reappropriated way. With the latter, they claimed "Heeb" was highly disparaging to persons of Jewish descent when the word was printed on t-shirts (the magazine was fine though, and they received a trademark registration for that service). Eventually, Dykes on Bikes overcame their refusal (after many years of fighting), so we decided to follow their legal strategy. But they didn't win on appeal, so it didn't set a precedent; they overwhelmed the Trade-mark Office with evidence and convinced the director of the Trademark Office to withdraw the rejection before an appeals board could examine it.

Heeb Media didn't have as much luck. While they had a lot of momentum, including the support of many prominent Jewish or-ganizations and leaders, they ultimately lost their appeal. They gave up the fight pretty early on because they were afraid that pressing the case might jeopardize their other existing trademark registrations.

As we looked at other people who tried to appeal a rejection for being disparaging, we found a common pattern. The applicant would gather expert reports and letters from community leaders to show broad support. The applicants making an appeal never attacked the law itself, just how it was interpreted in their specific cases. They asked for a more careful review of the evidence because they wanted their community's voice to be heard. We followed suit.

Over the next few months, I started reaching out to organizations that we worked with throughout Oregon. We collected legal declarations (the equivalent of a testimony or affidavit) from respected leaders in the Asian American community. We also provided evidence that the band had performed at the largest Asian American festivals in the country, we gave examples of other groups who had been using "slant" in a reappropriated way (like the Slant Film Festival), and we showed how nearly every Asian American media publication in the country had celebrated the work of our band.[17]

Spencer thought it was inconceivable that someone would seek to register a trademark that disparaged his or her own ethnic background and stated that in the argument. We felt confident in

---

[17] Shout out to Angry Asian Man, Disgrasian, TaiwaneseAmerican.org, the Asian Reporter, Asian American Press, Slant Eye for the Round Eye, and Asian Week for covering us in our first few months as a band!

the appeal. We worked tirelessly to ensure that the views of actual Asian Americans across the country were included. Unlike the Trademark Office, we didn't use questionable wiki sources and photos of Miley Cyrus. These were actual voices from the affected community. How could they dispute that?

In December 2010, just twenty days after we filed our appeal, the Trademark Office responded with another rejection, again citing UrbanDictionary.com. This time, they also referred to a misleading article that suggested my keynote appearance at the Asian American Youth Leadership Conference (AAYLC) was cancelled because of our name. I couldn't believe it: anyone could look up the AAYLC website and see photos of me speaking there and our band featured as entertainment. How could they present such an obvious falsehood? Why wasn't there any accountability for that kind of misinformation? The rejection sent me into a depression.

I was sulking, thinking about the few thousand dollars I had just wasted trying to register our trademark. I was still trying to personally pay off the loans I took out in order to produce our band's most recent release, *Pageantry*. One of the downsides to managing your own band is that you get all of the bills when there's no money in the band's account. The debt was threatening to drown me. I guess what they say is right: the captain goes down with the ship.

I was in Charlottesville, VA when all of this was happening—that's where Lizzie lived. We started dating after hanging out in Nashville, Chicago, and Huntsville—places where neither of us actually lived but where we both happened to be working at conventions. After seeing her in Huntsville, AL, I started sending her postcards and letters from every town we played in while I was on tour. Eventually, we found ourselves in love but living on opposite corners of the country. I couldn't afford to visit her. It's hard to understand how difficult a long-distance relationship is unless one you've been in one. And the person who knew me better than anyone else also knew what it was like: Perla. While Perla was dating her husband Dez, she lived in Riverside, CA while he lived in Newark, NJ. She only moved in with him a few months before their wedding—having been in a similar situation, she was sympathetic to my cause and wanted to help out.

Perla had recently started working for an airline. As an employee, she received "buddy passes," or extremely discounted tickets meant for friends and family that would cost little more than the taxes and fees. Perla gave me almost twenty of them so Lizzie and I could visit each other on a regular basis. There were no direct flights from Portland to Charlottesville, so I would usually need two or more flights followed by a two-hour bus ride. For me, it was worth the effort. Sometimes, I'd surprise Lizzie by flying across the country overnight and then asking her out to dinner in person after she got out of her classes at the local university.

On one of these trips, Lizzie wanted me to meet her father. She had started reconnecting with him again shortly after we started dating and thought it might be a good idea.

"Hi Simon, I'm looking forward to meeting you. I heard you like sushi, is that right?" he asked on the phone.

"Yep, the sushi in this town is pretty good. A lot better than the dim sum for sure." It's true, maybe it's the combination of being near the water and a distinct lack of Chinese population in Charlottesville, VA, but here's an inside tip if you ever visit: avoid the dim sum.

We made plans to visit a favorite sushi restaurant of ours. As I drove us there, I was briefed about the man I'd be meeting. I learned a bit about his past, how he used to play drums in his younger years, and how he was now selling computers for Hewlett Packard. I also learned that he spent a pretty good amount of time traveling and was a bit more conservative than her mother, whom I had already met.

I pulled up to the sushi restaurant, which was nestled into a parking lot next to a pawnshop, between the main downtown area and the university. The inside reflected many other sushi restaurants: dark wood furniture with paper panels, a brightly lit and chilled sushi bar, and tatami mats near each of the booths. Like most other sushi restaurants in the U.S., it was probably owned by a Korean family.

Jim, the father, was a large man in his sixties. He had thinning grey hair and strong features. He wore a light navy blazer with beige slacks and had an air of confidence. He smiled and extended a firm handshake.

We sat down and without opening his menu, he declared, "Well Simon, you're the expert here, so why don't you order for all of us?"

Unsure of what he meant or what he intended with that kind of a statement, I replied, "Well, I'm not sure what you like or don't like, so how about we all pick out a couple of different things, then share?"

"OK, but go ahead and order in your language."

At this point, I felt conflicted. I wanted to make a good first impression, but at the same time, I wanted to address the fact that I was just as American as he. Almost every Asian American experiences this moment multiple times in their life: people look at us and assume that we're from another country; in their eyes we don't belong here. It was almost as if I were back in elementary school again, being asked to be the sole cultural representative of the most diverse continent on Earth. Despite being here for over two centuries, Asians are often still seen as foreigners. Hence, why some of us get frustrated when we're asked, "Where are you from?" or "Where did you learn English?" Yo, we belong here too.

Asian immigrants began settling in the United States in the late 1700s. Larger waves, especially the Chinese laborers, started migrating during the 1800s, and helped build the infrastructure for the country to expand to the West Coast. Yet, we've always been seen as a temporary work force that isolated ourselves into Chinatowns because we didn't want to assimilate into American culture. However, Chinatowns weren't created because we wanted them—the Chinese (and later, other Asian immigrants regardless of country of origin) were forced to live in ethnic enclaves because we were not welcome anywhere else. We were treated like vermin, only useful for building railroads, doing laundry, or providing cheap labor for jobs that others weren't willing to do. Laws like the Chinese Exclusion Act of 1882, the World War II incarceration of Americans of Japanese descent, and immigration quotas on Asians show the long history of treating Asians as unwanted outsiders.

So, even if there is no ill intent, these constant reminders that we don't belong may sting. They create pain similar to when someone accidentally bumps into your sprained ankle. Sure, they didn't mean to, and they probably didn't even know about the ankle, but it hurts nonetheless. I didn't have the social justice vocabulary to describe what I was feeling at the time, but we now call this a microaggression, a slight or indignity that is pushed on others, regardless of intent.

The funny thing is that we had been speaking in English the entire time. The menu was also in English (there wasn't even Japanese text next any of the items, not that I could read that anyway). Nothing about the restaurant suggested that there was anything non-English about it. Besides, he didn't even know my heritage. How could he know what "my language" actually was?

I decided to give him another pass, but with an explanation.

I said, "I was born and raised in San Diego, so English actually is my main language. My parents are from China and Taiwan, and while those places have great food, they're not known for their sushi. Sushi is really Japanese."

I looked over at my partner, who gave me an approving look: good, friendly, safe answer. I didn't call him a racist, I didn't get irate. And I even provided a mini-lesson on how these were all distinctly different cultures. Ten points for Gryffindor![18]

"Yeah, but they're all just the same, right?"

At this point, the waitress came by for our order. We learned that she was from northern China, so technically, I could have ordered using Mandarin if I wanted to. But obviously, that wasn't really the issue.

Throughout life, I've experienced moments just like the sushi incident. Experiences that reside in the amorphous zone that some people don't consider to be legitimate racism. Systemic issues that are demeaning, like having some non-Asian bureaucrat tell me what words are appropriate for my community, fall into those murky areas. The problem is that these microaggressions compound exponentially with other demeaning experiences that involve institutional uses of power. But when people don't see pitchforks and burning crosses, they don't believe it to be a serious enough transgression. Ironically, this "racism scale" is often set by people who never experience racism themselves so we can see why disagreements on what actually constitutes harm are divided along racial lines.

Most polls and research show that whites in America overwhelmingly do not believe racism is a significant problem in our country. However, most people of color do. Whites tend to believe

---

[18] In all actuality, I'm a part of House Slytherin. But don't hold it against me— at least I'm not a Hufflepuff.

that racism belongs to the distant past: slavery and maybe segregation if they're feeling especially generous. Many unconsciously believe that racism disappeared during some moment between the "I Have a Dream" speech and the inauguration of President Obama. For these folks, the discrimination that people of color face is our fault: we are not trying hard enough to overcome institutional barriers or we are not grateful for the rights given to us. And according to many of these folks, we only make things worse by trying to talk about racism as a current issue.

Interestingly, no other social issue makes whites want to drop down the cone of silence like racism. Marijuana laws? We can debate this. Rectal cancer? Let's race for a cure! Imagine if we could only solve the world's problems by ignoring them like we do with racism: stop talking about hunger, and food will appear in the most impoverished areas! Unlike other issues though, systemic racism was created by and for whites, who continue to benefit from it whether they choose to address it or not.

We have to acknowledge that racism is part of a shameful history in the United States. Our country was built on the genocide of Native Americans, the African slave trade, and railroads constructed by indentured servants from China. Whenever subjugated minorities challenged the dominant group, our country resorted to depriving people of basic rights and dignity: for Asian communities this meant laws banning the Chinese and incarceration camps for those of Japanese descent. But instead of educating students on these egregious events so we don't repeat them, we simply pretend that none of this happened and that the United States is the shining beacon of freedom in the world.

At least we have sushi. While I wasn't going to make a fuss, I certainly wasn't going to order it in Mandarin like some kind of on-demand entertainment. I ordered in *my language*. I ordered in English.

* * *

Christmas was a big deal to Lizzie's family. They had deeply ingrained traditions like opening presents while in pajamas first thing in the morning and watching a marathon of *A Christmas Story*. The "fa-ra-ra-ra-rah" scene in the Chinese restaurant always made my skin crawl, but it was also nice having some kind of celebration. Everyone in the family was so sweet; I would be reluctant to bring up things like being called an Oriental or weird questions involving chopsticks. For most of my life, I've had to juggle whether to point things out or not, figuring out if people wanted to be educated on the nuances of respectful cultural exchange or if they would just be defensive, annoyed, or embarrassed . . . unless we had solid rapport, it was usually a combination of the latter.

After opening our restaurant, my family didn't do Christmas—not in the traditional sense at least. While most families identify December with time off to spend with loved ones, we always saw it as a time to double down on work: the restaurant was busier and more opportunities would open up. My dad also worked at Albertsons as a side hustle to help supplement our income when business wasn't doing well, so he always picked up extra shifts during the holidays. Holiday pay in a union job often meant double or triple pay. While he worked, my siblings and I would watch the Star Wars trilogy back to back. In our family, working hard for other people so that they'd have an easier time was how we said, "I love you." As a kid, that meant getting to watch two Death Stars blow up in one day.[19]

Now I was experiencing love in a different kind of way: opening presents up next to a fireplace while Jean Shepherd's movie was on repeat in the background. I could almost time it: every 102 minutes, the family would be eating "Chinese turkey" in a Chop Suey restaurant. "'Tis the season, to be jorry, fa-ra-ra-ra-rah, ra-ra-ra-rah." I never said anything about the movie. I knew it was made in a different time and experienced much differently by people who didn't grow up working in a Chinese restaurant, but it was one of those microaggressions where pointing it out would stir up more conflict than it was worth. Was this like fighting for a trademark registration?

Over the holidays, I focused on spending time with Lizzie and her family and friends baking cookies, playing board games, and watching marathons of holiday films. I genuinely loved it. It felt lighter to not think about the legal situation at all. As I boarded the

---

[19] You might be thinking, "What about that third destructive weapon in *Star Wars: The Force Awakens?*" Well, we only had the original trilogy back then. Also, Starkiller Base was a terra-formed planet and not technically a death star class mobile space station.

plane back to Portland, I made the decision to just drop the case. It wasn't worth it: even with a generous discount on Spencer's well-deserved attorney fees, I was barely able to afford the fight. I had more important things to focus on.

I figured that we could always just change our name or continue on without a trademark registration, like we had done before. As I mentioned earlier, trademark holders don't need a registration to use their names, slogans, or logos. They even still get some protection for their intellectual property. The registration just offers an enhanced set of benefits, like providing nationwide notice of ownership (otherwise your rights are limited to the geographic regions where you've used your mark). It helps prevent others from diluting or stealing a brand identity. It's one of the reasons why even if the efforts to cancel offensive trademark registrations for sports teams were successful, none of those teams would have been forced to change their names. Some legal experts have argued that their brand equity would be significant enough to give them robust legal trademark protection, while others have said that the loss of the registration would be significant enough to warrant dropping their names. But no one really knows since a registration has never been cancelled after it was issued. The courts haven't weighed in on it much at all.

But I wasn't thinking about any of this. I was just looking at the ever-increasing legal bills. What was the point in fighting for a band name if we couldn't even afford to do the work of a band? Yes, it was degrading to have the Trademark Office use UrbanDictionary.com and other questionable sources to trump voices from the Asian American community, but I didn't consider that my war to wage.

Nobody starts a band thinking that they're going to go to the Supreme Court. Legal proceedings are slow and expensive, and the results aren't guaranteed. It's hard to think about creating social change when you are struggling just to keep the lights on. Most of the time, people are set on that path through the judiciary system because of factors beyond their control. Often, they just want to enjoy the dignity of their basic rights.[20]

In early 1900s, the United States passed a number of anti-miscegenation laws[21] in order to preserve racial purity. These were laws that criminalized interracial marriage and were primarily used to target Black Americans, though other racial groups (including Asian Americans) felt the impact as well. However, the only "race" that the government wanted to keep pure was the white race: laws did not prevent people of color from marrying each other. The number of these Jim Crow-era laws applicable to Asians doubled

---

[20] It should be mentioned some organizations or individuals deliberately look for "test cases" in order to use overturn the law, set new precedent, or to clarify the intent of a law. These substantial efforts originally won some of the greatest victories in civil rights law. But in recent years, they've been used to undo civil rights.

[21] Stein, Edward. "Past and Present Proposed Amendments to the United States Constitution regarding Marriage." Washington Law Review 82, no. 3 (January 2004): 611-85.

from 1910 to 1950.[22] Unlike many other forms of legal segregation, these laws targeted relationships desired by both groups, including whites. They have arguably spanned the longest time frame of any modern form of statutory racial discrimination.

Loving v. Virginia, the Supreme Court case that declared anti-miscegenation laws, or bans on interracial marriages, unconstitutional began when Virginia police raided the Lovings home in the early morning hours of July 11, 1958. Despite the fact that the couple had their marriage certificate hanging on the bedroom wall, the state charged them with a felony punishable with a prison sentence of up to five years. The couple pled guilty and were forced to leave their home state. They appealed five years later only because they wanted to visit their families together. The Supreme Court made a unanimous decision for the Lovings in 1967—nine years after the couple was arrested in their own home—but anti-miscegenation laws remained on the books until 2000, over forty years later. Of course, even though they won, the Lovings still had to deal with the day-to-day challenges of living in an area that deeply resented their actions. Little did they know, but their act of courage would open doors for other marginalized groups nearly fifty years later.

---

[22] Karthikeyan and Chin's Asian American Law Journal piece, *Preserving Racial Identity: Population Patterns and the Application of Anti-Miscegenation Statutes to Asian Americans, 1910-1950* explores these issues brilliantly.

In 2015, the Supreme Court heard another controversial case involving bans on marriage: *Obergefell v. Hodges*.[23] This challenge to laws against same-sex marriage consolidated six separate lower-court cases representing sixteen same-sex couples, seven of their children, a widower, an adoption agency, and a funeral director. Many of those cases had originated a decade before they reached the Supreme Court as well. In each of these instances, some version of "separate but equal" existed. They were the embodiment of a system that would make the oppressed feel guilty or burdened for wanting to push back. *What's the big deal? You can still ride the bus, even if it's in the back. You can still love whoever you want, you just can't get a marriage certificate. You can still use a band name, you just don't get the trademark. If you want to change things, you're going to have to pay for it in more ways than you can ever imagine, and you still might lose.*

In many ways, government regulations are designed to uphold the status quo. Who was I to appeal to the government over something as trivial as a trademark registration? This wasn't about the right to love. Freedom of expression was important to me but not *that* important. I had already spent more time, money, and energy than I wanted to. We tried and failed. The lack of a trademark registration didn't affect me that much—I could always change the name of the band. And fighting the U.S. government (rather than an anime convention who cancelled their payment) seemed much

---

[23] Fortunately, the Supreme Court ruled in favor of Obergefell, requiring states to recognize and license marriage between two people of the same sex.

more daunting. Besides, my priorities were shifting, and I had an upcoming tour to focus on.

CHAPTER 6
HOW THE WICKED LIVE

IT WAS NOW 2011. A new year. I had just gotten back into town again after spending the holidays in Charlottesville with Lizzie and her family. Maybe it was the relentless marathon of Christmas cheer by way of Turner Classic films, or just taking a small break from the trademark stuff, but I felt better. I came to the conclusion that it wasn't worth continuing our fight against the Trademark Office. It was exhausting, both emotionally and financially. Spencer was trying to help by keeping his legal fees at a flat rate rather than billing me hourly, but when I stared at the newest invoice of $1,500 in my email, I only felt despair.

I didn't have a regular day job—I was laid off during the summer because the recession was impacting the nonprofit where I worked. Conveniently for them, they laid me off *after* I wrapped up final fundraising events and brought in over a few hundred thousand dollars. I was struggling to make ends meet, only surviving off of the combination of unemployment benefits and any cash I made under the table when playing gigs with the band. Lizzie and I moved in together, and I was helping with her expensive medical bills. How could I be thinking about a costly legal battle over a trademark when someone I loved needed help?

I told Spencer that I needed to drop the case. *I really appreciate your help, but I can't afford to keep fighting this thing.* It was true. After investing in our new album, the band didn't have very much money left, so I was funding the Trademark appeal with maxed out credit cards and ever-increasing debt. I was already skipping meals, but I refused to skip on Lizzie's prescriptions.

"Simon, I understand but you have to know that this case is a lot bigger than your band. Look at that newest refusal, they are straight up lying about the band and just trying to use whatever they can to make you give up."

"Well, I think it's working."

Spencer started telling me about a conversation that he had with one of his mentors, a law professor named Keith Aoki. While Aoki specialized in intellectual property law, he was also a respected voice in racial justice and immigration reform. Aoki pointed out the potential larger impacts of our case—namely, that we had an opportunity to address the disparate impact of the law being used against us.

Disparate impact in the legal system refers to unintentional discrimination that is caused by an otherwise facially neutral policy.[24] In other words, the focus is primarily on the impact of the law rather than the intention behind it. For example, the New York City Police Department implemented stop-and-frisk policies, the practice of temporarily detaining and searching "suspicious"[25]civilians. Over 685,000 people were stopped in 2011, during the height of this policy. Studies showed that 90% of the people stopped were young black and brown men even though whites had significantly higher rates of possessing contraband.[26] Despite claiming to be facially neutral, New York City's stop-and-frisk policies disproportionately impacted young people of color in practice.[27]

---

[24] A law that seems neutral as written. In 2014, The Supreme Court ruled that even facially neutral, evenly applied policies may be discriminatory (*Young v. UPS*)

[25] Read: black and brown people

[26] Mason, Melanie. "Stop-and-frisk's effect on crime is hotly debated. Its disproportionate impact on minorities is not." *Los Angeles Times*. September 26, 2016. https://www.latimes.com/politics/la-na-pol-crime-debate-factcheck-20160926-snap-story.html

[27] In 1968, The Supreme Court reached a decision in *Terry v. Ohio* allowing a "*Terry* frisk." This provided the legal justification for NYC's stop-and-frisk policy. In 2014, the Second Circuit Court unanimously declared that New York's policy was used in an unconstitutional manner via *Floyd v. City of New York*. The attention brought by that case (thanks ACLU!) helped provide a turning point, but it took

In a truly just system, laws would be judged on their impact as well as their intention. With Section 2(a) of the Lanham Act, Aoki believed that the "scandalous, immoral, and disparaging" component was being disproportionately applied to minority identities, especially people of color and the LGBTQ community. Because marginalized groups have a tendency to use reappropriated terms, it made us prime targets for the disparagement provision. Aoki believed that the law was possibly unconstitutional under the First Amendment as well. He wanted to get more directly involved with our case, but he was struggling with a prolonged illness. His insights on this definitely gave me a lot to think about.

Meanwhile, Spencer challenged me to look up trademark registrations for Asian American slurs or other charged phrases. He said that not only were the rejections inconsistent, but more often than not, the people being rejected under 2(a) were the ones trying to use stigmatizing labels in a self-empowering or even mocking way. It was true, registrations for the terms violently used against me as a kid (chink, jap, gook) were all registered by non-Asians.[28]

---

a lot of community organizing and new leadership to really effect change, which shows the limits of the courts can or can't do.

[28] Can we also take a moment to recognize that "slant" on the "racism Richter scale" would barely register a 2.0? There are far worse terms. Besides, people usually use the phrase "slant-eye." And if "slant" was as inherently bad as the Trademark Office claimed, why did they approve it hundreds of times, especially to non-Asians?

"This is really important. I know it's hard to pay for this, so I'm willing to do this pro bono. You don't have to pay me for my time I'm just asking that you help cover the filing fees or other legal costs and that you help me with some of the legal work."

He then told me about a conversation he had with Mark Shiner, the examining attorney at the Trademark Office. Spencer called him to see what was going on with our application and to talk candidly about any misunderstandings.

"It's coming from above," Shiner explained. "They're afraid of political controversy. If you want this objection lifted, you're going to need more experts—like a dictionary expert. You will need a national survey of Asian Americans. And you need to deal with this article I found that says the Slants' concert was cancelled at that Asian Youth rally. If you can get all of that, then I don't see why we can't make this all go away."

This became my homework. Spencer assigned this to me as my to do list. "You're the one with all of the connections. You've been working with these communities doing all kinds of work for them so maybe you can ask for a favor in return now."

I felt guilty for wanting to walk away. How could I give up while knowing that the Trademark Office was putting other artists, nonprofits, and small business owners of color through this long, expensive, and degrading process? Spencer seemed really passionate about this. I trusted he would help me, but I was intimidated by what was being asked of me. Where could I find all of these experts in such a short time? I couldn't even afford to pay Spencer, how was

I going to hire academics who could produce all of that work? It was overwhelming.

It's no wonder that most people don't appeal a decision when they're rejected for possible disparagement: the cost and the amount of work could bury a person. Most of the applications being filed at the Trademark Office are from small business owners who don't have the resources to fight. The system is set up for them to fail. Unlike criminal law, if your trademark is interpreted to be disparaging by an examiner at the Trademark Office, you are guilty until proven innocent. And the receipts show that no one has ever been proven to be innocent.[29]

If someone is looking for something offensive, they'll find it. I already knew that they didn't actually have to find a single person for proof: the rule was that it "may disparage," whether it actually was or not. "But we're not offensive to ourselves!" is not a good enough defense, even if the government is using flimsy sources. It was humiliating and demeaning that our work with community leaders fighting racism across the country counted for nothing while some joke website that anyone could edit would be considered a reliable authority on the matter.

For the past year, our battle with the Trademark Office was kept a secret. We didn't want anyone to think that we were being opportunistic about it. I also worried that having the government

---

[29] Our legal models, HEEB and DYKES ON BIKES, never shook the claim that they were disparaging.

accusing us as racist towards Asian Americans would hurt our work in the community. However, we needed to rally a lot of support in a very short amount of time, and we needed to keep the Trademark Office accountable for their actions. So, I wanted to make it clear that we were going to make it public.

"OK, let's do this. But let's blow the doors open on this. Everyone should know what's happening."

* * *

I was now speaking to Spencer multiple times a day. I had him on speed dial, and I sent more messages to him than everyone else in my life combined. Losing my job was a blessing in disguise: while I sorely missed having a regular paycheck and health benefits, the extra time allowed me to spend over fifty hours a week on our legal case. I didn't think my parents would understand, so I didn't even tell them about this. I ramped up booking and consulting work to take care of the bills, unemployment benefits helped cover the rest. The rest of the band showed some slight concern but weren't interested in helping with the case. It wasn't their battle. They just wanted to play music.

Whenever I wasn't playing a show, I was pretty much glued to my laptop. I sent messages to every organization that I worked with over the years, trying to see if they'd be willing to help us out by filing a legal declaration. It often meant long phone calls or presentations explaining the nuances of trademark law and why their involvement was important. I also combed through legal archives and read every law review article I could find about trademarks, especially around the disparagement clause.

Even though Spencer was writing the actual legal argument, I wanted to be able to personally answer every question possible about our case. I had piles of textbooks, dictionaries, and articles in every room of the house. Soon, I knew the names of almost every applicant, attorney, and expert who worked on trademark cases involving the disparagement provision. It was almost ironic how badly my parents wanted one of their kids to become a lawyer—I was pretty much doing all of the same work now. And, just like Spencer, I wasn't getting paid for it either. I was hoping that all of that research would pay off, that it might provide a clue as to our next step.

The Dykes on Bikes case was my gold standard since they actually received their trademark registration. As a lesbian nonprofit organization that advocated for gay rights, it seemed absurd that the Trademark Office would reject them under Section 2(a), but they did, saying that "dyke" was scandalous to lesbians. Dykes on Bikes only received their registration after petitioning the director of the Trademark Office, while providing a barrage of expert reports and testimonials.[30] As I combed through their case, I found contact information for an expert who understood the power of reappropriation: Dr. Ron Butters of Duke University. Dr. Butters was one of the top linguistics experts in the country. He was the former president of the International Association of Forensic

---

[30] Dykes on Bikes succeeded because the Trademark Office withdrew its rejection instead of reviewing their appeal. This meant no legal precedent was created.

Linguists, on the advisory board of the New Oxford American Dictionary, and testified before Congress on a regular basis. I wrote him an email pleading for his help, and he graciously agreed.

Then, I started looking for organizations that could conduct surveys using the scientific method. I believed it was really important for any survey to be statistically valid—I didn't want our evidence to be frivolously rejected by the government. I found two professors who specialized in that work. Charlton McIlwain and Stephen Caliendo had published extensively on statistical surveys, race, and inequality in America. Congress used their work on multiple occasions. They were perfect!

As I emailed the professors, I was nervous and excited. It was the first time that a survey would be used to appeal a false claim of disparagement. Even though we had almost no budget to provide (the original estimate they gave me was over $250,000), they agreed to do it pro bono because they believed it was important to have Asian Americans weighing in on the issue of race, something nearly unheard of in national debates at the time.[31]

I was sure that the survey would help tip the scales. However, the professors were a bit more reserved. Working with the government over the years gave them a different view of things.

---

[31] Frank Wu tried highlighting this with his 2002 book *Yellow: Race in America Beyond Black and White*. Despite being the fastest growing group in the country, not much has changed since then. In 2017, TIME published an article titled *Asian Americans and Pacific Islanders Are Often Ignored*.

Before conducting the survey, their research found that the problem with how the Trademark Office approached the law was one of power. Professor McIlwain said that the Trademark Office was "fully embodying the White power structure . . . [they get] to determine who controls the meaning of a term that Whites created to denigrate APIs. That is F****** maddening!" He suggested that we might approach this as a civil rights case later down the road since it appeared that the Trademark Office was singling out ethnic minority groups from being able to reclaim terms. But Spencer wanted to maintain a narrow focus on the intellectual property law issues. He believed that our appeals process would be fine without bringing in constitutional arguments, which could potentially dilute the strength of our appeal.

With the linguistics expert and the survey confirmed, things were looking very good. No one, not even Dykes on Bikes, had an expert survey in their corner to aid with a trademark registration. This gave us some hope. It was our last chance to appeal directly to the examining attorney before things would be escalated to the Trademark Trial and Appeal Board (TTAB); we wanted everything just right. Of course, we still needed address the misleading article about our concert being cancelled.

In their second refusal, the Trademark Office dug up an old article that referenced an event described by a blog on Myspace.com. The article claimed our concert and my keynote speech at the Asian American Youth Leadership Conference (AAYLC) were cancelled due to massive outrage that our band's name was offensive. The Trademark Office examiner said it was the most damning the piece of evidence being used against us. In fact, it was the only thing that he had indicating any Asian Americans took issue with our name at all. Of course, that wasn't the complete story.

The AAYLC is an annual event that brings together high school students from throughout the Portland Metro area for a series of workshops on identity, celebrations of pan-Asian heritage, and a fair to meet representatives from colleges and universities. Each year, there is a committee of volunteers who helps put together the event. In 2009—one year before we applied for our trademark registration—they selected me as their keynote speaker, thinking my work with the Slants was appropriate for their "Aspire to Inspire" theme. They also wanted the band to play since it would be new and exciting. Unfortunately, having a loud rock band play at the event proved a bit too edgy for some of the elders on the committee, and they opted for a "safer" option instead.

There seemed to be some misunderstanding about what actually happened, so I set up a meeting with a member of the AAYLC steering committee, a local minister and community organizer named Joseph Santos-Lyons. We reviewed all of the email exchanges and notes from conversations around having the Slants perform. He recalled there weren't any formal complaints received—in fact, the biggest concerns were shared by Portland Catholic High School over the secular nature of our lyrics. In the committee meeting, they noted that hosting a concert wasn't logistically feasible with their limited budget that year, so they decided to have students create short films around the theme and showed those instead.

In a short, but powerful legal declaration, Reverend Santos-Lyons directly addressed the objections of the Trademark Office by stating, "The decision was not in any way based on the band's name." He also further explained:

There were no formal complaints or protests over the Slants' name by other event sponsors, supporters, or members of the Asian American community. Simon Tam and the Slants remained involved with the youth leadership conference event as sponsors and their names were printed in the 2009 program guide without hesitation. Even after printing the Slants' name in the program, no complaints were received.

The AAYLC chair also remarked that the decision to replace me as speaker was a mistake since having someone from the Slants as a keynote would have elevated the experience for all of the Asian American students involved. To cap it off, we also sent copies of later programs that prominently listed the Slants as performers and me as their keynote speaker to further prove that this was not an issue in our community, especially not to the AAYLC. We refuted the strongest piece of evidence from the Trademark Office: unlike the Myspace article they referred to, this all came directly from the organization itself.

The thousands of emails and calls that I was sending out, combined with a long history of working with our community, were finally paying off. People were willing to go out of their way to help us by writing legal declarations, doing research, or helping us where they could. It was so encouraging to have Asian Americans from across the country reach out in solidarity. We were finally making some real progress and felt confident about it. Even a board of Asian American leaders appointed by the Governor of Oregon wrote a letter in our support (The Oregon Commission of Asian Pacific Islander Affairs).

Everything fell into place a few weeks before our filing deadline. We had everything that the Trademark Office asked for and then some! More important than all of the evidence we amassed, I felt genuine solidarity with my community of activists. They supported our anti-racism efforts, our battle for identity, and our catchy synth pop music.

Dr. Butters came back with his linguistics report. After conducting some extensive research, he found that *slant* was an obscure racial slur even during the height of its abuse. More often than not, he found contemporary uses of the term to be self-empowering to Asian Americans.

He wrote:

> While dictionaries may continue to label slant as a pejorative term, this is readily explained by the fact that dictionaries in general lag somewhat in updating entries with respect to linguistic change, and, particularly with the treatment of ethnic labels a desire to do nothing that could possibly provoke controversy. Moreover, the evidence of the history of entries in New Oxford American Dictionary

supports the contention that the empirical data demonstrate: even if some Asian Americans in the last century may have felt slant to be an objectionable epithet, the term has been reclaimed by contemporary Asian Americans for use as an informal term representing racial and ethnic pride.

To demonstrate how obscure *slant* was for a racial slur, he showed that the 2010 edition of the New Oxford American Dictionary recognized the amelioration of the word to the extent that the editors removed the reference to offensiveness from its definition. In fact, not even the printed version of Urban Dictionary listed *slant* as an offensive term for Asian Americans.

A couple of days later, we received the results of our survey that put all other doubts to rest. The professors found that only 16% of Asian Americans found *slant* to be disparaging. Moreover, when survey respondents learned that the use of *slant* was by an Asian American group, that number fell to only 8%. This was significant because, according to the rules, the Trademark Office could only reject a registration if a "substantial composite" of Asian Americans thought it was disparaging. The problem was that no one knew what constituted a "substantial composite." The only guideline was from another case involving the potential cancellation of the Washington Redskins' trademark registration (*Pro Football, Inc. v. Harjo*).[32] There,

---

[32] *Pro-Football, Inc. v. Harjo* was a case where Suzan Harjo and other Native American activists petitioned the Trademark Trial and Appeal Board to cancel six trademark registrations owned by Pro-Football, Inc. (for the Washington Redskins) based on the disparagement provision of the Lanham Act. A federal appeals

a sample survey showed that 36.6% of Native Americans found the term *redskin* to be disparaging. In that case, the Trademark Office argued that 36.6% did not constitute a substantial composite. The range in the survey on *slant* was well below 36.6%. Even in a worst-case scenario, we were still less than half of that number.

The survey also challenged some of our own assumptions that elders in our community would be more likely to take issue with our band name due to generational differences. We discovered that age, geography, and education were not a substantial factor in determining if people found our name offensive. The professors wrote:

> Given that language usage and meanings change over time, it would be reasonable to expect that people of different age cohorts might have different opinions about a term like SLANTS. However, these results demonstrate that age is not a factor. Given that the mean age of the survey respondents was thirty, we compared those thirty and under with those over thirty. Doing so showed not statistically significant difference.

With the two expert reports and the many legal declarations, our case file ballooned into a massive stack of paper. I started getting worried because of how much it would cost to scan the documents.

---

court rejected the cancellation, claiming that the Trademark Office lacked substantial evidence to find disparagement and that the petitioners waited too long to file a claim (the doctrine of laches).

I was barely able to keep up with the bills, and the idea of paying for something like a digital scan in addition to the legal filing fees made my stomach turn.

Spencer wanted to something much more symbolic. He told me, "The amount of evidence is ridiculous. We need a special box just to contain everything. I think we should pay for shipping this box over to the examining attorney so he'll have to hand scan every one of these pages. Maybe then, he can feel the weight of the Asian American community."

That level of bureaucratic subversiveness was unreal, I had to go halfsies on that! I started the Slants because I wanted to challenge assumptions about Asian Americans, it was always about asserting our own approach to things. I was grateful to have a trusted friend working in the trenches with me who understood that: we wanted to disrupt the system by adopting unexpected, symbolic tactics. That was the point of reappropriating the Slants to begin with! This fell right in line with that philosophy.

Reappropriation, or the process of reclaiming disparaging terms, isn't something that is universally understood or appreciated. That's because it's messy. It involves shifting cultural norms, and like any kind of social evolution, will leave people in different degrees of acceptance. Usually, disparaging terms are reclaimed by an in-group. For example, Southern comedian Jeff Foxworthy humorously co-opted the term *redneck*, essentially putting him on the map for his "You might be a redneck if . . ." jokes. Sometimes, the reclamation process is so powerful that it shifts discourse for the general population as well. For example, the term *queer* is often the preferred umbrella term for sexual and gender minorities in the LGBTQ spectrum. Yet other terms, such as *the n-word* remain controversial, with some embracing it while others reject its usage altogether, even within in-community contexts.[33]

Because there's no cut-and-dry standard for what is acceptable, some don't believe reclaiming language is effective at all. But every published social and psychological study conducted on reappropriation has confirmed that reclaiming terms results in a shift of power from dominant groups to those they've oppressed. This shift even occurred with terms that weren't embraced as self-empowering. That's the subversive nature of it: dominant groups have to check in and get some kind of social permission from the affected groups first, lest they face some kind of social disfavor or retribution for its use. When communities co-opt terms for self-reference or self-empowerment, it's saying *you can't use that word against me. It belongs to me now.* In that sense, refusing to be defined by others is an act of creation. It is both activism and art.

Sometimes, you need to work within a system in order to have justice. We were doing that with the traditional appeals process

---

[33] A lot can be said of this word. In fact, many books have been written about the complexities, intentions, and impacts of it. When Harvard law professor Randall Kennedy published his book *Nigger: The Strange Career of a Troublesome Word*, it received widespread attention but no media outlets would verbally share the title. In one famous C-SPAN interview, Brian Lamb remarked "How am I going to get through this interview?"

at the Trademark Office. Other times, we need to be able to flex our creativity to make sure our values are experienced in unexpected ways. That was the name of our band. That was shipping a box of hundreds of sheets of paper.

Our community had spoken: leaders, experts in linguistics and surveying, organizers, activists, and artists were joined in concert to say ASIAN AMERICAN VOICES MATTER. The paternalism the Trademark Office expressed through the deeply insulting use of Urban Dictionary and photos of Miley Cyrus didn't hold a candle to what we were doing.[34] It was time for the second part of my plan to kick in: getting the message out.

Before we shipped our appeal to the Trademark Office, my publicist Alex sent out a statement that finally let the world know what we were doing. We thought we could put public pressure on the government and recruit some more help with the appeal. Ironically, the headline in our press release read: "Asian Dance Rock Band the Slants Continue Long Battle With US Patent and Trademark Office Over the Group's Name." We were only a year into legal purgatory; we had no idea that it would be another six and a half years before we'd reach the final boss stage.

---

[34] A phrase and a gesture can be dramatically different. For example, the words "middle finger" are not inherently insulting (e.g., *I cut my middle finger*) whereas a photo of someone flipping the bird could be seen as scandalous or offensive. Not coincidentally, "middle finger" is a description with a neutral definition, just like "slant" is. Context matters.

The press release became a rallying cry, inviting community organizations and other people who were interested to help on our campaign. Until then, no one even knew we were fighting this obscure battle against the government (beyond the organizations we were working with directly). It spread quickly with Asian American newspapers and bloggers, then alt weeklies and the national press picked up the story.

As I was kicking off a new tour for our latest single, "How the Wicked Live," I woke up to a text message from my sister. It was a photo of the Oregonian, our local newspaper. The front page read: "What's in a name? That's up to feds" with our photos and story. I couldn't believe it: we made the front page! Word was spreading quickly. Later that night, we played a sold-out show at Dante's, our favorite club in Portland. That concert was also the inaugural for the newest member of the band: Thai Dao.

* * *

I first met Thai, a Vietnamese punk musician, at a Slants' show in Seattle. His band, Veritas, had just moved up there from Los Angeles, and he was trying to connect with musicians in the region. We kept in touch, and I'd throw contacts his way whenever he needed help putting a tour together. He was smart, driven, and just an all-around cool guy.

When Veritas disbanded, I reached out to Thai to see if he'd be interested in joining our band. He hesitated at first—we were both bass players and he didn't want to displace me. But a month before we left on tour, he changed his mind and decided to join as our keyboardist and second guitarist. With only one rehearsal under his belt, he bought a one-way Greyhound ticket to Portland to join us on the road. To be honest, that rehearsal was shaky. But I believed in him and vouched for him. The band reluctantly agreed and during the two weeks before our tour, he worked on our material like crazy so he'd be ready for that first show.

If the release of our new album was a spark that signaled more rock and punk into our show, having Thai join was the giant flare. His bright red Mohawk and energetic stage antics fell right in line with what Jonathan (guitar), Aron (lead vocals), and I were doing at the front of the stage while Tyler pounded on drums behind us. Jonathan and I built several custom boxes for the tour that triggered 1,500 watts of pure light underneath us whenever we jumped on them. It was orchestrated chaos on the stage, and our fans loved it. More importantly, the band finally felt like a family. We were genuinely having fun on stage, and that enthusiasm was contagious.

The "How the Wicked Live Tour" was also important because it locked in our involvement with community projects and issues. The Fukushima Daiichi nuclear disaster was unraveling at the same time. A tsunami and massive earthquake rocked Japan and triggered three nuclear meltdowns. The entire country was in upheaval. I wanted to use our platform for good, so anytime press reached out about our trademark case, I'd use that attention to talk about what was happening in Japan. As a result, we collected donations for the Japanese Red Cross Society at every show on tour and gave out free music in exchange. We also donated merchandise to a number of silent auctions and other fundraisers too, raising over $34,000 for the effort.

When I think about my favorite tours with the Slants, that tour is definitely near the top of the list. Our band was never more unified in the work that we were doing. During the day, we'd scavenge towns for the best regional foods and thrift shops we could find. At night, we'd take the stage and raise money for a cause that we were passionate about. There wasn't any bickering like on some of our other extended tours, we were all on a mission. It reminded me why I started the band to begin with. It was also the first and only time I got to share a stage with Perla.

Perla was playing guitar with her husband for a project called Dez Cadena and the Broken Down Bitches. When he wasn't on tour with the Misfits, it was his punk band for the New York and New Jersey area. They thought it'd be fun to host us and have their band play with us in Brooklyn.

Staying at their place on tour felt like coming home to family. Their cozy Newark apartment was filled with guitars, records, and vintage horror movies. There was always Italian food in the kitchen: leftover pizza slices from Lombardi's, cannoli, or homemade red sauce. It gave us a home base where we could explore NYC on our day off without worrying about parking. Both Aron and Thai were fans of Dez's bands too, so they deeply appreciated having breakfast cooked for them by a punk rock legend. Of course, I was just thrilled to spend some time with my best friend.

Perla and I had been talking almost every day for the past year, leaving a permanent chat window open on our desktops to catch up on music, our families, and our respective relationships. This would often involve sending ridiculous things to each other just to keep our spirits up, as I was dealing with my case, and she was trying to get settled with her job. I found an old chat from about two months before the tour:

> Me: I'm so freaking stressed! Lizzie's really sick right now, fighting US Trademark Office everyday for the band name, booking tour right now . . . my band members are being idiots, not wanting to practice even though we're adding to our lineup for the tour.

> Perla: Oh boy. You need a vacation. I have something that will make you feel better!

She then sent me a video of a horse named Patches who enjoyed to riding in cars with cowboys. Keep in mind that this was way before memes or animated gif responses were a thing. Perla was always a head of the curve.

Our chats were great but nothing could beat being there in person, feeling the genuine and warm embrace of a lifelong friend. I never had to explain myself with Perla. She just got me. She knew where I came from, understood my intentions and my dreams. Seeing her in person reminded me how special our friendship was.

On the day of the show, we met up with Perla after she got off work. Together with Dez, we drove our van and trailer into the Park Slope neighborhood of Brooklyn for an intimate show at a venue called Union Hall. Parking in New York City is challenging enough as it is but having an extra large van with an oversized trailer filled with equipment is an entirely different level. It's like trying to park a train of cars linked together. When we pulled up to the club, we saw enough space to fit two cars in: just enough room for our tour rig but not enough to drive into. I pulled the nose of our van in and left the trailer in the street so we could unload all of our gear onto the sidewalk. Then, we all hand lifted the trailer into position behind us, giving us a few inches of space in front and behind. It was parallel parking by manual labor.

The venue portion of Union Hall was actually underground, with stairs leading to their basement. It had a tight stage and ceiling so we couldn't run around or jump onto our light boxes like normal but the intimate stage also made everything feel more exciting and fun. It had been four years since Perla and Dez saw us at the Whiskey A Go Go during our first tour, and the band had come a long way.

When Perla took the stage with her band, I was beaming. She was rockin' out! She was playing a beautiful Gibson Les Paul guitar through her Fender Tonemaster amp, and the band ripped through several songs from Black Flag, played some new originals, and ended with a cover of *Louie, Louie*. She handled every song gracefully, using all down strokes just like I taught her when we were younger. She'd also come a long way.

After the show, I ran up like the world's biggest fan.

"You were amazing, I'm so proud of you!"

"TAM! I did it! And I looked pretty hot too," she half-joked. "I wish you boys could stay but I know you gotta get to Nashville." We were planning to drive all night after the gig. We often did this for shows over eight hours away so we wouldn't need to pay for a hotel room after the show. Since I wasn't on deck to drive first, I asked to see if Perla and her husband wanted to hang out and grab some drinks.

"Oh, Dez and I are sober now. We had some problems before, so we're taking it easy for a while."

"No worries, you can have all the iced tea you want on me!"

The rest of the band generously offered to load the gear so we could spend more time together. We walked upstairs and watched patrons playing bocce, an ancient sport that involves rolling metal balls down a long and narrow court. As we sipped on our teas, the occasional metallic clang would cut through the electronic dance music playing overhead. We talked about the show, shared some of our favorite memories, and discussed upcoming plans. Before long though, it was time to go.

"I have to visit you again soon. I want to bring Lizzie to New York so she can meet you!"

We hugged tightly. If I knew that it would be the last time I'd ever see her again, I wouldn't have ever let go.

Nashville was the last stop of our tour. We were playing the same anime convention, MTAC, where I first met Lizzie. It felt great to be back—the show was even better than in previous years, and our band was really connecting. As we drove home from our last show in Nashville, it felt like riding on an effervescent wave of good things: the stories being written about our case showed broad support, the shows went better than imagined, and I got to spend time with my best friend. On top of that, we were crushing it with our recent trademark filing so that ordeal would finally be over. The euphoria didn't last long.

Within a day of getting back, I got a call from Perla. She was staying with some friends, trying to figure out her next steps because she had gotten into a huge fight with Dez the day after our show together. While she was at work, he met up with some friends and started day drinking. When she talked to him on the phone that afternoon, she could already hear it in his voice. She felt betrayed. When she confronted him about it later that night, the result was explosive. She immediately left because she didn't feel safe around him anymore. The details that she shared with me over the next two hours left us both feeling broken.

"I don't want to go back . . . alcohol made him Dr. Jekyll and Mr. Hyde. And I am hurt beyond any hope of recognition. Like even if he never drank again, I can't look at him the same. Is that wrong?" She felt lost.

"I don't think it's wrong. There are consequences to our actions, even if we aren't completely aware of what we are doing."

"You think you know what the rest of your life is gonna be like and then overnight it's completely changed and you have to come up with plan B fast."

"Well, according to one cult group the world is going to end on May 21st anyway. That's only next week! Some so-called Christian radio guy swears it's true, even though he was off on his 1994 prediction."

She laughed, perhaps for the first time since we were together in Brooklyn. It was nice to hear her smile, knowing that some bit of our dark, sardonic humor could bring a glimmer of happiness back.

"Wouldn't that be funny?" she said. "I'm going to mark my calendar!"

A month later, she filed for divorce. I tried convincing her move to Portland or back to San Diego to be with her family, but she had already found a new place in Manhattan. New York City was a magnet for her. She told me how she would one day love to see more places with mountains and waterfalls, but for the moment, it was all about the Big Apple.

CHAPTER 7
OPERATION GRATITUDE

IN 2011, I got a message about the Slants from a branch of the U.S. government that wasn't the Trademark Office: the Department of Defense. The Pentagon wanted us to perform for troops serving overseas in a series of shows that they dubbed *Operation: Gratitude*. They were hoping that we could help them with some of their Asian American outreach. It was about the same time as the suicide of Danny Chen, a U.S. Army soldier who served in Afghanistan.

An investigation revealed that Chen had been subjected to repeated physical abuse and ethnic slurs by his superiors, who appeared to single him out for being Chinese American. For the six weeks before his death, he suffered from daily abuse, enduring taunts and slurs like "gook," "chink," "Jackie Chan," and "Soy Sauce." He was assigned excessive guard duty to the point of exhaustion, forced to do push-ups while holding water in his mouth, pelted with stones, and dragged across gravel, leaving cuts and bruises all over his body. After almost two months of torture, he was found with a gunshot wound to his head.

Chen's story paralleled another suicide from a few months earlier: Harry Lew, a Chinese American Marine serving in Afghanistan, shot himself in the head after being subjected to repeated abuse from his fellow Marines. In both instances, the most serious charges—involuntary manslaughter and negligent homicide—were dropped, and the offending service members essentially received a slap on the wrist.

I learned that the Asian American presence in the military is fairly small but significant; about 4% of all enlisted men and women are Asian American, many of whom report racial discrimination and harassment. Asian Pacific Islanders (API's) have played a role in every major American conflict of the 20th and 21st centuries; during World War II, one of the most decorated units in military history was comprised almost entirely of second-generation Japanese Americans (the 442nd Regimental Combat Team). Despite this history of military service, our community members have always been seen as foreigners who don't belong among American troops. The military thought having us perform would help change that perception. Against this backdrop, we flew to Eastern Europe for a series of shows on military bases across Sarajevo, Bosnia and Herzegovina, and Kosovo.

Everyone in the band was excited: not only would this be our first overseas tour, but it would be a chance to honor those serving our country while sharing our own Asian American experiences of harassment and prejudice. After the requisite background checks and paperwork, I received the military's first draft of the poster they wanted to use to promote our shows. The poster said, "Funkytown Meets Chinatown: Pacific Coast wunderkids the Slants cook up wok-fried beats with a distinctly Asian flavor." No. Just no.

* * *

Before heading to Eastern Europe for our military tour, I was wrapping up loose ends for the next step of our trademark appeal. Spencer called me to go over the final details. Over the past couple of months, we would check in daily to go over all of our evidence and legal arguments in the appeal. We condensed our file from a couple of thousand pages down to 270. We wanted to focus on a tight legal argument that was built around all the evidence we had gathered: the dictionary report, the national survey, the Asian American Youth Leadership Conference committee declaration, and broad support from Asian Americans that came in at every level. He was very confident about the appeal, but his excitement was tempered with something serious. Finally, he broke the news: he wanted to quit being a lawyer.

"I'm walking away from all of it—the case, everything. Working in law has been so stressful for the past year, and it's really expensive to renew my license. I just got offered a general counsel position with a local company and for my sanity, I'm going to take it."

"This must be my fault. This case has been so hard, and all of my messages haven't been helping." I was riddled with guilt. "I wish I could have been paying you for your work, I'm so sorry."

"Don't apologize, it's not your case. It's all of the other work. You are doing a GREAT job with this case so far. I can honestly say that I have never had a client who has done so much work on their own to help a case. You should be very proud of all the time and energy you put into this on your own behalf and on behalf of the Asian American community. I have always been very, very proud to represent you guys. But you will need to find a new lawyer and I can help you with that."

I couldn't believe it. For the past eighteen months, Spencer and I had been working so hard on this case. He was the one who helped me see how important it was to deliver a symbolic victory at the Trademark Office and provide a path forward for other marginalized groups who wanted to register reappropriated terms. We were about to deliver the most exhaustive appeal on a 2(a) rejection! I wanted to cross the finish line together, but I also understood how the law wore him out. In many ways, I felt the same, but I couldn't walk away when we were so close to winning.

"What about that Ron guy?" I asked. A few months before, I came across an article about our case on an intellectual property blog called *Likelihood of Confusion* written by a trademark lawyer named Ron Coleman. He had a "Top 50 Law blogs" logo displayed proudly at the top of his site. When I looked through his credentials, he seemed to really know his stuff. His writing had incisive humor. More importantly, he seemed sympathetic to our cause. When I showed the blog to Spencer, he told me that Ron was one of the best intellectual property guys in the country.

"Well, that might be a long shot, but you should send him a message and if he's interested, I can talk to him more about our case and see if he's willing to help you out pro bono."

Not one to give up, I went back to the website and clicked the contact button. I wrote a short message explaining our plight and asked if he might be interested in working with us.

Two hours later, I received a reply saying, "Thanks for the note. I'm in and, yes, I am very motivated over this issue. Can I call you later this afternoon?"

It seemed a lot easier than I thought it would be. Spencer and Ron talked on the phone, and they agreed to transfer ownership of the case, on the condition that it would continue to remain pro bono. After signing some of the paperwork, I spoke to Ron on the phone for a few minutes. I was confident that we were on a winning streak, that we just needed an attorney to finish things out with this final round.

"Look, you guys have done a hell of a job here. But the system isn't designed for you to win." Ron was cheerfully pessimistic about our chances. He said, "Don't be surprised if you don't get the registration. In fact, I'm almost certain we're going to have to appeal this to the Trademark Trial and Appeal Board, and probably kick it up above there too."

"But we gave them everything that they asked for." The examining attorney assured us that if we delivered on that checklist, they would remove the objection. Our 270 page appeal was more than they asked for. I continued, "It's even more than the Dykes on Bikes case, and they won their registration!"

"They didn't win on appeal. The objection was withdrawn, so there's no precedent or anything like that. What you've done is really impressive, but I know these guys and mark my words, if we continue the case like this, it's going to be an uphill battle."

A few weeks later, Ron's prediction came true.

The Trademark Office quickly issued another crushing rejection. They dismissed our survey and disparaged Dr. Butter's report as only "the opinion of one linguistic expert." They ignored all of the new evidence we supplied, including the letter from the Asian American Youth Leadership Conference. They also found a couple of British dictionaries from the 1930s that listed *slant* as a derogatory term and misrepresented quotes from some of our social justice partners, like the Japanese American Citizens League.

The examining attorney wrote that our extensive effort was "laudable, but not influential . . . The Office maintains that the applied-for mark is disparaging to a substantial composite of Asian-Americans. Accordingly, the request for reconsideration is denied and the Section 2(a) refusal is maintained." In other words, *nice try but you lose.*

I was pissed off and filled with shame, but I wasn't about to go down without a fight. It was degrading to have the government say that our efforts were in vain, and to go around begging for help to prove that our name wasn't as provocative as the government claimed. They even had the audacity to suggest that I was trying to be a self-appointed representative of all Asian Americans, even though that's exactly what they were doing themselves (without actually consulting any Asian Americans).

I started combing through their newest refusal and picking it apart, line-by-line. I sent my notes to both Ron and Spencer. I knew that we had six months to file a new appeal with the Trademark Trial and Appeal Board. I went to work immediately by contacting local elected officials, the organizations whose quotes were taken out of context in the examining attorney's response, and other groups who might be able to support us. I wasn't going to let them get away with lying and abusing our communities like this!

One month turned into three. I still hadn't heard anything back from Ron other than a couple of cursory "we'll talk soon" emails. I went from working with an attorney who was speaking with me nearly every day to someone who went M.I.A. I'm sure he was busy with paying clients, but I was definitely getting impatient. Finally, he shot me a message saying, "I believe we need to start fresh on this application. In its current posture, we are staring into a brick wall; there is no chance of getting the registration or getting meaningful review of the issues. I believe there is a way to get this registration but it is not the way we started out."

I looked up our case in the Trademark Office database. They had dismissed our application for failure to file a brief at the Trademark Trial and Appeals Board. Ron told me this was all part of the plan; the appeal needed a fresh start: "same trademark, but a different, er, SLANT. I will explain." I was frustrated and confused, but at this point, I had no choice. I had to trust Ron with whatever would happen next, especially because Spencer couldn't help me at all. The next few weeks were a flurry of paperwork as we rushed to file a new application for trademark registration before the Christmas holidays and our overseas tour.

* * *

I spent that Christmas with Lizzie's family, then flew to Ronald Reagan airport the following day and met up with the band. We grabbed some lunch at a brewery while we waited for our flight to Munich. There, Aron pulled out a large ziplock bag with multi-colored slime inside.

"Gross. What is that?"

"Vodka-soaked gummies! I read about it on the Internet and learned you can take them on the plane. So now I can get wasted instead of paying for drinks!" He demonstrated by scooping his hand inside the rainbow liquid, grabbing a wad of the gummy slime, and slurping it down. "What some?" We just shook our heads.

Our band's reunion didn't last long, as most of our seats were scattered by two's throughout the middle section of the plane. I spent most of the overnight flight reading Sung J. Woo's novel *Everything Asian* and talking about future plans with Tyler, who was next to me. At one point, a middle-aged white man sitting across the aisle turned and yelled at us: "Hey! Can't you guys just shut up for a little while? Some of us are trying to sleep!"

This roused Aron from his drunken sleep.

"Why don't you just shut the fuck up and let people talk if they want to? If you say one more thing, I'm going to go over there and punch you. I swear I will break your nose."

The guy sized Aron up and decided it would be best to put in his headphones and sleep. That was the strange duality of Aron: he could totally have your back or make your life completely miserable, especially when drunk. He did all kinds of terrible things to us when he was in the wrong mood. He kicked out the windows of our van when he was upset for breaking his own laptop, constantly peed on the hitch for our trailer out of amusement, threatened to sue us for a bigger cut of royalties . . . the list goes on. But when he was feeling generous, he would do anything for his friends. Or maybe he was just pissed from being woken up.

After spending some time in Munich, we boarded a plane for Sarajevo, Bosnia and Herzegovina. I sat next to the daughter of a famous soccer player from Sweden who was excited to practice her English. She told me that I was the third American she had ever met. The irony wasn't lost on me: while most Americans' first impression of me was "Asian," hers (and most people outside of the U.S.) was "American."

The views flying over Austria and into Bosnia were breathtaking: sweeping landscapes of snow-capped mountains, frozen lakes, and villages could be seen below. We were greeted by a group of soldiers when we landed. As we drove to Camp Butmir, the NATO base we were performing at, they talked about the complicated history of Sarajevo and pointed out buildings on the side of the road that were patched together due to tank shells. Signs of previous wars were everywhere in the city: scars from mortar shells marked sidewalks and buildings alike. I watched as a group of b-boys danced in front of a perpetual flame memorial to the war in Bosnia.

On our first night in Europe, we set up for our concert in a venue located on the military base, called The Millennium Club. It looked like nearly every other dive bar in the U.S.: a small stage with a small bar in the back. The only difference was that the customers were heavily armed soldiers who represented a peacekeeping force comprised of nearly two-dozen countries. They were especially excited when we launched into a cover of Joy Division's "Love Will Tear Us Apart."

A few hours into our show, the Military Police (MP) stormed the venue and tried to shut it down while we were still on stage. But the crowd wasn't having it. The many drinks they consumed made them brave—and loud. The soldiers watching kept yelling "Encore!" as more MPs came in. We decided to listen to the guys with the guns and stepped off the stage.

The MPs tried to clear out the room, but many of the soldiers there wouldn't budge. They wanted us to stay and sign autographs. Several of them were pushing back, saying, "I'm waiting for my signature! I'm not leaving this place without it!" We quickly gathered whatever posters we had on a table and began handing them out as the MPs watched. Finally, one of the MP officers sheepishly asked, "May I have one too?"

None of our other shows that tour were crashed by the Military Police, but each one had some unique experiences that let me better understand what life on the base was like, especially for the local civilian contractors in the area who were working for the U.S. government. I was surprised to find statues of Bill Clinton (on "Bulevardi Bill Klinton") and replicas of the White House in Kosovo. As a teenager, I was often told that the U.S. military intervention in Kosovo during the 1990s was a pretext to distract the American public from the Monica Lewinsky scandal. But many ethnic Albanians credit Clinton for ending the conflict with Yugoslavia, and with it, the ethnic genocide of their people. Each conversation I had illuminated the many perspectives and experiences of Eastern Europeans who experienced the war, the military, and American culture differently.

At our final appearance, we were booked to play an outdoor show at a NATO base in Film City, Kosovo. It was named for the amount of (mostly pornographic) films produced there. Since it was below freezing, we played in full winter coats and tried to stay close to the gas lamp heaters when possible. Only a handful of American soldiers showed up as we started our set, mostly out of courtesy. They kept warm by aggressively jumping up and down and screaming to our music. The commotion eventually caught the attention of Belgian soldiers walking by, who also joined in. Soon after, soldiers from Romania, Germany, Poland, and Albania were hopping, yelling, and singing along too. After the show, we spent time talking with different soldiers about our band name and our experiences with stereotypes about Asian Americans. I spoke frankly about

Private Danny Chen's suicide and how I identified with some of the bullying he experienced.

As we were loading our equipment into the van, the base commander approached me and said, "We've had a lot of acts here—big names, too—but I've never seen soldiers from all of the different countries dance together like that." He seemed genuinely pleased about the event, even though we ran a few hours past curfew. Then, he apologized, "As the commander of the base, I'm expected to make appearances at these kinds of things. But when I first saw your poster, I didn't know what to make of this Oriental band. However, now I know I should never really judge these things on the surface."

"Thank you so much. It's an honor to be here," I said. "Also, you shouldn't use the word *oriental*, because it makes you sound like a racist. But thank you." I quickly jumped into the van and we sped off while he looked perplexed. That night, fighting stereotypes of Asian Americans didn't come in the form of a lecture or a workshop on the model minority myth or a debate over "Asian privilege." It happened through sincere fellowship powered by Chinatown dance rock. That night, the victory happened simply by showing up and having meaningful conversations.

CHAPTER 8
TOO ASIAN

～

I SPENT NEW YEAR'S EVE WITH THE BAND on an active military base in the capital of Kosovo. Instead of alcohol, the tables were filled with "near beer" and alcohol-free wine (there were also large piles of pistols, M16 assault rifles, and pieces of armor). Everything felt like a fantasy: for the soldiers, it was a night of live music and dancing instead of patrol duty. For us, it was like playing inside a heavily armed summer camp, complete with a secret prison that resembled Guantanamo.[35] The surrealism of the moment allowed us to temporarily ignore reality and work with the government instead of against it. It allowed us to be perceived simply as American (at least by the Europeans we encountered), without any qualifiers or hyphens. When we returned to the United

---

[35] At the time, The United States Army denied having such facilities, but the prison was visible from several parts of the base, and it was pointed out to us by a few soldiers. Later investigations found that prisoners would be locked for months without trial in conditions similar to Guantanamo.

States, it was already a new year. And that meant it was time to get back to work.

Ron's new approach to our trademark application was simple: file a new application but remove anything that could be tied to Asian or Asian American culture. This included album artwork, flyers of our shows that seemed to have Asian imagery, and photos of our band. Because *slant* could mean so many different things, he thought we might be able to reapply and get a new examining attorney, one who wouldn't associate the name of our band with our ethnic identities. He nicknamed it the "ethnic neutral" application. Essentially, we were starting over again. We filed the application just before the holidays and our Department of Defense tour. Two days after I got back from Europe the U.S. Trademark Office had an answer waiting for me.

The novel idea of getting a different examiner to look at our application failed miserably. We were assigned the same examining attorney, Mark Shiner, who basically copy and pasted his previous response into the new application. I stared at the bold text in his response:

SECTION 2(A) – MARK IS DISPARAGING

"Registration is refused because the applied-for mark consists of or includes matter which may disparage or bring into contempt or disrepute persons, institutions, beliefs, or national symbols."

The examiner didn't even bother introducing new evidence—the same screenshots of UrbanDictionary.com and Miley Cyrus taken from two years before were being used again. I could feel my temperature rise with each passing moment as I read the words before me. Then, I saw a repeated, blatant mischaracterization: "a band performance and a speaking engagement for the lead singer were cancelled because there had been concerns over the name of his band."[36] Never mind that the examining attorney couldn't tell two different Asian musicians apart (I've never been the lead singer), but recall that we had representatives from the Asian American Youth Leadership Conference refute this erroneous claim with a signed legal declaration just a few months before. This correction wasn't even acknowledged. It was simply ignored.

To add insult to injury, Shiner wrote,

"while applicant may not find the term offensive, applicant does not speak for the entire community of persons of Asian descent and the evidence indicates there is still a substantial composite of persons who find the term . . . offensive."

Who did this guy think he was? If I couldn't speak for my community, despite working with Asian American organizations across the United States, why did this one employee at the Trademark Office have the right to do so? We followed all of the rules,

---

[36] They mistakenly identified me as the lead singer. The Trademark Office repeated this mistake so many times, including at the Supreme Court, that the final opinion from the high court repeated it. Now it's in many law books. They also misspelled my name (the literal name of the case) and "The Slants" a few times over the years. You can tell how much they care with that level of attention to detail!

addressed every wiki-fueled concern they raised, yet it was still not enough. With just a few keystrokes, a single attorney in a government office could brush away the voices of thousands of Asian Americans who wanted to reclaim this outdated slur. To me, it was even more ridiculous that the government had already registered "slant" over and over again for other people. It was like the rules were different for me.

After beginning my legal journey, I started doing more research into conflicts that Asian Americans had with the law. The results were troubling but not surprising. I found a pattern where litigants of Asian descent would be treated differently than non-Asians. Sometimes, the government would change how they applied laws specifically to work against marginalized communities. For example, I learned that in 1875, Chae Chan Ping legally came to the U.S. to work as a laborer in San Francisco under a treaty that guaranteed Chinese people the "natural right" to immigrate to the United States. In 1882, Congress passed the Chinese Exclusion Act, the first federal law to suspend immigration for a specific nationality; it was created to address concerns about the large number of Chinese entering the country. Cities were afraid that it would upset the "good order" of their localities. The Exclusion Act allowed Chinese nationals who were already present to remain in the U.S., but they could not become citizens; these residents could visit China and return to the United States only if they obtained permission from the U.S. government first. After working here for twelve years, Ping obtained a government certificate to guarantee his return and visited China, but a week before his return to the U.S., Congress voided the certificate and customs refused him entry.

Chinese benevolent societies raised money for a legal defense fund in order to deal with immigration cases; Ping was able to hire the best lawyers in the state who took the case to the United States Supreme Court. In addition to rejecting the arguments for Ping's right to return in *Chae Chan Ping v. United States*, the high court used broad language that led to the establishment of the "plenary power" doctrine, which would allow the government to ban any foreign immigrants, even if legally admitted, and even if unconstitutional. The significance of the case can not be overstated: it has been quoted dozens of times by the courts and used to shape future immigration policy, including President Trump's Muslim ban. The Chinese Exclusion Act and the laws that followed it prevented my great grandmother from being able to reunite with her husband for forty years and displaced my father for nearly seven years until he could enter the United States. The U.S. government has no problem using Asians when needed—for labor or doing some outreach on their behalf—but are just as quick to strip of us of our rights when convenient.

We'd like to believe that the courts are fair, and that the government is objective when dealing with basic legal processes, but justice is only as strong as our laws and the people enforcing them. With each exchange I had with the Trademark Office, I believed that the government would act responsibly and fairly. After all, these documents were all available as public records. Why would they deliberately use misinformation? Even if this wasn't a major civil rights issue or a matter of criminal law, surely there must be some kind of accountability. I fired up my computer and began writing a detailed, line-by-line rebuttal of the newest rejection. Unlike Spencer, who would always be available with an immediate call, the working relationship I had with Ron was far less collaborative. I thought I could provide some insight into the appeal, especially since I knew the application history better than anyone else. We could bring back the experts, we could call out the Trademark Office on their misleading claims, and we could show them that our name was not disparaging.

Ron had other ideas. He believed that the dismissive nature of the Trademark Office created a weakness that we could exploit: a procedural and evidentiary oversight. In other words, Shiner screwed up when he copy-pasted the language from the last appeal. The Trademark Manual of Examining Procedure (TMEP), the Holy Bible of trademark rules, dictates that every new application warrants a fresh search to see how a trademark is being used in the marketplace. Ron argued that the Trademark Office's most recent rejection violated TMEP guidelines because all of the evidence provided was out-of-date (not "fresh")—it predated our application by two years. So, while I was filled with anger by the newest rejection, he was chuffed. Either way, it didn't matter since we were appealing to Shiner himself. He would have to acknowledge these issues for us to win since we weren't at the Trademark Trial and Appeals Board level yet.

The newest exchange with the Trademark Office also allowed us to make new, different arguments. Ron argued that the examining attorney improperly claimed *slant* was disparaging:

nothing in our "ethnic neutral" application suggested that "The Slants" was a reference to Asian people at all. In fact, records showed that every other trademark application for "slant" was approved without any concern that may be disparaging. This contradicted the examining attorney's argument that the term "slant" was inherently racist. Ron wanted to hang his hat on this highly technical argument, which meant that we wouldn't include any information to refute the Trademark Office's claims, since the procedural issues took precedence before any arguments regarding disparagement. In other words, there were no grounds for the examining attorney to interpret "The Slants" as disparaging, so we didn't even want to dignify those accusations with a response.

"Can we at least correct them on the Asian American Youth Leadership Conference issue or bring up the survey results again?" I asked. It really bothered me that they would perpetuate the (false) assumption that Asian Americans throughout the country had issues with our name.

I could hear Ron sigh over the phone. "That would dilute the argument. I know it's hard, but we have to stay focused on this." Over the past few months, we had probably spent a total of fifteen minutes talking. At this point, I didn't feel like I had any choice. Part of me still wanted to believe in our old strategy—that if we simply addressed their points strongly enough, we'd be able to win. But Ron knew what kind of results that approach would bring. He reminded me that every single appeal for a trademark rejected under the disparagement provision lost. It was like he was *Star Wars'* Gold Five, chastising me: "Stay on target!" The only chance that the Rebel

Alliance had against the death star was not a direct, large-scale assault, but rather a small thermal exhaust port. A precise, subversive hit made all the difference. *Stay on target.*

The argument we presented was so different and unexpected, legal experts weren't quite sure what to make of it. Instead of going back and forth on whether our name was disparaging or not, we changed the question altogether: we asked *why* they interpreted our name to be offensive when the term *slant* had an inherently neutral definition and had been approved for registrations by the government hundreds of times before. It was like Ron was playing chess while Shiner was stuck in a game of freeze tag. I didn't want to play any games at all; I just wanted a straightforward and fair process. But I also wanted to know why I was being singled out, so I went along with it.

When we got our answer, I couldn't believe it.

I blinked.

I refreshed the screen.

I checked again.

The United States Patent and Trademark Office said that I was *too Asian.*

Instead of relying on their previous argument that *slant* was an inherent racial slur, the examining attorney said that in the absence of any proof of inherent offensiveness, they needed to rely on context—and the context of *slant* in a group of Asians made it disparaging. He wrote, "Here, the evidence is uncontested that applicant is a founding member of a band (the Slants) that is self-described as being composed of members of Asian descent . . . thus, the association of the term SLANTS with those of Asian descent is evidenced by how the applicant uses the mark—as the name of an all Asian-American band." He connected the dots by using my ethnic identity against me, saying people would assume our name was disparaging because of my eyes. Instead of Miley Cyrus' photograph, it was now my own. In their attempt to prove how "Asian" we were, they referred to our album artwork and photographs of Asian people on our website. They literally included pictures of me.

There were many issues with their evidence. For example, they only found offensive content in relation to *slant* when they combined it with the phrase *derogatory* and the *n-word*[37] in their searches. They also used unverified, anonymous sources that suggested our band name might be offensive, and they continued to cite the inaccurate blog article about our appearance at the AAYLC. I was annoyed but relatively OK with that. It was expected. What got me was how blatant they were about improperly conditioning my registration on my ethnic identity. They were implying that anyone could register THE SLANTS as a trademark . . . anyone except Asian Americans. By suggesting the evidence that we were an Asian band was "uncontested," the only way to rebut such a statement would be to prove that we were not entirely Asian, a ridiculous and patently offensive proposition. Besides, how many Asians would be considered too many to be able to register the Slants? And, if we are

---

[37] Except that's not how they wrote it!

to rely upon context in how we use a mark, under the government's rationale, it would be forever impossible for me to register the trademark because I can't change the context. I was born Asian American. I will always be too Asian.

I went back to the Trademark Office database and looked at other slurs used against Asian Americans again: jap, chink, slope, gook, oriental, nip, coolie. They were all registered trademarks. I dug a bit further and looked at the ones that were rejected and stumbled on a pattern: whenever an apparent Asian applied for the mark, they were rejected for being scandalous, immoral, or disparaging. CHINK PROUD was applied for by Randall Loo—too Asian (but the trademarks from white-owned companies like PERMA-CHINK, TIMBER-CHINK, and DURA-CHINK were all perfectly fine). Spencer's mentor, Keith Aoki, was right all along.

This problem with Section 2(a) of the Lanham Act was always hinted at, but no one ever explicitly stated it: it allowed the Trademark Office to deny rights based on race, gender, sexual orientation, or unpopular political beliefs. It chilled speech. Most legal analyses dealt with the inconsistencies in how Trademark Office decisions were made.[38] Several law articles discussed possible First Amendment implications, but no one dared point out the

---

[38] See Megan Carpenter and Kathryn Murphy's *Calling Bullshit on the Lanham Act: The 2(a) Bar for Immoral, Scandalous, and Disparaging Marks* and *Self-Disparaging Trademarks and Social Change: Factoring the Reappropriation of Slurs into Section 2(a) of the Lanham Act*

constitutional question of how the Fifth Amendment's equal protection clause was applied in trademark law.[39] They might not even have thought about it. In one of our appeals Spencer included a small footnote that suggested the Trademark Office's refusal was a violation of our First Amendment Rights because it was an unlawful content-based burden on our speech, but that argument was never fully developed because professor Aoki died from his illness while we were still working on that submission to the Trademark Office. It would be another couple of years before that argument would appear again.

It was as if, for the first time, I truly realized the full extent of how genuine government ignorance in this area could further inequity. Of course, there were far worse examples of injustice like police brutality, but I also realized that we needed to use small victories in order to build momentum so we could address the larger complexities of systemic racism. Dr. Martin Luther King Jr. once stated, "Injustice anywhere is a threat to justice everywhere."[40] In

---

[39] Both the Fifth And Fourteenth Amendments provide equal protection. The difference is that the Fifth Amendment provides it under the due process clause, or the assurance that legal proceedings are fair and reasonable.

[40] From "Letter from a Birmingham Jail [King, Jr.]," (April 16, 1963). Dr. King wrote, "Injustice anywhere is a threat to justice everywhere. We are caught in an inescapable network of mutuality, tied in a single garment of destiny. Whatever affects one directly, affects all indirectly. Never again can we afford to live with the narrow, provincial "outside agitator" idea. Anyone who lives inside the United States can never be considered an outsider anywhere within its bounds."

the name of fighting against racism, the government was denying me rights based on my race. Perhaps if we could show the absurdity of how one seemingly innocuous government office could get things so wrong, it could highlight how our intricate system of laws built on slavery, genocide, and oppression could easily further injustice. Could we start a chain reaction? Maybe I was just hoping for too much.

The rest of the band was annoyed—they didn't care about the issue nearly as much as I did. They mostly just wanted to focus on our music. We started writing new material for our third full-length release, *The Yellow Album*. If the Beatles could have *The White Album* and Jay-Z *The Black Album*, then why not? It was a playful nod to the idea of ethnic pride in music. The new songs sounded like a bridge between our synthesizer-charged debut *Slanted Eyes, Slanted Hearts* and the harder hitting rock sounds from *Pageantry*. Many of the lyrical themes reflected a struggle: dealing with a lineup change, personal relationships that were falling apart, and working to support charities in our community while still fighting the government. That was the context which we were writing in.

Because we spent so much time on the road, and because Thai lived three hours away, we stopped rehearsing. Almost all of our songwriting began with riffs that Jonathan and I would create and circulate via email. Soon, Thai started uploading song fragments as well. Aron would then take those ideas and send back demos of vocal melodies that he recorded on his phone for me to stitch together. Within a year, we wrote almost twenty songs before narrowing them down in the studio. Thai and I also started writing lyrics while our drummer Tyler would arrange beats and additional guitar parts. It was only after we received the final album in hand that we got together and learned how to play the songs. Music was like a soothing balm for battle wounds. My friendships were like the sutures.

Perla and I started talking more often. Usually, it was just general chatter about our day and things that we were working on, but I started making plans to bring Lizzie to New York so that they could finally meet in person.

"It seems only appropriate that you meet her, especially since I'm going to propose."

". . . Oh my God. I'M SO EXCITED!"

"Can you be like the best woman? I don't think there are any rules about the person having to be a man. Besides, there's no one else in the world I'd rather have up there . . . and I need your help to pick out a ring!"

I planned to propose shortly before Christmas by presenting Lizzie with a refurbished vintage typewriter along with the ring.

"It's adorable!" I could hear the excitement in Perla's voice carrying across all 3,000 miles between us. "You gotta have a speech though!"

"A speech?"

"Yes! Like you've got to have nice things to say!"

A few weeks later, the plan was in motion. Lizzie had no idea what our plans were; I told her that I wanted us to enjoy our own Christmas before heading to Charlottesville to spend it with her family. The only guidance I gave was to dress nicely. We headed down the street to The Armory, a historic building with two theaters inside. That afternoon, we caught a matinée black box theater showing of David Sedaris' *The Santaland Diaries*. I spent previous Christmases reading the book to her whenever she was sick, so watching the work brought to life was particularly meaningful (and funny).

After the play, we enjoyed a nice dinner, drinks, and dessert at the hotel before checking into our room. When we made our way upstairs, she walked into a room that was decorated with roses and chocolates. A bottle of chilled champagne sat on the desk with a large wrapped present. As she sat down and removed the colorful paper, she found a dark, heavy case. She opened it and saw the restored 1938 Underwood typewriter gleaming inside.

"Oh my god! It's so beautiful! I can't believe you got me a typewriter for Christmas!"

I started to show her the different mechanisms that made it work, and how the different levers would pop the ribbon into place.

"You can write your novel on this! I even took the liberty of starting a story for you, too."

"What do you mean?"

"Scroll down."

She turned the large knob on the side of the typewriter. The sheet of paper that I preloaded started appearing. As she continued to scroll, I started to sweat with nervous energy. Then, the words I typed out appeared on the page:

> Lizzie,
>
> Will you marry me?

Her eyes opened wide, her hands raised up to cover her mouth. As she turned to me, I presented her with the ring. She looked at me, then back at the typed words. She was completely speechless—it was then that I remembered Perla's advice to have something nice to say. I told her how much she meant to me, how she had brought so much joy into my life, and that I wanted to spend the rest of my life with her. Tears were streaming down, but she was still completely silent. She hardly took a breath.

Finally, she nodded as she typed her first word on the page. Yes.

She tried to add a smile to the page but didn't know how to work the punctuation keys yet, so we ended up with a few extra characters.

> Yes.;:) ' b

* * *

That same winter, I did an interview with *Travel + Leisure Magazine* about Portland, Oregon. They wanted to profile our city for a piece about America's Best Cities for Hipsters. I thought it was fascinating because a hipster is defined by actions and attitude: tall bicycles, artisan beer, progressive politics, and so on. Yet because of the negative connotations, many would shy away from the label even if they embodied the characteristics (people always believe that they're the exception). It reminded me how we've demonized the idea of racism so much that some pretend it doesn't exist in our communities, houses of worship, or government even if the actions and attitudes fit the bill—and even after massacres like the Charleston church shooting. People like to believe those are isolated incidents rather than see them as evidence that racism is deeply rooted in our society. Denial is a powerful force.

The government believed that they were protecting Asian Americans from ourselves. They were imposing their own ideas of justice and order on us, without actually consulting what we wanted. This is why they never once asked the opinion of Asian American organizations on the matter—they claimed it was due to limited resources—but it was really because their attorneys assumed they knew what racism meant for our community. When a Governor-appointed board of Asian American leaders wrote the Trademark Office asking if anyone from our community helped with these decisions, a simple form letter was sent claiming their "commitment to diversity" by "hiring many Asians" in the department. Despite what some people might think, racial awareness and understanding doesn't come through osmosis. Just because Kevin the Asian works a few cubicles down doesn't mean you truly get him. That's the ultimate privilege: being able to live in a world where you can determine what racism looks like for other people.

I didn't learn the term "white privilege" until Lizzie showed me a video from Tim Wise speaking about it.[41] She was taking a class on representation and asked what I thought. I felt like I was waking up for the first time, that many of the things I intuitively felt were finally articulated. While I knew that skin color and hair type could affect things like being able to move through life with or without being racially profiled and unfairly stereotyped, I didn't fully grasp how the lure of whiteness could also be a legacy and a cause of racism, that it could both be the result of conscious acts as well as embedded into historic (and current) inequities.

The term "white privilege" has received pushback in the past decade, both because it creates discomfort for those not used to being defined by their race and because some (especially poor, rural whites) feel like "privilege" implies a lack of struggle. But it isn't that—it's the power of normalcy, which can be something as basic as having hair products or groceries catered to the cultural traditions of most white people. It's the ability to receive the benefit of the doubt rather than being seen as representatives (or exceptions to) a stereotyped racial identity. It's being less likely to be presumed guilty of a crime. In my case, it's not being expected to be a sushi expert and being able to register the same trademark as anyone else

---

[41] The Pathology of Privilege:

https://www.youtube.com/watch?v=J3Xe1kX7Wsc

SIMON TAM

without the additional questions about my race. People of color
don't do anything to receive unequal treatment, just as whites do
not "earn" disproportionate societal benefits—they receive it as a
byproduct of systemic racism and bias.

The most pernicious and least discussed articulation of
white privilege isn't just being able to walk through a department
store without being followed or "randomly" stopped by police
though: it's the ability to preserve and perpetuate the normalcy of
racism. It is the power to remain silent or "neutral" in the face of
racism, to stop the conversation when it becomes too uncomfortable. It is being able to create a policy, to call it objective and fair,
even if it can be qualitatively and quantitatively demonstrated to unjust. It is the privilege of being able to choose when and where to
stand up, and more importantly, make decisions about who to stand
up for, even if the affected people are asking you to sit down.

Section 2(a) of the Lanham Act was the perfect articulation
of privilege: the ability to define for others what would actually be
considered "scandalous, immoral, and disparaging," simultaneously
denying them rights as well as any recourse for appealing any mistakes made. The more that I thought about it, the more angry I got.
*The government doesn't have the right to determine what's best for me. That
right should belong to our community!* Even though Ron was working pro
bono, the court fees were pushing me further into debt. Still, I felt
like I couldn't walk away at this point. I saw how the government
was denying rights based on race, gender, and sexual orientation.
"Rebellions are built on hope," as Jyn Erso told the Rebel Alliance
in *Rogue One*. "This is our chance to make a real difference!"

Meanwhile, the examining attorney's response seemed to echo Darth Vader's chilling sentiments: "Be careful not to choke on your convictions."

CHAPTER 9
LIFE'S A GAS

~

IT WAS 2012, and the band was finally getting some momentum. Our newest release, *The Yellow Album*, was doing very well. Our music video for the first single, "Con Kids," was premiered by IFC, the television channel best known for *Portlandia*, who said that it was "providing the soundtrack to some insane dance parties . . . with a message. Much like Public Enemy and N.W.A., the Slants, who are all Asian American, are co-opting what was once a racial slur and making it their own." The preview for the video helped raise tens of thousands of dollars, enough to rescue a family of refugees, through a special collaboration with Liberty in North Korea (LiNK). I was on a media blitz, doing countless interviews to talk about our music and providing an update on our fight with the Trademark Office.

My balancing act of music, a legal battle, and a relationship were all starting to get out of control. Our tour bus that we recently acquired (a major upgrade from the van and trailer in terms of comfort) was constantly breaking down and required neverending maintenance. It turned out to be a rust bucket—literally. The entire drivetrain was covered in rust so we had to replace nearly every moving part on it. Because so much money was going into our bills from the bus and new album, very little was going into any of our pockets, which meant everyone in the band had to pick up regular jobs. Regular jobs meant that we needed to become a "weekend warrior" band for a while: work during the weekday, tour on nights and weekends. Each person would save up his or her vacation days or request time off without pay in order to tour—it's actually the most common way of life for active musicians. It tends to burn people out.

Jonathan was the first to go. He met someone.

He met her at one our shows. When they started dating, everyone in the band was genuinely happy for him. But as we kept touring, we noticed that he was getting further and further detached from the band.

After over half a decade of touring with the Slants, Jonathan's priorities were shifting. Understandably so—he used up almost all of his hard-earned vacation time from work in order to tour. We all did. But now there was someone else in his life who wanted some of that time too. As one of Jonathan's oldest friends, we had history. I knew his family, where he came from. I helped him get a job, move to Portland, and tour around the world in the band. In the last several years, I had spent more time with him than anyone in his family. For years, our band considered itself a family, but he was starting to feel like a stranger.

Jonathan started distancing himself as we were talking about touring Asia. We got invited to a couple of major music festivals in China, and the idea was to connect our tour with appearances in Japan and Taiwan as well. While the band eagerly discussed potential shows and gorging ourselves on Asian delicacies, he was notably absent, even more than our previous tour, where he spent most of the time texting on the phone. I met up with him to find out what was going on.

"How are you doing? You don't seem like yourself. On our last tour, it was like you weren't even there, and now you aren't even responding to our messages about China."

"Yeah . . . I don't think I can go."

"What do you mean? You already told us that you could get the time off if you wanted."

"I don't know . . ."

"Playing in China would be a huge deal, they don't let just anyone play. We're being invited in to do this!"

"I love touring. It's the best, but I don't think my heart is into it anymore."

"Like into touring? Or being in the band?"

"Being in the band. I think you deserve someone who really wants to do this."

We sat there quietly. I reflected on the memories that we shared, from ditching school for our first tour to our most recent national trip to Nashville and back. If our nomad band lifestyle was really like being in a pirate ship, he was my first mate. He always had my back and trusted my judgment when others questioned my decisions.

Just like that, he was out. The lineup that released *Pageantry* and *The Yellow Album*, that began the legal journey with me, and toured around the world was fractured. I didn't have time to dwell on it. I just wished him well and continued booking shows.

I was laying out plans for another tour. This time, we'd drive across the country to Atlanta for an event called Dragon Con and back. In the months leading up to it, we had a few flyout shows to get Will, our new guitarist, up to speed. After some solid touring, I planned to take some time off later in the year with a Thanksgiving trip to New York City. Finally, Perla would be able to meet Lizzie, about whom she had heard so much.

"Oh my God I'm so excited!" Perla always spoke like every sentence ended with an exclamation point whenever we made plans. "I can't wait for you to see my new place!"

"And I'm looking forward to meeting Troy, too. We'll see if he's really good enough for you."

For the past several months, Perla had been seeing Troy. He was a DJ on satellite radio and had gotten her into skateboarding, hiking, and electronic music. With the dust settling on her recent divorce, she was finally moving on and enjoying life in the city.

"I can't wait to finally have this year behind me and just have some fun for once. It's been three years since I've been fighting in court, but now that we're going to the Federal Circuit, a lot of it is out of my control."

"You boys are ALWAYS fighting! Don't forget to take care of yourself too!"

I was filled with excitement. I felt like I could finally breathe again. Touring without Jonathan was tough, but Will was bringing a new, different dynamic to our shows. The band's music was leaning harder than ever—Will preferred a traditional, heavy distortion on his guitar rather than Jonathan's Britpop tones. He also moved around more, displaying glam rock moves borrowed from Motley Crue, and he would also sweat like a beast. If anything, it just added to the raw power of the band.

That summer, we were booked to play at Otakon Matsuri, an outdoor festival in Baltimore that had an impressive lineup of Asian American performers. As the headliners, we had the final slot. But dark clouds rolled in and covered resplendent sunshine during the afternoon. Intermittent thunderstorms would drench the grounds for about ten minutes, scattering crowds, only to completely clear up moments later. People would slowly come back from under tents at the edge of the festival. It was ominous and surreal.

When we finally took the stage and started setting up, the rain came back, even more fierce than before. I watched as the stage began to flood—we scurried to pick our equipment off the ground. We were rained out! The organizers arranged for us to play locally that weekend, but it was definitely a let down.

While were in Baltimore, we drove up to Amish country and performed at a birthday party for Will's cousin in Jersey, Pennsylvania. I walked through cornfields and chased cows before we took the stage. The gentle terrain and family gathering was a welcome contrast to the chaos of the crowded events we normally played. It was great reminder that all of our shows, no matter the size or location, had something special to offer.

On the final day of our trip, I checked my phone while we were waiting in the lobby of our hotel for the airport shuttle. As I was scrolling through comments on photos from our recent tour, I noticed an unsettling one from Perla's mom. "O dios, mi Perlita esta muerta (Oh God, my little Perla is dead)." I called Perla to let her know that her mom's account was hacked by some creep, but no one picked up. I looked at the misplaced comment again and checked the account for any other updates, but there weren't any. Then, I looked at Perla's profile and saw posts from her new NYC friends ominously saying, "I'll miss you." NO, NO, NO. This couldn't possibly be real!

I called Perla's older brother, who picked up right away.

"Hey Phil, it's Simon."

"Hey, what's up?"

"OK, this might seem strange but I got a weird message from your mom about Perla. I don't know what's going on, she isn't answering her phone, so I wanted to call in case there was an emergency."

He sighed.

"Yeah . . . Perla is dead."

The words broke me. I crumpled to the floor when he told me the details. I could barely hear him over the sound of my pounding heart, racing and bleeding sorrow into the pit of my stomach. This couldn't possibly be true, it couldn't be happening.

Phil told me that she was hiking near a waterfall with her boyfriend Troy when the ground gave out from underneath her, causing her to fall forty feet. It took nearly two hours for emergency workers to reach her. She was initially responsive as they carried her on a stretcher down the gorge. She died as they were taking her out of the park. She was less than two hours away from me when we were playing in Pennsylvania.

I hung up the phone as our shuttle pulled up to the front entrance. All I wanted to do was be alone but I had to cram into a van full of band members, music gear, and anime convention guests. I fell silent as the people around me loudly joked and shared stories about their weekend. My chest felt heavy and I had trouble breathing. My ears rang, my eyes blurred. Shortly after, I went through the familiar motions of checking into the flight and going through security. Soon, I found myself on another oversold flight, full of crying babies and people complaining of delays. I just thought, What do you really have complain about?! Don't you know that it's all in vain? Despite being surrounded by people, I never felt so alone. I didn't want to say anything to anyone. It felt like verbal expression would be acceptance, that it would make it real.

A few hours later, the band was taking a dinner break during a layover. They noticed I was eerily silent the entire trip, so I finally said something.

"Perla . . . passed away. She fell to her death yesterday when we were playing a 100 miles away. My best friend is gone."

"Oh God, I'm so sorry."

"Wow, that sucks."

"Are you OK?"

I didn't say anything as I walked away from them. I needed to get away. I know they meant well, but none of them knew what I was going through. They couldn't possibly know the heaviness that I was feeling, the cancerous sorrow that had only taken root inside. I called Dez, who was on tour with the Misfits in Europe. I figured that after the divorce, no one else in Perla's family was going to let him know. The last time I talked to him was at our show in Brooklyn. I felt like he was a monster for hurting Perla and causing her to leave, but he deserved to know. Everyone who knew her, who loved her should know and should celebrate her life. At the very least, he knew how special she was.

On the final flight home, I wrote an open letter to Perla and shared it on social media. Her family later asked me to share it, delivering it as her eulogy. When I finally got home to Portland, I was in state of deep depression. I felt completely detached from everything and everyone, including Lizzie. Lizzie tried her best to console me but she never got the chance to meet Perla, she only knew about her from all of the stories I told. She didn't know. No one knew.

The invitation for her memorial service said that it would be a celebration of life, but the dark church organ sounds made it difficult to hold onto the small bits of joy from shared memories. I knew that the Ramones had to be played at some point. I selected the acoustic version of "Life's a Gas" by Joey Ramone, a posthumous work where his signature crooning brought as much melancholy as it did comfort.

So don't be sad
Cause I'll be there
Don't be sad at all
Life's a gas

The words embodied Perla's constant, exuberant optimism. A slideshow rotated photos of her smiling radiantly as the guitar strummed, and Joey's voice rang out. When the song ended, the quiet sobbing of a mother who had to bury her child cut through everyone in the room. She knew.

I didn't shed any tears that day. It wasn't that I was devoid of feeling—I was overwhelmed with it. The grief had enveloped me like a heavy blanket and consumed everything in me. I didn't have the energy to cry. The outward expression seemed futile; it would never fully capture the profound sadness inside. For weeks, I couldn't do anything except sleep and dream. Memories would swirl in my head at night, transforming into nightmares that would tremble and shake my body. Sleep became a poison for me.

Then one night, I dreamt I was inside an old diner that resembled the Denny's on Sunset Blvd. in West Hollywood. The place was devoid of people—no customers or staff. Everything had a strange amber hue to it. I went over to a booth in the corner. The glistening maroon vinyl sounded like a peeling orange as I sat down on. A faceless waitress appeared and poured me some hot tea. I held the warm mug as I watched the front door open. Perla walked in and took a seat across from me.

"Perla . . ."

"Tam!"

She was smiling, radiant as ever. She took my hands, her skinny fingers wrapping around mine as they unfurled from around the cup.

"Perla. I can't believe you're gone. I miss you so much–"

"What are you talking about? I'm right here!"

"But you fell. Your funeral . . . It all happened."

Or was that just a dream? Could it be that everything that had happened was a nightmare? This vision felt more real than the numbness that was my daily waking life over the past month.

"Oh, that." She shrugged. "Don't you remember? We agreed that we would never let anything stop us from being there for each other or from changing the world."

"It's hard to remember that now. It's hard to feel anything at all."

"I know, sweetie. But just because you don't feel something doesn't mean that it isn't there. You have everything that you need.

You don't let anything stop you because you care so deeply. You care too much to give up."

"Maybe that's why this hurts so much. I don't want to give you up."

"Hon, I'll always be here when you need me. Just check your messages"

I snapped awake, shaking with cold. I sat up in the empty bedroom. It was early morning. I could hear Lizzie getting ready to leave for classes in the other room. After taking several deep breaths, I walked into the living room to tell her about my dream. I wrote everything down in a journal so I wouldn't forget it. Then, I stepped into the shower and wept with such a tremendous and heavy sadness, I thought I would melt away in the drain with the water. I cried out in frustration and slammed my first against the shower wall. Then, I knelt down and asked God for guidance. I felt like the answer was the same: I'll always be here when you need me. Just check your messages. Like, literal messages?

After drying off, I grabbed my laptop to look for answers. I had an email from Ron letting me know that we were officially filing an appeal to the Trademark Trial and Appeals Board and another from Alex asking for content to create a press release. I didn't want to deal with either at the moment.

I scanned my bookshelf and picked up the Bible, the first time in a long while. I flipped through the tabbed pages and saw a highlight I made from years ago, while working in Murrieta. It was Deuteronomy 3:16: "Be strong and courageous. Do not be afraid or terrified because of them, for the Lord your God goes with you; he will never leave you nor forsake you." It seemed very appropriate.

I went back into the bedroom and grabbed my phone, flipping through dozens of old texts from friends and family who sent me messages of concern or sympathy. I stopped when I saw Perla's name. It was our last message exchange. The last words ever typed out by her fingers to me.

"Don't forget Tam . . . you're a fighter! Give them hell! xoxo"

. . .

Lizzie was wrapping up her final few semesters before finishing grad school. Meanwhile, wedding magazine subscriptions were piling up in the office—her mom started sending them to us immediately after our engagement even before we had a date in mind. We didn't have time to plan though, we were just trying to keep up with our work. On most days, we sat next to each other working on our respective laptops. We needed a vacation. The stress was a stranglehold.

In February, I was scheduled to speak at a conference about Asian Americans in entertainment at the University of Pennsylvania's law school, PennLaw. After the conference, Lizzie and I planned to spend Valentine's Day weekend in New York City.

At PennLaw, I finally met Phil Yu, the blogger also known as Angry Asian Man. We had been trading emails for seven years, mostly about the Slants and issues around the Asian American community. He even wrote legal declarations in support of our case. I also sat on the panel with Alvin Lau, a spoken word poet whose work I had long admired. There was an incredible sense of solidarity in the room, especially with those of us who engaged in arts and activism. Later that night, I ran into Pamela Chen, the first openly gay Asian American federal judge in the country. When she heard my story about fighting the Trademark Office, she didn't mince words: "They're idiots. You should win."

Lizzie flew up to meet me in New York City, but I felt like there was a great distance between us. She spent most of the time hanging out with new friends while I wandered the city alone, bitter that I would never be able to see Perla again. Lizzie wanted to move to New York. For her, it represented boundless opportunities with literary organizations and new friendships. But I only felt loss. Still, we made plans to move there after she finished school and we got married. She would move first, and then I'd follow after selling the house and working on loose ends. I'd figure out what to do with the band and our wedding later on. It didn't matter to me; I'd follow her anywhere. The excitement of moving consumed us and distracted from what was actually happening in our relationship. A rift started growing. We were changing.

One weekend back in Portland, we walked to get brunch at our favorite neighborhood spot, The Arleta Library. It was a beautiful afternoon. The sun warmed the earth beneath our feet and playfully created intricate shadows with the leaves of plants around us. Birds chirped along the walk. For the first time in months, maybe even years, everything felt weightless. She started talking about her plans again.

"You know, I've been thinking a lot about this move. I think . . . I should move by myself."

"Well, of course. I can help you but I still have to sell the house so I'm not sure how long that will take."

"No, I mean I don't think you should move there too."

I was silent as she continued.

"I really appreciate you. You saved me. You are the most amazing person I've ever met, but I need to know I can do this on my own. So maybe we should just take a break from our relationship."

"So you want me to put my life on hold and wait until you figure out who you are? That doesn't really seem fair." I was hurt and needlessly cruel.

"You're right. That's asking a lot. You deserve better than that."

We had both been feeling disconnected for some time. I was stuck in my own desert: feeling emotionally lost while I was grieving, mired in an endless legal battle, and trying to keep my band together. How could I really be there for her? She was looking towards a future of standing on her own. She would still rely on me for a little while longer; she needed a place to live until the move. I couldn't refuse. I still cared about her deeply. We were still friends.

"I just want you to be happy. Of course, I'll do everything I can to help you."

Over the next few months, Lizzie would continue to live with me until she could finish her degree. When she told her family about her decision, they expressed extreme disappointment and stopped speaking with her for some time. Not long after that, my parents visited to attend my graduation ceremony. I didn't have it in us to tell them what happened, we just maintained the illusion that we were still together until she bought her one-way ticket. I helped her box everything up and shipped everything over once she had a fixed address.

. . .

As my engagement with Lizzie was disintegrating, tension in the band continued to build. In public, things were going well: the David versus Goliath aspect of our legal battle curried a lot of favor with our fans. We started getting press coverage from all over the globe. Whenever there was an update to our case, I would often have to do interviews eighteen hours a day for several days in a row because I was speaking with journalists from nearly every time zone. But attention didn't always translate to album sales, especially since most of the stories were on our legal issues and not our music, which meant we were still struggling financially. Some of the band members also resented that I was usually the only one interviewed.

One day, I was asked to meet with a representative from a major label. In fact, it was the record company that I dreamt of working with since I learned anything about music. When I was a kid, I would write them letters asking for the mailing addresses of my favorite bass players. I couldn't believe that this was the company that I was speaking with! I allowed myself to get excited again.

When I got to the coffee shop, I was greeted warmly by a slender white man, in a band t-shirt and blazer. He was in his early 30s and looked like a quintessential A&R rep in his fohawk haircut. He had a laptop open on the table with a small, leather briefcase next to it. I had my shoulder bag with multiple press kits and CDs ready to go. I sat down and answered questions about the direction of the band.

"Let me cut to the chase because I don't want to waste your time. I have an offer valued at four million dollars here for you— you get to keep all the rights to your music, your merchandise. There's a nice signing bonus too."

He slid a stack of paper over to me and continued.

"You can definitely have your attorney look it over. I know you've got plenty of legal things going on so we wanted to make it easy for you. You'll find that this is a really good offer. We really love what you're doing. It's really special! We just need to make a small, but important change."

I couldn't believe it. I finally had a way out of the endless debt. The band was going to be thrilled when I told them of this unbelievable offer! Most recording contracts have stipulations about decision making around choice of producer or direction of music but I was pretty sure that we could make things work. At that moment, I was feeling very flexible. I asked what they wanted to change about us.

"You need a new lead singer."

I reflected on the past year that I spent with Aron. He was my crazy punk rock brother from another mother. He brought an edge to the band that no one else in our lineup had. He once performed a show on a broken foot. He got wasted far too often and could be a selfish prick, but he had a heart of gold.

"Wait. You just told me that you liked everything about our band. Why do we need to replace Aron? Couldn't we just get him a vocal coach?"

"Well . . . I'm just going to level with you and be honest here because I don't know who else will tell it to you straight. You need to replace your lead singer with someone who is white."

"I can't believe you're saying this to my face right now."

"I'm trying to do you a favor here. Asian doesn't sell. I think we can make it work with the band being mostly Asian but we need something more marketable here. You're never going to see an Asian American band featured on the cover of Rolling Stone, covered by Pitchfork, or on the Billboard charts. That's just a fact."

I looked at the contract in my hands and looked back up at him. It was almost like he was reading me. He chose his next words carefully.

"I know this is your dream. A dream you've had your entire life. I've heard you talk about it in interviews. You could still do something amazing for your community but on a much bigger scale! Don't you want to be able to take care of your family? If you sign this, your parents could retire right now. You could take care of them and they wouldn't have to work ever again."

I started thinking about everything that I owed my parents. Each of them worked so hard their entire lives; my dad had been working two jobs since the age of eleven. I remember that they let me drop out of college to tour in a punk band just because they wanted to see me be happy. My mind flickered to the many non-profit organizations and causes that I cared about. I could do a lot of good with this. I could take care of my band—even Aron, by giving him a huge share even if he wasn't in the band. I'm pretty sure he wouldn't mind receiving royalty checks for the rest of his life.

But then my mind drifted to the letters I received from Asian American kids who wrote me in those early years, thanking us for our work. I started the band because of representation, because I was tired of watching Hollywood whitewash roles meant for people of color. I wanted to create an opportunity for Asian American musicians to be their whole selves, to live their values without compromise.

My parents wanted me to be a doctor. Instead, I got into rock n' roll. They wanted security and stability. I wanted social change. But when I thought about what kind of person they wanted me to be, regardless of vocation, I knew the answer. They wanted me to be a man of values, one who followed his heart.

I stared intently across the table as I firmly held the papers in my hands.

"Yo, that's racist. And you're wrong. I'm going to prove you wrong one day."

I tore the contract in half, stood up, and walked out.

* * *

I never told Aron about what was discussed. I just told the band that it didn't work out, that it was another false promise just like the other offers we'd received in the past. No one questioned it; they were used to being let down. I don't know how I would respond to such an offer today. I'd probably try to find a creative way to use the money, perhaps help fund the work of many other Asian American acts, especially if I knew that one day the Slants would eventually come to an end. Maybe it was easier for me to display stubbornness and bravery because I felt so bitter about the losses I was experiencing. I had already lost Jonathan, I really didn't want to lose Aron as well.

We were all strapped for cash, especially Aron, who was bartending at a restaurant that was on the verge of being sold. He started canceling shows on us, sometimes with only a week's notice and even if we had flights booked. It forced our new hired guitarist, Will, to step up and sing for several shows instead. When Aron did make it to shows, he'd often get in heated arguments with other band members because of his excessive drinking. Nobody in the band was happy: every band member told me that we needed to let him go. Should I have signed that contract?

Just when we thought things were getting better, Aron's self-destructive behavior was getting worse. On one trip, he kicked the windows of our tour van out and refused to pay for the damage. On another, he threatened a tow truck driver who was helping us out when we were stuck in Moab, Utah. Whenever band members tried to intervene, he would get even more aggressive. *Shut the fuck up. I'll do whatever I want.*

Everyone in the band confronted me: Aron needed to go. Either fire him or they'd all quit.

I needed time to think.

Everything was falling apart. I knew without a doubt that we needed to find a new singer, but I hated the notion of the Slants without him. Since his first audition, I had stuck by him when others doubted his abilities. When he got drunk and did stupid things, I'd defend him and blame the bottle. He instinctively knew how to put on the kind of dynamic, chaotic show that I always envisioned when I first thought of the band. I even turned down millions of dollars because I believed in him. But at this point, I knew that this kind of behavior was dangerous. Our lives on the road could be at risk if he decided to take the wheel. It could hurt all of our social justice efforts, especially the students we worked with. I came to terms with it: we'd have to let him go.

I broke the news to Aron but he took it surprisingly well. Everything went better than we could have imagined. After booking his final show where we could celebrate our years together, I announced his departure online. We told our fans we was leaving for his new job—we agreed we didn't want anything that would make him look bad or imply he got fired. I started posting ads to look for a new lead singer. We could finally move on.

A week later, everything changed.

Something snapped in Aron. He started stewing over the situation, getting more upset the longer he thought about everything. First, he posted long rants on our Facebook page saying that I was a manipulative backstabber, that I fired him without his consent. He then took the same posts and started sending them to individual fans and mutual friends of ours. In his mind, I had convinced the band to turn against him.

The entire situation made my stomach turn. He stopped responding to any of my messages, except ones related to him being paid royalties for our work. He continued to vent about the band wherever he went, especially to anyone who was still working with me. To him, I was the person ultimately responsible for the misery caused by losing the band. It wasn't anyone else in the band and it certainly wasn't himself. I was the target. Now, I was dead to him.

Jonathan. Perla. Lizzie. Aron. In one year, the four people closest to me disappeared. Now all I had left were a couple of lawyers and a lot of debt.

CHAPTER 10

LEGAL UNICORN

I WAS FEELING MORE ALONE THAN EVER.

The quick succession of losing so many important relationships at once caused me to start erecting emotional walls unconsciously. When I first moved to Portland, it was a chance for me to change how I presented myself to others. Instead of being the shy, withdrawn kid, I would host dinner parties and events in my home to make friends. When I first started the Slants, we'd have regular outings that weren't tied to rehearsals or band meetings. We would just get food or enjoy cultural experiences together. But over the past few years I had gotten busy. First, touring with the band kept me away from home most of the time. Then, I went back to school full-time to get an MBA; I was hitting the books at least twenty hours a week. After Lizzie left, any remaining hours would be filled with working on my legal case or volunteering with community organizations. At one point, I was serving on the board of eleven organizations at the same time. I filled my life with tasks and responsibilities instead of relationships.

People would often ask me when I slept. It was easy—I didn't have kids or Netflix! I didn't tell them that I didn't have any close friends. Even though I was often around other people, I only saw them when it involved work of some kind. It was great to be able to help others, but I felt like most of my relationships were built on me doing some kind of work. Even when connections were made through service, they could still feel empty or draining. During this time, my favorite thing to do was to draw a hot bath and sit in it until the water turned cold. Sometimes I'd bring a book but never my phone. It seemed to be my only solace.

Shortly after Lizzie moved out, I walked back to have breakfast at our neighborhood café. A couple was breaking up at the table next to me. It conjured up images of a spider web. Relationships and webs are alike in that they are intricately complex, require a great deal of attention, and can appear in the most surprising places; but they are frail and can come quickly undone with a thoughtless or malicious gesture. Sometimes, it all seems to be in vain. But spiders keep spinning, and people keep loving. Maybe I just needed to take a break and focus on my music. I needed to rebuild that web. Little did I know that parts of it were already coming undone.

Thai decided to leave the band. He wanted to focus on his career and spend his time off with his girlfriend instead of only using it for our tour schedule. I couldn't blame him. There were no hard feelings, and I truly appreciated that he invested four years of his life in our band. His last show with us was on the same stage where he first started, at Dante's in Portland. Just like that first night, it was a packed venue of flashing lights and sweaty bodies moving to our music. We played most of the same songs, too.

A few months later, Will left the band too. He was the most vocal about replacing Aron but ultimately decided to focus on his own project back in Seattle after Thai left. He committed to doing one last show with us—a diversity and equity training for City of Portland employees followed by a lunchtime concert from the band—before calling it quits for good.

Just like that, the entire front of our stage show changed in less than a year. All of our performances had to be put on hold while I figured out the lineup once more. But there wasn't a shortage of things to do, I still needed to work on our legal matters.

***

The Trademark Trials and Appeals Board flatly dismissed our claim that it was improper for them to use my ethnic identity in their decision-making process. Put simply, they said that they found our arguments "unpersuasive." How could they do this?

"Well, no one is holding them accountable," Spencer told me. Even though he wasn't legally representing me, we continued to talk about the case as it developed. He read everything that I sent him with interest. "It's really a shame that all of that work, all of those organizations, experts, and surveys were just ignored. But they just want to use the ends to justify the means, even if they aren't showing an accurate picture."

"I can't believe they still claimed our concert at the AAYLC was cancelled even though we sent them that legal declaration and proof that we continued working with the organization," I lamented. "That's just unethical!" This was a sore spot for me. If they wanted to actually have a debate on whether or not the Slants was disparaging, fine—but at least don't use dirty tricks to do so. If we were constantly being booked at the largest Asian American festivals and covered by every Asian American media outlet in the country, wouldn't there be more evidence that a "substantial composite" of people found our name disparaging? It had been years, but the Trademark Office still couldn't find a single Asian American willing to publicly go on record against us. Not one Asian American group opposed our name. Instead, the examining attorney based his rejection on a few anonymous comments on message boards.

When I spoke to Ron about these concerns, he simply shrugged it off like it was no big deal. To Ron, those were all just extraneous details that were distracting us from the main argument: the Trademark Office had no right to claim our band was disparaging to begin with. We were moving to the federal appeals court where it would be reviewed by three judges, and he said that only a highly technical and procedural argument would be persuasive. Going to a federal court was a pretty big deal because they could finally consider our legal arguments that the Trademark Office was ignoring. I tried bargaining with Ron and suggested that we at least address the false allegations about our concert being cancelled, but he refused. Instead, he asked me to get amicus briefs. The problem was, I didn't know what amicus briefs were.[42]

With our trademark case moving into the Federal Circuit, I started getting messages from Ron's associate attorney, Joel Mac-Mull. Our communication was always brief, with calls lasting only a few minutes long and emails a few sentences at most. It was such a different working dynamic than what I had shared with Spencer. In fact, I had never met Ron or Joel in person. Everything was done remotely. I usually had to do lots of research on my own to understand where we were in the legal journey and why we chose to appeal to that specific court.[43] I thought that was all part of being a pro bono client.

To my chagrin, I learned that an appeal at the Federal Circuit meant that no new evidence could be introduced. The court would review what had been presented as evidence in our appeals to the Trademark Trial and Appeal Board. That meant any final chance to rebut the claim that the Slants was disparaging was lost. I was

---

[42] Amicus briefs (or *amicus curaie*) simply translates to "friend of the court." They're legal briefs filed by someone who is not a party in a case and offer information or insight into the issues in the case itself.

[43] When trademark cases move out of the Trademark Trial and Appeal Board (TTAB), or the administrative arm of the Trademark Office, applicants can choose to appeal to a District Court (such as the Ninth Circuit for those of us who lived in the West Coast) or the Court of Appeals for the Federal Circuit (CAFC, also referred to as the Federal Circuit).

extremely frustrated by this, but my attorneys earnestly believed that the procedural and evidentiary arguments would prevail. Because the Federal Circuit usually only cared about highly technical issues, our brief was positioned perfectly for them. Besides, Ron and Joel wanted the evidence record locked in to show how my ethnic identity was being used against me and that the highly biased searches for *slant* were problematic. It was like a carefully laid trap but it would only work if the court agreed with the premise.

Before we submitted our legal brief, Joel threw in a couple of constitutional arguments as an afterthought. He told me, "This is just in case this thing ever goes up.[44] It won't . . . but this is just in case."[45] First he argued that Section 2(a) of the Lanham Act violated my First Amendment rights. Then, he suggested that the Trademark Office violated my Fifth Amendment rights of due process. He explained that their law firm was in my corner until we exhausted every possible option for appealing. To me, it just sounded like many more years of my life and even more money that I didn't have.

Unlike the Trademark Trial and Appeal Board, arguments before the Federal Circuit took place in person, so we started making plans to be in Washington, D.C.[46] But a few weeks after our brief

---

[44] To the Supreme Court

[45] Attorneys often will do this to "hold the argument." If you don't submit the argument, it's too late to do so later.

[46] The TTAB does not have oral arguments. Everything must be a submitted brief.

was filed, I started receiving invoices for thousands of dollars. I was shocked. The expenses had grown tenfold! I learned that it was all for appellate printing. Appellate printers specialize in meeting the very precise format of indexing and binding required by the court. It was yet another thing that, had I known about it from the beginning, I probably would have dropped the appeal. Thankfully, the law firm allowed me to pay in installments. This gave me time to sell most of my records, DVDs, and comic books I had held onto since childhood to pay for it. But it also meant I'd have to get a loan out just to be there.

I'm not sure if Joel knew how much I was struggling financially, but a few weeks after our court date was set, he called me to let me know I didn't need to be there in person. He said he'd hate for me to fly all the way to Washington, D.C., just to be disappointed by the thirty-minute argument before the three-judge panel. I wasn't sure if they also suspected that I might be disruptive or make their job tougher with all of my questions. It was just as well since I needed to focus on filling those empty positions in the band.

* * *

Auditioning people for the Slants was a lot tougher than what one would think. The process took a lot longer than what most bands go through when trying to replace someone. Finding Asian American talent was tough in a place like Portland. When I first had the idea for the Slants in 2004, it took me two years before I could find enough people to put a band together. I would post ads on

Craigslist and Myspace regularly.[47] I even hung posters that said ASIAN MUSICIANS WANTED at restaurants and Fubonn, our local Asian shopping center. Ten years later, the band had a much higher profile so it would seem to be easier, but I wasn't just limited by how people identified themselves; I wanted to make sure that they had similar values as well. To do this, I created an online application that included some short essay questions on personal goals and issues of Asian American representation. I cast the net wide with a national search, but it was only the first step.

After the responses started coming in, we'd hold auditions at a local venue. The applicant would be given five songs to learn on their own. Then, they would perform the set on stage with us as if it were a live concert while we filmed it. Not only would they be judged for their musical talent, but also for their charisma on stage. Afterwards, we'd sit with the candidates for a casual conversation about their life goals, experiences, and values. If they had a significant other, we'd meet them and talk about expectations for how often we'd be gone on the road as well. Ken Shima was the first to go through this entire process and, after a six-month probationary period, ended up being our new lead singer. A year later, Joe X. Jiang joined as our guitarist. Tyler was still on drums so that left me as the only original member. Over the years, our band sometimes swelled to seven people on stage, but I decided to keep this version as a four

---

[47] Remember, this was 2004. Facebook wasn't around yet. R.I.P. bulletins and top 8 friends.

piece. A leaner crew meant we could tour more easily with fewer logistics to worry about.

Once Joe joined, I didn't wait long to get things moving again. I scheduled our first photo shoot and started booking a national tour. We also began recording another album. Alex, our publicist, suggested that we get something out reflecting the new lineup as soon as possible, so we took seventeen of our most popular songs and created a "best of" release, rerecording everything under the title *Something Slanted This Way Comes*. For the liner notes, I wrote a history of our first ten years as a band. Looking back, it reads like I was ready for everything to end:

> There's no way that I could have predicted all of this to happen as I was watching Kill Bill on that fateful night many years ago. I just wanted to start a band to provide some representation for Asian Americans and to share our culture, not fight a legal case. . . . But honestly, I wouldn't take any of it back. It's been an incredible journey and there have been so many amazing people that we've met along the way. It's been said that we are defined by what we care about. As we share our music with you that has carried us through the past decade, I hope you'll hear how it is ingrained with the passion, spirit, and struggles of this band over the years. More than any 80's music or film with yakuza, our band has been defined by the community that we serve: The Slants Army. And whether you're just joining or you've been in our ranks for years, we salute you.

* * *

Joel called me the day after oral arguments were held at the Federal Circuit. I was on the road, playing a set of shows down the West Coast. He seemed energized by the hearing even though things took a very different turn than expected. Apparently, the court was apathetic about our technical arguments regarding procedural and evidentiary issues. The Presiding Judge, Kimberly Moore, seemed to care about only one issue: the First Amendment. Within a few minutes of the oral arguments starting up, she wanted to focus entirely on whether the disparagement provision was constitutional or not.

"To the extent that the Office Action made any reference whatsoever to the ethnic identity of the applicant himself . . . that is entirely improper," Ron argued. He tried steering the conversation back to the original focus of our appeal. "But we don't want to push that too hard. We don't think it's necessary to address that issue. We want to focus on the far more obvious issues, the evidentiary issues." I later found out that he was so confident that the court wouldn't care about the constitutional arguments that he didn't even bother reviewing them. He was caught off guard and began stammering when he tried to answer their questions about the First Amendment. He definitely sounded different than his normal confident and jovial self that I was so used to hearing over the phone.

At one point, Judge Moore snapped, "Do you even have a First Amendment argument? I'm having a hard time grasping what your argument actually is." Ouch.

When it was time for the attorney representing the Trademark Office to make her arguments, she also tried focusing on whether the Slants was disparaging or not. Within a couple of minutes, another judge intervened, asking, "What about the First Amendment argument here?" She tried sidestepping the conversation by referring to an old trademark case where the same court ruled that denying a registration for a trademark did not violate First Amendment rights.[48] Judge Moore immediately jumped on her for that.

"What about the unconstitutional conditions doctrine? Which, I'm sure you're familiar with . . . So you may not be prepared to discuss this with me and you can say so and I'll let you sit down without further questions if you're completely unprepared . . . I'll let you off the hook."

I listened intently with headphones while band members were relaxing in our hotel room after the show. Both attorneys were harshly grilled for not being ready to answer questioning about the constitutional issues related to our case. I wasn't quite sure how we did, but it was obvious that neither side came prepared to answer so

----

[48] *In re McGinley* was decided in 1981 and often referred to by the Trademark Office to deny registrations. However, free speech was a rather minor and unexplored point in that case and was referred to in just two sentences in the entire opinion. In fact, the Trademark Act of 1988 further clarified that trademark rights were substantive and not simply procedural, which meant the application of *McGinley* should have evolved over time as well, and that the substantive issues of my case could only be decided *en banc*.

many questions about the First Amendment. A few months later, the court issued their unanimous opinion.

We lost.

In a short, eleven-page opinion, the court affirmed the Trademark Office's position. They rejected all of our procedural and evidentiary arguments as well as our constitutional ones about free speech and due process, saying that as a three judge panel, they were bound by the precedent set by *In re McGinley*. Curiously, the court's decision was followed by twenty-four pages of "Additional Views" from Judge Moore. She had voted with the majority (against us), but her "Additional Views" read like a powerful dissent.[49] It was confusing to say the least since no one really knew what "Additional Views" were. Ron, Joel, and I decided we'd take a couple weeks off to reflect on the opinion before reconvening to discuss our next steps. But we weren't even able to do that.

A week after the opinion was issued, the court changed their mind: I received a notice that the Federal Circuit wanted to rehear our case; this unusual step was called a Sua Sponte Hearing En

---

[49] Judge Moore wrote, "It is time for this Court to revisit McGinley's holding on the constitutionality of § 2(a) of the Lanham Act. Under § 2(a), the PTO may refuse to register immoral, scandalous, or disparaging marks . . . More than thirty years have passed since McGinley, and in that time both the McGinley decision and our reliance on it have been widely criticized."

Banc.[50] The court ordered that the decision on my case, *In re Tam*,[51] would be vacated (everyone would pretend that it never happened) and that the court would hold oral arguments again en banc (before all the judges of the court) instead of only a panel of three judges. Basically, the court was saying, "Oops! Let's have a do over!" In addition, the court requested that we file new legal briefs to focus only on one matter: did the bar on registering disparaging trademarks violate the First Amendment?

This immediately excited legal scholars because it was exceptionally rare for a federal court to rehear a case on its own accord—the odds are close to one tenth of one percent—and it's usually a patent case, not a trademark ruling, that triggers that kind of response.[52] Or, as Joel told me in an email exchange,

---

[50] Our legal system can never seem to decide which language to use, English, Latin, or French. The phrase *Sua Sponte Hearing En Banc* has all three. *Sua Sponte* is Latin for "on its own accord" and *En Banc* is French for "in bench."

[51] As a case moves through the court system, it will often change names. My first two applications began as numbers. At the Federal Circuit, it was called *In re Tam*. When it first got to the Supreme Court, it was known as *Lee v. Tam* (named for the director at the U.S. Trademark Office, Michelle Lee). By the time the decision was issued, it became *Matal v. Tam*, because Joseph Matal replaced Lee before the opinion was released. It's a little confusing but probably not much more so than how the Star Wars films are sequenced.

[52] Alexandra Sadinsky, Redefining En Banc Review in the Federal Courts of Appeals, 82 Fordham L. Rev. 2001 (2014).

A few things here are truly incredible. First, this Court of Appeals almost never elects to revisit issues sua sponte, i.e., by its own doing. Typically, an application for a rehearing en banc has to be made by a party and even then is it rarely granted. Second, as we have long said, this Court doesn't usually pass on constitutional issues. While they have the authority to do so, they typically don't go there.

This is a legal rarity in its truest sense.

Great. A legal unicorn. Legal wonks weren't the only people interested. Within minutes of the opinion being issued, a few dozen journalists contacted me and asked for a response. As word spread, I started getting emails from high-profile lawyers at large firms offering their services pro bono. They could see what I couldn't, that this case was already making history, and they wanted to be a part of it. It only frustrated me more. Where were these people when I needed help years ago? Were they only contacting me now because it was getting so much attention? Then, I got word that the American Civil Liberties Union was finally interested in getting involved.

For years, I sought help from groups like the ACLU, the Public Interest Law Center, and the CATO Institute, but they always turned me down, saying my case was too obscure. The ACLU of Oregon told me, "it's more of a matter of where we deploy our scarce resources in an uphill fight than any reflection of the justness of your cause . . . if the Slants case makes it to the Supreme Court we would of course take another look to see if we should weigh in." Other groups shared a similar sentiment or didn't bother responding at all. Now that we were shaking things up, it was like I was suddenly the star of a high school prom movie. My case just needed a First Amendment makeover so we would finally be noticed by the cool kids. The glasses are off! How do you like me now?[53]

It is understandable for public interest groups to remain on the sidelines until a case becomes more prominent. With so much litigation in the United States, the demand for help can overwhelm groups with limited funding and time. They have to be selective so they can make the most impact with each particular case.

A few years ago, I learned about Daniel Bernstein, a cryptologist and programmer who wanted to publish the source code for an encryption system that he developed as a student in college. However, the National Security Agency (NSA) threatened to prosecute him as an arms dealer if he ever shared his code. It was only after the Electronic Frontier Foundation, a nonprofit dedicated to civil liberties in the digital world, intervened that Bernstein had a chance to expose the ridiculous government policies that were encroaching on his rights. Against all odds, they successfully argued before the 9th Circuit that the NSA's policies violated the First Amendment. *Bernstein v. United States* became one of the most important legal battles of the internet age, ushering in new levels of privacy and encryption for all users.

---

[53] Kudos to Isaac Asimov for critiquing the "ugly girl with glasses becoming popular" trope in his essay, "A Cult of Ignorance." He wrote, "Is there a person alive so obtuse as not to see that the presence of glasses in no way ruined [her] looks?"

We need champions because the legal journey is long and full of terrors. It is expensive to get outside help from organizations even if you have legal representation (each amicus brief may cost $50,000, not including appellate printing). If I didn't have help through pro bono representation, I would have easily spent a half million dollars at this point. Most people don't realize how emotionally draining it is to be constantly looking for outside help. At this point, I didn't have a choice. I needed to recruit more organizations to join our cause in order to have a fighting chance.

* * *

I started getting invited to speak on panels at law conventions around the country. Most of the time, I agreed to do so because it could expose the facts of our case to more people. The event I was looking forward to more than any other was the annual convention for the National Asian Pacific American Bar Association (NAPABA), where I would be joined by a number of prominent attorneys to discuss whether the U.S. government should be involved in determining what is offensive. It was the largest gathering of Asian Americans in law and would provide me with a chance to win their support. But there was also something very personal about this event for me: it would be the first time I would meet one of the attorneys representing me in person.

When Joel first greeted me in the lobby of the W, I thought he looked like younger John Oliver with a very strict side part but less prominent nose. He was sharply dressed with complementary patterns in his suit, shirt, and tie. It was almost as if our respective hotels reflected the state each of us were in: the W was luxurious, hip, and filled with spaces for socializing. It was within walking distance of the convention. On the other hand, the best feature of my motel was the free granola bar I got for checking in. It required a bus to get to the convention.

Joel spoke very quickly about our panel, like the legal disclosures at the end of a pharmaceutical commercial. It was only when he slowed that I could detect a faint Canadian accent, particularly when he said "about" and "house." He wanted me to share my story, but I could tell he was concerned that I might muddle up the legal issues. Considering the number of slides in his PowerPoint deck, I was worried he'd go over his allotted time.

It turned out that we didn't need to worry. The panel went better than we could have imagined. As we fielded questions, each of the panelists started to demonstrate support for our position. Some were initially concerned that our case could inadvertently be used to help the Washington Redskins, but once they saw how the government's trademark policies could create disparate impact, that skepticism disappeared. One of the panelists called my effort an "intelligent . . . quiet, dignified revolution." The audience resoundingly agreed and began calling on NAPABA to support us with an amicus brief. By the time I was introduced to their president, George Chen, he told me they were already exploring options to support me and said, "You have many fans within NAPABA." He also suggested he'd help arrange a follow-up panel for their national conference the following year and possibly book a concert performance from our band as well!

Finally, it seemed that things were starting to move in our favor. I had two new band members and a couple of amicus briefs in the making too!

* * *

I received notice that oral arguments for the en banc hearing were going to be in October; our briefs would be due in July. The months leading up to that deadline were a blur. I was working on a social justice boot camp for high school kids, reviewing the legal briefs, and revving up for a late fall tour with the band. I was so busy that I didn't have time to do as much follow-up work as I wanted with each of the organizations we were courting for amicus briefs.

In July, Joel forwarded me the last of the briefs that were filed. His email included the government's own brief as well as amicus briefs from people who supported their position, including Amanda Blackhorse.[54] Blackhorse was a social worker known for being the lead plaintiff in the legal efforts to get the Redskins' trademark registrations cancelled. It wasn't surprising that she submitted a brief, given the rising concern that my case would inadvertently help the Washington football team retain their trademark registrations. However, I was shocked to find NAPABA's brief among those in support of the government, especially after the conversations we had about them supporting me. For five years, I had

---

[54] Amanda Blackhorse belonged to a group of Native American activists who were in litigation against Pro Football, Inc. to cancel six trademark registrations for the Washington football team under Section 2(a) of the Lanham Act.

worked with their members on a variety of issues, both with the band as well as with my roles in a number of Asian American organizations. What happened?!

I felt a wave of nausea as I read their brief, each word like a small dagger being twisted into my back. This wasn't a disagreement over the application of a law like the Blackhorse brief. The Blackhorse brief provided a cautionary tale about allowing disparaging trademarks and argued that a registration amounted to government endorsement of a trademark. The NAPABA brief downplayed the wide support from the Asian American community, even among their own members. There was clear animosity present. Instead of holding the government accountable for using my ethnic identity against me or for failing to apply laws in a culturally competent manner, they called my band's work racist thirteen times. Statements like, "Mr. Tam cannot wield his First Amendment rights as a sword to compel the Government to aid him in spreading racial epithets to every concert hall and record store in the nation or to enrich him in the process" stung. They even implied that our band was equivalent to a group of Caucasians "made up to look Asian." I was filled with so much anger and deep sadness that I physically felt sick throughout my body.

It hurt, deeply. I thought it worse than the kicks to the belly I received as a kid for being Asian. It was worse than repeatedly being called a jap or a gook. It was more degrading than having the record label of my dreams ask me to replace our lead singer with someone who was white. It was a different kind of pain because NAPABA claimed to represent the interests and values of my community.[55] Just like the government, NAPABA was eager to use me when it suited their purposes (as a speaker and panelist, to raise money or awareness, or to sign autographs at their events, etc.) but also just as quick to throw me aside when it didn't.

I tried phoning and emailing their president, who I had been corresponding with, but was ignored. Radio silence. There was no justification, no clarification as to why they'd lead me on about working together only to submit this degrading brief instead. Several of their members started calling me since they assumed that the organization was enthusiastically behind us. No one could explain what had happened.

I started publicly venting my frustration at NAPABA. Many of their members did the same. News sites like the Huffington Post and community blogs like Angry Asian Man asked me to write guest pieces calling for accountability. A petition for NAPABA to withdraw their brief was circulated, and thousands signed. I even did a TEDx talk on the story, explaining how betrayal challenges us to

---

[55] I understand that no community is monolithic and as the most diverse racial group in the world, Asian Pacific Islanders are no exception. I wasn't asking for erasure of all voices, but rather, the representation of them. Just as I argued that most, but not all, Asian Americans were in our support, they too could have argued from a more comprehensive perspective and provided support for their position.

better demonstrate our values.[56] I was overwhelmed with notes of encouragement from people who believed in our work and by members who said NAPABA did not represent their views. Several NAPABA state chapters even shared some of my Op-Eds that rebuked their parent organization. I was striking out in pain. Some of it seemed pretty extreme. Yet looking back, I'm not sure if I'd do anything different. At least it was honest—I don't think the organization could say the same.

The backlash caught NAPABA off guard. They didn't expect to receive criticism from so many voices in the Asian American community. In a subsequent press release, they substantially softened their tone, claiming that they were trying to protect us against harmful terms. Publicly, they realized that rebuking my work wasn't a good idea—clearly, their own members railed against them for that. Instead, they referred to their legal brief as a line in the sand against racism. To that end, they propped up the litigation of the Washington Redskins as a demonstration of why the disparagement provision was necessary. In order to attack symbols of hate, efforts of reappropriation—no matter their intention—had to die as collateral damage. They used the football team's name as a shield to protect themselves from criticism. After all, what kind of monster could support such a racist name in professional sports? A prominent Asian American legal scholar reached out in an attempt to connect me with their president and board, but NAPABA declined

---

[56] "Losing the Line Between Art and Activism" was about NAPABA and my legal journey. It was shared at TEDxErie in November 2015.

any attempts at mediation. For them, the monster wasn't actually Dan Snyder[57] or the people actually using racist terms and logos. It was me. Because my case might inadvertently perpetuate racist iconography, they needed to stop me.

* * *

As all of this was developing, I was working with a local theatre group to do a staged reading of *Citizen Min*, inspired by the life of Minoru Yasui. While I was familiar with some of the legal cases that challenged the constitutionality of the incarceration camps during World War II, this play helped bring to light details that were relatively unknown. Yasui, as well as Fred Korematsu, bravely fought against laws that stripped Japanese Americans of their dignity and their rights. Both of them ended up at the U.S. Supreme Court as well. But one thing I didn't realize was that the Japanese American Citizens League (JACL) originally denounced their efforts. The JACL was afraid that Yasui and Korematsu's efforts would provoke the government into doing more to harm the community, so they refused to help. It was only years later that both men were lauded as heroes by the JACL for their work.

After our reading of *Citizen Min*, the attorney who represented the Yasui family spoke briefly. I didn't know it until they shared their own background, but they were also on the board of directors for NAPABA. When they opened the floor to questions,

---

[57] Dan Snyder is the billionaire owner of the Washington Redskins. He has vowed to never change the name.

I was the first to ask one. I stood up in front of the audience. "If there was an activist today who was fighting for something that they believed in, but an organization like the JACL or NAPABA was against them, what would your advice be to them? Should they follow the example of Minoru Yasui and defy orders?"

"You should always follow your heart, especially if that fight brings justice to more people than only yourself," they told me. "Sometimes organizations are slow to understand, sometimes they have different competing interests, and sometimes they can be wrong. Minoru was driven by a strong sense of justice, we should all follow that example and never give up."

When I introduced myself later in private and explained the context of my situation, they admitted that they weren't familiar with my case. They told me that what the organization did should have never happened. Members of NAPABA's staff and board have told me the same thing. Even though it's been a few years, and I've spoken at other NAPABA affiliated events since this all happened, I still feel a tinge of pain.

It isn't uncommon for there to be differences among organizations in the same community. In recent years, Asian Americans have been seemingly divided over issues related to affirmative action (taking different sides on a monumental Supreme Court case that challenged Harvard University's admissions processes), accountability for police violence,[58] and even support for presidential candidates.[59] That's because we are not a monolithic group. There's nothing in our DNA that binds all Asian Americans together. No group identifiable by race, gender, sexual orientation, or religion is unanimous in terms of how they approach justice, even if they share the same values. We're far more diverse than stereotypes allow.

* * *

As I started making plans for Washington, D.C., our guitarist Joe asked if he could join so that he could film a documentary about my journey through the courts. I set up a number of interviews for him with scholars in the area. A few Asian American organizations and teachers also asked me to speak at their schools; we ended up with a packed schedule that would keep us busy from

---

[58] Peter Liang was a Chinese American police officer who fatally shot Akai Gurley. Some Asian American groups argued Liang was being treated as a scapegoat and that the charges should be dropped as in the case of nearly all instances of white cops shooting unarmed victims. Others disagreed, arguing that all police officers should be held accountable for their actions.

[59] We were originally invited to perform at the inauguration ball for President Trump that was being thrown by the Asian Pacific American Advisory Council and National Committee of Asian American Republicans. Deciding whether to play at all or not had us divided as a band! In the end, they decided to go with a local dance troupe to "focus more on an act that represents cultural heritage."

morning to night. It felt like we were going on tour since I was trying to fill every minute of the day with something productive.

Joe would pepper me with questions for his documentary while I drove the rental car. It was like I was constantly "on." It felt a bit uncomfortable, even though it was a friend behind the lens. Sometimes, a television crew or journalist would meet us on location for one of my appearances and ask even more questions. It was mentally and emotionally draining. I'm fairly certain that I just stopped answering questions at one point because I wanted some kind of reprieve.

In the middle of our trip, Joe's cousin Yin drove up from North Carolina to come hang out with us. When he mentioned how hungry he was even after we had already eaten two back-to-back meals, I knew we'd get along. At one point, I was doing an interview with a newspaper in China and was asked for my written Chinese name. I didn't know how to type Chinese characters so I wrote out my name on a piece of paper and asked for Joe's help. Joe was born and raised in China for most of his childhood whereas I was denied being able to learn the language while I was in school.

"What is that?" He stared, rotated the paper, and laughed. Yin looked over but couldn't make sense of what I had written either.

"I only know how to write a few things in Chinese—my name, the numbers one through four, mom, and food—that's it. Or at least, I thought that was it."

"Some of these aren't even real characters! Say your name."

"Tom shi wun? Tam siu wun? I know, my pronunciation sucks."

We then called my dad to try and make sense of it. He tried explaining it as well but the intonation wasn't very clear over the phone. Shù as in number? Or are you saying shū as in book? Or is it shū like unique? With so many variations and possible combinations of characters in Chinese, it seemed impossible to decipher what was happening. It was ironic that while I was trying so hard to fight for my identity, I couldn't even figure out how to write out my name even with the help of three other men who were born and raised in China. Finally, after about thirty minutes, we figured out my name: 譚仕文 (Tánshìwén)

I think we often forget the importance of names. I was born "Simon Hsiao Tam" on March 31, 1981—at least according to my parents. Growing up, I had a couple of different middle names. My paper trail through the public school system will sometimes list it as "Hong," like my father's, and sometimes "Hsiao," from my mother's side of the family. I didn't really know which to choose, I just knew that no matter what, it began with an "H," so that my initials of "SHT" would either be a badass proclamation or a target for ridicule.

But this wasn't exactly the whole story: my birth certificate revealed that both my birthday and my name were wrong—at least according to the state. I was actually born "Simon Shiao Tam"[60] on March 30, 1981. I was no longer the "SHT," but "SST," something that sounded like a large, antiquated cargo barge.

There was a lot going on at the time, I could see how mistakes could be made. On the day I was really born, President Ronald Reagan and several of his staff members were shot in broad daylight. But the reality is that this wasn't the first time the government screwed up names in my family. As different relatives entered the U.S. and dealt with different officials, our family name was interpreted and recorded differently. That's why my father, his parents, his grandparents, and his siblings all have different last names: Tam, Tom, Tong, Tan.

Identity matters. When simple mistakes are made due to ignorance or poor translation, these can create difficulties later on for families trying to communicate, share resources, or navigate government systems that often require accuracy. Identity is inherently tied with dignity. We should be able to define ourselves based on our own terms and to identify ourselves as part a community. Yet, what we find is that people from marginalized groups often have others defining their identities for them: the status of their citizenship, the categories for racial and ethnic groups as defined by the dominant population, or as in my family's case, how names are spelled and pronounced.

---

[60] Ultimately, this was the name recorded by the Supreme Court since it was in our original application.

The simple, lighthearted misunderstanding with the Chinese journalist reminded me of the importance of names. Some names are sacred, passed through generations for thousands of years. Through laziness and misinterpretation, our family name was butchered at the hands of immigration officials and getting further lost with each passing generation that was forced to assimilate. I vowed never to forget my family name again. Some names are worth fighting for.

Over the next few days, I visited schools in the area. Spending a few days with students was just what I needed before heading into the courtroom. As I opened up about my own personal story and answered questions about the Slants, many of the Asian students shared their own stories about being bullied or feeling invisible. Some of them came up to me privately afterwards, telling me that they even considered taking their own lives, but that our band's story helped them feel seen. It was overwhelming, and I could see that even some of the teachers had tears in their eyes. Even if things didn't go how we'd hope in court, I felt like the trip was worth it just for those moments alone.

* * *

As the date of our Federal Circuit appearance got closer, I was filled with nerves. I laid out my outfit the night before carefully: my cheap H&M blazer and vest, a pair of dinosaur socks gifted to me, a crushed maroon tie made by friend Rachel, and a silver watch that I inherited from my great-grandfather. I combined the nicest stuff I owned with as many things from loved ones as possible, like I was assembling a bit of armor. I mindlessly used the lint roller, in a vain attempt to remove the dog hair on all of my clothes. Outfit complete.

We left early the next morning to beat any traffic. As we walked to the court, Joe and I paused in front of the White House, which was across the street from the building we were heading to. I projected some thoughts towards President Obama, asking for any kind of help or recognition for what we were trying to do with our work. Then, I walked through the gates of the Court of Appeals for the Federal Circuit, while Joe followed with the camera rolling. Security quickly dampened that effort: no filming was allowed.

As we took the elevator up, I could feel my stomach rising to my throat. The doors parted and I walked into a large lobby. Joel walked up with a large smile and extended hand as he told me, "Before we go into the courtroom, we need to take a second to really appreciate this moment." He ushered me into a smaller courtroom where a portly man was pacing back and forth with animated hands, as if he were rehearsing an important speech. Dressed in a fine wool suit, he resembled a grandfatherly Paul Giamatti. Of course, I recognized him right away—it was Ron Coleman, the attorney whom I'd been corresponding with for several years!

Ron was exuberant and gave me a large hug. He had a kind face that sometimes gave way to a sneaky, mischievous grin. On social media, the initial perception is that he is a snarky, hard-line conservative who takes no nonsense from any bleeding heart liberals. But in person, he was gracious, had a sardonic sense of humor like mine, and was deeply considerate of others.

Introductions to others were made and pictures were taken, despite signs saying no cameras were allowed. The air felt electric. I could tell Ron was really excited to be there. For him, it was a career-defining moment. After some polite chatter, Joel told us it was time. "Gentlemen, let's do this!" We walked down the hallway and into the large en banc courtroom like it was a Quentin Tarantino movie, our own respective theme songs playing in our minds.[61] My attorneys walked right up to their table, briefcases in hand.

Before we sat down, I was introduced to two attorneys from the American Civil Liberties Union. Lee Rowland, their senior staff attorney on speech, privacy, and technology was granted ten minutes to argue as amici, or "a friend of the court." Esha Bhandari, another staff attorney who worked on the legal brief, was also there to support. They were enthusiastic about supporting our case, especially because we made more sympathetic clients than the Washington Redskins, who were dealing with some parallel issues in their trademark case. I always saw the two cases as distinct, but those subtle complexities are often lost when trying to simplify and discuss legal issues.

"Who are all of those people?" I asked, looking at the dozens of suits to our left. In addition to filling all of the extra chairs at the table, the men also filled the two rows of seats behind them as well. Each one of them carried large folders and a small stack of

---

[61] Of course, I was thinking of Tomoyasu Hotei's "Battle Without Honor or Humanity," the song that introduced the world to the Crazy 88's in Kill Bill.

books with colorful slips of paper sticking out like little tongues. They looked more like a preppy fraternity than anything else. They seemed to be lightly joking and giving each other high fives when they glanced at our table.

"That's who we're up against."

I took another glance to size them up. For every attorney on my side, they had three. They weren't taking any chances. Working together, the Department of Justice and the Trademark Office sent some of their best and brightest. Even though only one person could stand before the court, they had an entire team of attorneys doing research and preparing notes for them throughout the arguments. I wouldn't be surprised if some of them were hired just to sit and intimidate us. They might have tripled us, but I liked those odds. My attorneys weren't being paid to win—they weren't being paid at all. They were here because they believed in me. They had heart.[62]

Joel looked serious, like he was putting his game face on. He said, "Listen, no matter what happens today, we're with you all the

---

[62] One of my favorite chapters in *The Tao of Wu* by The RZA is Heart. He says if someone "has the will and courage to do something difficult, even if it's just surviving . . . he got a lot of heart . . . This relates to the Heart Sutra, one of the shortest but most important sutras in Buddhist writings . . . it's only a paragraph long, but you might look at it like the illest verse ever spit—simple, tight, and incomparably profound."

way. If we don't win, we're going to appeal. We're going to use every option for you, even if this has to go to the Supreme Court."

The room began to fill up quickly. Every seat was taken, including rows in the balcony that peered over us. I looked up at the twelve empty leather chairs raised above us. Each had a small placard bearing the name of the judge to be seated there. One name in particular jumped out: Chen. Raymond T. Chen was the only Asian American judge serving in this court. Originally, it was speculated that he would be asked to recuse himself in our case for fear of bias. They said it was because of his past experience with the Trademark Office, though almost everyone could see right through that.

When all twelve judges walked in wearing their robes, it felt like we were attending mass. We were told when to sit or stand, and it seemed to require a bit of understanding Latin.

"The case for argument this morning is 14-1203 In re Tam."

The gavel struck and the countdown clock began.[63]

The next ninety minutes flew by as twelve judges hurled their questions at whichever attorney was standing. Ron was up first. Despite the occasional slips, he sounded far more confident than the previous three-judge hearing as he began articulating arguments why Section 2(a) of the Lanham Act should be considered

---

[63] The lectern which the attorneys argue from has a small digital clock that counts down the available time left for them to make their arguments or answer questions.

unconstitutional. I rolled my eyes as one of the judges refused to say "the Slants," but tried to add dramatization by calling it "the S word" instead. Perhaps he forgot that unlike other terms, "slant" is not an inherent racial slur. Besides, isn't there an actual vulgar term that children refer to as "the S word" already? Twenty minutes in, Ron stepped down to save some of his remaining time for rebuttal.

Lee Rowland from the ACLU was called up and immediately jumped in to answer questions brought up by one of the more reserved judges. Lee was fully confident as she quoted Supreme Court opinions and cases from memory. It was like watching Neo after he realized he was The One: bullets were dodged, attacks from multiple angles were parried with one hand. When it came to the First Amendment, she knew the system inside out. There is no spoon. She also had no problems calling out the government for using my ethnicity against me saying, "We have a written record of the government saying 'We don't like what the Slants have to say. We know they are Asian and therefore their viewpoint is impermissible."

Boom. Mic drop. I wanted to give her a standing ovation!

Then, a thin middle-aged man in a navy blue suit walked up. It was now the government's turn to speak. He walked with an air of privilege like he was untouchable. But after a few tough questions from the judges, his nasal voice cracked, and he started taking the shape of a slinky, clutching the platform for balance or strength. He was crumpling under pressure. He was having trouble distinguishing between copyright and trademark law. The attorneys around him furiously flipped through their books and handed notes to him, but he only used them to pat his sweaty forehead. Judge after judge seemed annoyed at his inability to provide clarity on the government's position.

"I don't think you're answering my question . . . I'm just not following what you're saying."

"I don't quite follow either."

"I found your brief a little confusing. Can you clarify?"

"I don't understand why you think this."

He was taking such a pummeling, I started to feel bad for him . . . but not that bad. After all, the guy claimed to care about fighting racism but he seemed to have no problem with upholding laws that would perpetuate discrimination based on race, like the law we were fighting. He saw racism embodied in words, or racial slurs, and not actual systems that impact how people navigate our society. For him, this was just another day in court where he was hired to make an argument. Win or lose, he wouldn't be impacted by the decision.

Afterwards, the government's attorney came up and shook the hands of each of my attorneys before turning and walking away. Joe and I were ignored. Journalists and students started coming up to us, asking questions. I thought it interesting that we had a wide diversity of gender, age, and racial identities walking up to us while the other side of the aisle was composed of nearly all-white men. It was one of those things that could never be articulated as a legal argument in a court of law, but I really thought that it should have counted for something. In that courtroom, I didn't feel as alone anymore.

* * *

In the months that followed, our band hit the road to solidify our new lineup. We had a new album to support and were preparing for a tour across Asia. We also released a music video for "Sakura, Sakura" in support of the Oregon Nikkei Legacy Center, a museum that focused on the history of the Japanese incarceration camps. It was particularly meaningful for our singer, Ken, since members of his family were put into camps themselves.

Our publicist worked tirelessly to get people excited about our music and the new video, but the media only seemed to be interested in our legal battle. We were fighting to be seen, but the case cast a shadow over everything. I couldn't forge my own identity through our band's name, and now that struggle was creating a different identity for me. It seemed no one cared about our background, our intention, or our art. My band was just a footnote for a larger, looming story.

We often forget about the people behind the major events in legal history. Most legal scholars don't know much more than what is contained in documents published by the courts, even in some of the most influential and quoted cases in history. Consider *Yick Wo v. Hopkins*,[64] a case argued before the Supreme Court in

---

[64] The first case where the United States Supreme Court ruled that a law *de jure* administered in a discriminatory fashion would infringe Equal Protection

1886. The litigant, Yick Wo, just wanted to operate his laundry business despite the city of San Francisco making it illegal for most Chinese immigrants to do so. He was fined and jailed. It took six years before he won when the Supreme Court unanimously declared that even if a law is nondiscriminatory, enforcing the law in a discriminatory manner could still be unconstitutional. After the decision, he disappeared into obscurity despite being part of such a monumental case. He wasn't reimbursed for his fines paid or compensated for being unjustly jailed. Most likely, he continued to struggle with his business. The only information available on Yick Wo comes from sources related to his court case. Who gets to choose the identity and assumptions that come with being the named litigant in a high-profile case?

I hoped that no matter what would happen with our case, that we wouldn't fall into the same kind of obscurity. I worked hard for my music and our social justice work. I didn't want to be known only as the guy the government thought was racist.

Eight weeks after our trip to the federal courts in D.C., I woke up to a Twitter notification. It was Lee Rowland, who tagged me in a message saying, "I am delighted at the idea of you waking up to victory . . . "

We did it. We finally won.

---

rights. It also extended rights to non-U.S. citizens. Even though it had little application after the decision (*Plessy v. Ferguson* allowed discriminatory behavior), it's been cited in over 150 Supreme Court cases.

A solid majority of nine federal judges struck down the seventy-year-old Lanham Act's provision on disparagement, paving the way for us to finally receive the registration of our trademark. Writing for the opinion, Judge Kimberly Moore stated, "Courts have been slow to appreciate the expressive power of trademarks . . . Words – even a single word – can be powerful. Mr. Simon Tam named his band the Slants to make a statement about racial and cultural issues in this country. With his band name, Mr. Tam conveys more about our society than many volumes of undisputedly protected speech." It took nearly six years, but we were finally seen!

Then, people started talking about football.

CHAPTER 11
FROM THE HEART

~~~~

UNTIL THE FEDERAL CIRCUIT RULED ON OUR CASE, we enjoyed relative isolation from other legal issues. It didn't mean that the issue was simple. It just meant that people saw it as obscure and not something that could affect other issues. Generally speaking, that's how things work at the Trademark Office. That's one of the reasons for the vast inconsistency in how trademark decisions were made in the past. For example, the Trademark Office denied "Madonna" for wines in one application[65] but approved it for another. They found "Queer Gear" as fine to register for clothing but not "Clearly Queer" or the same kind of product. And imagine if you received a registration for one type of service only to have it denied for another. That's what happened with Jewish comedy magazine, Heeb Media (they registered the trademark for their magazine successfully, but were denied registrations for the same

---

[65] In re Riverbank Canning Co., 95 F.2d 327 (C.C.P.A. 1938).

trademark for other products and services). This was the random history of trademark rejections under Section 2(a) of the Lanham Act. Even if one person at the Trademark Office thought what you were doing was fine, it could still be rejected by someone else who decided that your trademark was scandalous, immoral, or disparaging. Why would anyone care how the Trademark Office ruled on the Slants?

This all changed when we were asked to argue the case before the Federal Circuit en banc. Unlike the Trademark Office, the court had the power strike down the law. The stakes were raised. On one hand, this meant we could truly disrupt a process that I saw as unjust; a process that allowed the government to use minority identities against people like me. On the other, it could allow more vile trademarks to be registered. Trademarks that might possibly be denied under the law I was fighting. I didn't take that choice lightly. I sought out advice from experts in social justice from many different backgrounds across over thirty states. From policy makers to activists, I shared the different possible outcomes and was repeatedly told the same thing: focus on whatever would create more options for those who had the least. For me, that was the power of expression.

Immediately after the Federal Circuit decision was published, the media shifted the lens from a story about the underdog Asian American band to the most hated man in football.[66] Six

---

[66] Dan Snyder has been named the most hated man in sports by various sources for about twelve years now. It isn't just because of his treatment of Native

months prior to the ruling on my case, a federal judge in a different district ruled that six Washington Redskins trademark registrations could be cancelled under Section 2(a) of the Lanham Act. This was seen as an important step for the Native American activists who had been working for years to get the team name changed. Now the Federal Circuit had found that Section 2(a) was unconstitutional: as a result, the Washington Redskins could potentially keep their trademark registrations. That's when it became difficult to find a news story that didn't link me to the team. And when that happened, all hell broke loose.

A group of Native American activists and some of their allies flooded social media with angry posts about the recent Federal Circuit decision. They were calling me out, denouncing me as someone who was enabling racism. To them, I was enabling people like Dan Snyder to profit from racist imagery. They believed that my case had just selfishly rolled back years of efforts to get the Redskins to change their name.

I tried responding by clarifying how trademark laws worked. Even if the Washington football team had all of their registrations cancelled, they would not have to change their name. They would still have trademark rights. Of course, this all came across as insensitive and paternalistic, especially when responses were limited to

---

Americans, but also his terrible winning record and price gouging as well. See "The Most Hated People, Places and Things in the NFL." Sports Illustrated, July 22, 2015.

140 characters. When I explained that I supported efforts to change the name, and that I met with numerous Native American confederated tribe leaders in the process, it only appeared to be pandering and tokenizing. This went on for several days. What would Perla do? Sure, I might be a fighter, but these weren't people I wanted to fight against; they were ones I wanted to fight alongside with.

My eyes drifted towards an old plastic car that Perla gave to me when we were young. I always kept it near my desk as a little artifact to remind me of our friendship. "It's just a silly little thing," she told me. "My mom and I found it in a thrift shop and thought of you." It had two small heads hidden in the sunroof in the center of the car. When it was rolled, one would pop up and the other would go down. With a heavy sigh, I rolled it back and forth and watched. One head would come up, the other down, as if they were trading places, but they were never up at the same time. That's when I realized that these online exchanges were never going to be productive. Everyone was trying to express something, but no one was listening. My responses only made people angrier, so I proposed to meet in person. Thank you again for your wisdom, Perlita. Jacqueline Keeler, co-founder of Not Your Mascots, took me up on the offer, and we decided to meet up in Northwest Portland.

My nerves were shot. I didn't really know what to expect. All I knew was that she wrote for publications like *Indian Country Today* and *The Daily Beast* and was extremely passionate about the issue. It was Christmas Eve—not that I had any plans, but it was definitely an unexpected way to spend the holidays.

When Jacqueline arrived, she held up a camera and took my picture. Smile! I was caught off guard. I didn't smile. Instead, I stared straight ahead with a blank face because I had no idea what was going on. Was this a setup? Did they want to know what the enemy looked like? Soon, we sat down, and she pulled out a small recorder and notepad. I told her that I wanted to meet in order to address any concerns that she had about my trademark case. I explained that I believed we didn't have different values, but rather, we differed in terms of where we saw solutions for problems of injustice. I hoped that by providing context, there'd be a more comprehensive understanding of why I was fighting so hard.

We spoke for hours. I listened as she explained how Native Americans were deeply affected by negative stereotypes, which were only aggravated by their use in professional sports. Native Americans suffered greatly due to inequality, especially with issues of mental health and high rates of homelessness, incarceration, and abuse. Additionally, the government was still stripping away Native people of their sacred lands.[67] Exploitation, rampant poverty, and other major issues that revealed deep disparities were often ignored

---

[67] Just a few examples: the Apache Nation has been fighting to keep Oak Flat from a land grab attempt by developers in Arizona; the Kanaka Maoli are trying to protect their sacred mountain Mauna Kea from the construction of a major thirty-meter telescope; the government illegally seized millions of acres of land in the Black Hills from the Great Sioux Nation, land that has the faces of Washington, Jefferson, Lincoln, and Roosevelt permanently etched into Mount Rushmore. The list goes on.

by news coverage that favored headlines involving mascots and ca-sinos instead. The recent ruling felt like another wound inflicted on a community that has never experienced justice. Many didn't care if cancelling the football team's name was only a symbolic victory—they just wanted a small taste of justice.

I shared some of the struggles faced by Asian Americans: like Native Americans, our community was far more diverse than simple labels would allow. Those overly simplified assumptions about Asian Americans often meant erasing the experiences of those who also faced injustice. I answered many questions about my own legal journey and expressed why, despite feeling that the federal court system hijacked my case when they turned it into a First Amendment issue, I believed it was the right outcome because of the disparate impact of the law.

I explained, "For me, I was put in this battle: Either I fought against a law that was allowing the Trademark Office to deny people based on their sexual orientation or their ethnicities or . . . I moved forward while knowing that some of my arguments might be poten-tially hijacked by a racist football team."

We agreed that the government pitted our respective com-munities against one another to fight for scraps instead of working together to challenge dominant power structures. In social justice circles, this is often referred to as "divide and conquer," or the act of dividing up potential allies and communities. This usually in-volves creating a narrative that blames each minority group for the other group's problems and fostering mistrust between different communities. Sometimes, benefits or rights are given to one group over another.

Asian Americans are often presented as the "model minority" and used as a racial wedge to divide us against other communities. Generalizations about Asian Americans as the most prosperous, well-educated, and successful group are shallow and inaccurate. Parsing the data about Asian Americans reveals that, as the most diverse ethnic category we face a host of disparities, especially between different community groups. Often, people don't realize that the "Asian" category also includes people from Afghanistan, Cambodia, the Micronesian Islands, and portions of the former Soviet Republic. But many people would rather use the most successful extremes of our community (such as the success of Chinese American students in Ivy league schools) as proof that perseverance can overcome systemic racism. They imply that other racial groups should follow suit. Frank Chin famously wrote in 1974, "Whites love us because we're not black."[68] That kind of attitude has built racial resentment. In some ways, the sharp divide in reactions towards my case seemed to pit Asian Americans against Native Americans, but the reality was far more layered and complex than that.

I tried to explain why I didn't think the government should be left to decide what was offensive or appropriate. I pointed out that even though the Trademark Office had recently cancelled some

---

[68] Lee, R.G.. (2010). *The Cold War Origins of the Model Minority Myth.*

of the Washington football team's trademarks, they recently issued another new registration for the term redskin.[69] That same government often got it wrong when it came to the rights of marginalized groups—from protecting protesters to making decisions about basic human rights—how could we trust them to get it right?

Jacqueline replied, "It's all we have."

It started getting late. The teashop was clearing out as people were trying to get home to their families for the holiday. It was clear to me that I needed to do a better job of listening before diving right into complicated legal arguments, justifying my intentions, and theories of change. People who are marginalized and oppressed don't want to be explained at. I should have known better. I promised to do whatever I could to help her cause, including introducing her to a number of other legal experts working to get racist sports teams to change their names.

A few days after Christmas, she published an article about our discussion and the text of the full interview. It was raw and frank. My lawyers were upset when they came across the article. They said I was throwing federal court judges under the bus, especially when I mentioned that the lead judge was a big fan of the Washington football team, but I thought it was important to provide the full context for everything. People deserved to have real answers. From the very beginning, I wanted to win based on principles

---

[69] ALL NATURAL MY DADZ NUTZ CARMELIZED JUMBO REDSKINS, Registration No. 3,792,438.

and a just process, not clever legal or political posturing. I told them "Let's make justice a process, not an afterthought." To me, every step needed to reflect values of transparency, honesty, and the principles that I fought so hard for. Besides, it didn't matter anymore. We won. It was over . . . except it wasn't.

It was March of 2016, three months after the Federal Circuit decision, and we still didn't have our trademark registration. The Trademark Office made the decision to refuse court orders and suspend my application, as well as all applications to their office that could be flagged as scandalous, immoral, or disparaging under Section 2(a) of the Lanham Act. They did this despite the fact that the Federal Circuit ruled the disparagement provision was unconstitutional. In response, my attorneys decided to try a long shot by filing a petition for a writ of mandamus.[70] Basically, we argued that the court should enforce its own decision and compel the Trademark Office to approve the trademark registration. Sure, why not?

A few weeks later, the court rejected our writ, and I was sent an appellate printing invoice for over $2,100. I should have known. Everything we did at this point was unaffordable. I'm surprised I

---

[70] According to the Legal Information Institute, a writ of mandamus "is an order from a court to an inferior government official ordering the government official to properly fulfill their official duties or correct an abuse of discretion." It's usually considered an extreme remedy, reserved for emergencies or matters of particular importance. I don't think anyone truly believed this would work, the effort was largely symbolic in nature.

wasn't charged tickets for attending my own hearing at the court, but I guess that was built into the thousands of dollars it cost to file. Thankfully, Joel went to bat for me and got his firm to take care of the bill for me. I had enough to worry about since the band was about to tour our way across Taiwan.

The Slants Taiwan Tour was—and still is—my favorite musical adventure. Tyler, Ken, Joe, and I had spent much of the past year solidifying our live show on stages across North America, so it felt like the right time to take Asia by storm. We were invited to perform at Spring Scream, an annual outdoor music festival in the southernmost region of Taiwan, and we decided to tour our way up and down the island. I had not been to the area since I was four; this could also be an opportunity to visit family members that I hadn't seen in years. We wanted something to capture the experience, so we launched a crowdfunding campaign that raised the money needed to film the adventure.

Unlike all of our previous tours, I planned plenty of days off so we could explore the country. It was the first trip in six years where I wasn't working on some kind of legal documents while traveling. I never felt so at ease! We spent most of the time hunting down the most delicious foods possible, especially in the sprawling night markets. In Taiwan, we were always known as the American band. All of the posters for our shows would say THE SLANTS (U.S.A.). No one called us the Asian band or even the Asian American band. Racial identity had an entirely different context there.

A few Taiwanese nationals were familiar with our band because they had read about our trademark woes in the newspaper, but they couldn't wrap their heads around why the government was so disapproving of our name. They would say, "Wo bù míngbái wèishéme zhè shì yīgè wèntí" (I don't understand why this is an issue). People in Asia never think that references to slanted eyes could be insulting. Why would they? Experiences with racism are vastly different when you're the majority population and in power.

* * *

Over the years, I would often meet up with Spencer. He was always eager to hear about any news of our case and would give me some feedback with our latest brief. "Well actually, this isn't legal advice because I can't legally give you legal advice but I can let you know what I think, like my personal thoughts, you know?" While talking, I think he sensed some of my loneliness and suggested I try online dating to meet some new people. Does that even work? He met his fiancé through a website, so it worked for him. For many years, I had been in a long-term relationship. I didn't know where to begin, but I liked the idea of being able to use filters to help narrow options. At least it would get me out of the house for a different reason.

Soon, I was getting all kinds of unsolicited advice from friends. They would tell me to try to get a date within three message exchanges so there would still be plenty to talk about, to wait seventy-two hours between any kind of contact so I wouldn't come across as desperate, and of course, my friends told me to drop my personalized compatibility chart. You see, I developed a list of twenty attributes, each with their own weighted values, to come up with a total compatibility score. I thought that this was practical. It was a great formula because it funneled right into a weighted decision-making matrix that allowed me to rank people by fit. People told me it was creepy and weird.

I decided to be more open and flexible. I started going out often, at least five or six times per week. Sometimes I'd pick a restaurant and book out dates every few hours, walking out after each one and coming back in like I just arrived. It confused the waitstaff but again, it was all about efficiency. To keep track of my dates, I had a spreadsheet complete with information like their sibling count, interests, and other notes. The problem is that most of the time, it didn't work out for a second or third date. There would often be some kind of deal breaker in the process, so there was a lot of work that seemed in vain. Once, a date drank four beers over dinner, then wanted race me on their bike while I drove to a different bar so they could get additional drinks. I only had hot tea. Then, there was the woman who sent me photos of herself when she was dressed as a geisha, complete with eyes taped back. Finally, there was someone who seemed to be great match but quickly deflated my interest when they told me that they were "dino-neutral" when I asked about going to the new Walking with Dinosaurs exhibit.

After dozens of bad dates, I was about to give up. I decided to try one last time by contacting a woman I was particularly interested in—but this time, I did it on my own terms. I didn't ask for a date immediately like people suggested I do. We traded long, deep emails asking about books, life stories, and interests. She was an artist. She loved adventures and trying new foods. I started filling out my compatibility chart (her score was off the charts!). After a few weeks, we met up for dinner.

Faina had a radiant, contagious smile and large, brilliant blue eyes. During our date, I broke all of the rules set by rom-com films. I openly shared my worst dating experiences and explicitly told her that I never wanted to have children. I wanted to be an open book. Curiously, she agreed to future dates, and we caught Walking with Dinosaurs LIVE the following week. I even bought front row, center tickets for the show!

When some kids behind us started complaining loudly because they couldn't see, I said, "Maybe if your parents loved you more, they would have bought you better seats!" Or at least, that's what I wanted to say. Instead, I did the proper adult thing by passively aggressively sitting up taller when they made more noise and easing up a bit when they didn't. Somehow, she was amused by all of this. Those dates turned into a few more. A lot more. In October of 2016, we flew to Shanghai, China where I proposed to her in a real-life fairytale castle. She said yes. We were engaged!

* * *

It seemed that I had several big announcements for 2016. Shortly after getting back from our Taiwan tour, Tyler decided to retire from the Slants so he could focus more on his life in Seattle. With his departure, our longtime roadie stepped down as well. This was bittersweet news, especially since I felt like we were finally starting to gel as a band! Every time we started gaining momentum, something would happen or someone would leave. I couldn't blame him, but things wouldn't be the same without him.

Tyler played in the Slants for nearly eight years, which was longer than anyone else except for me. There was no question that he brought a special, hard-hitting dynamic to the band. Even though we occasionally had creative differences, I could always count on him. His last official show with us was at the Jade International Night Market, a multicultural celebration in the heart of Southeast Portland. Since then, he's joined us on stage a few times. And each time, things felt right again.

During this time, I also learned that the U.S. Department of Justice and the U.S. Trademark Office had filed a Petition for Writ of Certiorari (the document that a losing party files) in order to appeal the decision from the Federal Circuit. That fall, we received notice that the Supreme Court of the United States had granted cert.[71] We were now officially going to the Supreme Court. This was the final boss stage! There were no other levels left.

Sensing an opportunity, the legal team for Pro Football filed a motion to the Supreme Court, arguing that their case should be consolidated with mine, and that they should be the ones to argue before the Supreme Court. In their brief, they threw some serious shade at my legal team, stating that our Federal Circuit filing was "an undersized brief that was barely half the word limit." In fact, they

---

[71] A Writ of Certiorari is a decision by the Supreme Court to hear an appeal from a lower court.

claimed they were better advocates. "The Team, not (the Slants), is the best suited to serve this function here." Thankfully, the Supreme Court denied that request, which meant that we were on our own. The last thing I wanted was to be mixed up with the Washington football team again!

Before the year's end, a representative from the Obama administration contacted me. They congratulated us for our social justice work in the community and wanted us to be a part of the new anti-bullying campaign sponsored by the White House Initiative on Asian Americans and Pacific Islanders (WHIAAPI).[72] To help bring awareness to the effort, we joined high-profile Asian Americans such as George Takei, Jeremy Lin, and other celebrities to release a special compilation. But they didn't want to just recycle any old song of ours, they wanted to have something brand new. We had just the thing. We had been working on a new song called "From the Heart,"[73] written about our own personal bully: the United States Patent and Trademark Office. In a delicious and symbolic ironic twist, the White House released our song.

These were the words:

> *Sorry if our notes are too sharp*
> *Sorry if our voices are too raw*
> *Don't make the pen a weapon*

---

[72] Gotta love those extremely long government acronyms.

[73] Fun fact: our working title for the song was "FUSPTO" but we wanted to soften the tone and approach it with a sense of resilience and compassion instead.

And censor our intelligence
Until our thoughts mean nothing at all

Sorry if you take offense
You made up rules and played pretend
We know you fear change
It's something so strange
But nothing's gonna get in our way

There's no room
For your backwards feelings
And backyard dealings
We're never gonna settle
We're never gonna settle

No, we won't remain silent
Know it's our defining moment
We sing from the heart
We sing from the heart
No we won't be complacent
Know it's a rock n roll nation
We sing from the heart
We sing from the heart

Sorry if we try too hard
To take some power back for ours
The language of oppression
Will lose to education
Until the words can't hurt us again

So sorry if you take offense
But silence will not make amends
The system's all wrong
And it won't be long
Before the kids are singing our song

CHAPTER 12

THE BAND WHO MUST NOT BE NAMED

WHO GOES TO THE AIRPORT TEN HOURS BE-
FORE THEIR FLIGHT? Apparently, that was me. I spent nearly a
decade fighting my way to the Supreme Court and I wanted to do
everything possible to make sure I would not miss one of the most
important moments in my life. A major blizzard was sweeping
across the Northwest in early 2017 and was closing down most of
the roads. Most flights were cancelled; the airport was eerily empty
with abandoned gates throughout the major terminals. At least the
Wi-Fi was still up. I found a remote station with rows of empty arm-
less seats we could sleep on and camped out until the morning. I
watched the snow flurries swirl furiously through the air before
landing on the ever-growing piles outside the window. I said a prayer
and crossed my fingers before closing my eyes. It felt like only a
blink before I woke up to the sound of announcements. Luckily, we
were one of the only flights to escape the storm.

Joe and I were flying to Washington, D.C. early, landing ten days before our oral hearing in order to attend our lawyers' final moot court session (the rest of the band would meet up with us later). A moot court is like a rehearsal session where law faculty and experts help attorneys prepare for oral arguments at the Supreme Court. In fact, there are moot court tournaments all over the country to help students become better at arguing, complete with competition rules and trophies. "Mooting," as they call it has even inspired entire lines of humorous t-shirts and bumper stickers. I later learned that my case eventually became a favorite one to use for mooting and have met student teams from all over the country who have argued for or against our position. For our upcoming hearing, my attorneys had scheduled three moot court sessions. I'd be joining them at the Georgetown University Law Center, who did their best to create a mini-replica of the high court, complete with a backdrop of velvet curtains and a golden clock hanging above nine leather chairs.

Despite our recent victory, the stakes felt so much higher. As soon as the Supreme Court granted cert, my attorneys retained a publicity firm and put me on radio silence. They didn't want me to talk about the case in public or to do any interviews unless they approved. They were afraid I would say something that would hurt our efforts. For months, I had to cancel multiple speaking engagements and forward all legal inquiries to the attorneys. I hated being restrained. I was fighting for freedom of speech but unable to speak myself. My attorneys were finally lifting that restraint with my trip to our nation's capital.

On the plane, I watched a boxing movie called *Hands of Stone,* based on the life of a Panamanian street fighter named Robert Duran who became the lightweight champion of the world. Audiences from barrios and slums throughout Panama cheered him on, especially in light of tense U.S.-Panama relationships. For them, he was the pride of the streets. His victories represented overcoming an unjust system—each punch he threw carried the hopes of these marginalized communities. For me, it was a reminder that when marginalized groups have to navigate an inequitable system, minor jabs carried more significance.

As soon as we landed, I turned on my phone and saw a backlog of 1,200 messages, mostly interview requests, in my email. Al Jazeera, HBO, ABC, NBC—those interviews would all be scheduled over the next week, but our plan for the first night was to sit down with Nina Totenberg at NPR's headquarters in Georgetown. I was scanning my inbox as I navigated my way through the airport when I heard my name being called.

"Mr. Tam? I thought that it might be you!" An older man dressed in an open-collar shirt and a navy blue suit extended his hand before me. It was a law professor who flew into Washington with the hope of being able to attend our hearing at the Supreme Court. "I've been teaching about you for years! My students would really get a kick out of this. Would you mind if we took a photo?" I smiled awkwardly as he took the selfie and then caught up with Joe to make our way across town. I looked out the car windows and saw all of the familiar buildings and monuments of D.C., but they felt bigger this time around, as if they were personally trying to intimidate me.

* * *

I spent most of the months leading up to our trip writing and recording a new release with the band. We couldn't make solid plans for going to D.C. because the Supreme Court didn't officially schedule our hearing until a few weeks beforehand. We weren't even guaranteed seats in the room. It was frustrating, but then again, I was used to these arbitrary rules set by the government.

We started auditioning drummers as soon as Tyler announced his departure. Once again, different prospects worked their way through our arduous audition process. Eventually, we settled on a Japanese American named Yuya Matsuda who had enjoyed some success earlier in his career. I was concerned that he wouldn't be able to keep up with an aggressive touring schedule since he had five children. Also, he had never been apart from his fiancé for longer than a day. I thought that level of codependency would create problems if we were on the road for weeks or months at a time. Despite those concerns, we ended up choosing him; he was the best drummer of the lot and carefully took the time to memorize the nuances of our material. Most of all, he was hungry for it.

In his late teenage years, Yuya's band was signed and joined the Warped Tour. But things quickly unraveled, and he was in and out of bands for the next decade. He was a top contender to join rising rock band The Offspring but was eventually rejected because he "didn't have the right look."[74] For years, he played drums for a popular country act but was often tokenized as "the Country Act with the Asian drummer!" They even asked him to wear a lab coat on stage. He was tired of the racial slurs thrown at him night after night and eventually just settled for being a hired gun for theatres or the occasional studio session. He could finally be his full, authentic self as a member of the Slants and feel certain he wouldn't be ridiculed. We could all relate to that experience.

Joe and I took the helm writing most of our new songs. He wrote lyrics and a vocal melody to a synth-pop tune I composed, which eventually became our song "Fight Back." He also wrote all of the music for a song we called "Jonesin," originally inspired by the Marvel Comics character and Netflix show, Jessica Jones. We eventually changed the name to "Endlessly Falling" but kept many of the inside jokes and references:

It's like a jump and then a fall
Crashing your way through my walls
And I'll watch you fly

It felt great to finally be writing new songs again. It had been four years since we wrote any new material. Our best-of album *Something Slanted This Way Comes* was really meant to hold fans over while we dealt with the many transitions in the band. The tumultuous legal work, grad school, and tour schedule had also drained me of any

---

[74] We all know what that means . . . maybe they felt their single "Pretty Fly For a White Guy" would lose credibility.

creative energy. It also felt strange to work on new material without Jonathan around, since he helped me write most of the music for our first few albums. We would constantly bounce ideas off of each other, but when he left the band, I was pretty discouraged and hardly picked up any instruments unless I was jumping on stage. Once Ken and Joe had been around for a while, I finally felt some semblance of stability again. It was freeing.

One night, I had a dream where I was waiting to meet up with Perla in our familiar diner. I would often dream of having elaborate conversations with her about everything that was happening in my life. She'd have succinct, wonderful bits of encouragement for me, but it had been a while. Maybe I got so busy and stressed that we weren't able to connect. In any case, it felt comfortable to be in that vinyl booth again.

As I waited for her to walk through the door, I realized that she wasn't going to come that evening. I picked up a pen and started scrawling a note on a napkin. I watched my hands write, "I called Death, it's true so I could ask her for a favor and trade with you." I was nervous that she wasn't going to show up ever again. I felt my veins pulsating. I continued writing, "My heart is strong but it won't beat this drum. My skin will crawl but can't run away from . . . tonight." I looked out the windows and could see the dawn breaking. I continued and wrote, "I want to give it all away . . . though I know that it'll fade into a new day without you."

I woke up in the middle of the night, shivering and drenched with tears and sweat. With the note still in my mind, I sat down and immediately wrote down all of the words as if they were a last letter to my best friend. Those words eventually became the song "Sutures":

I confess
The first breath, I drew
After your last was full of tears
'Cause I already knew

And yet
I called Death, it's true
So I could ask her for a favor
And trade with you

My heart is strong
But it won't beat this drum
My skin will crawl

But can't away from
But can't away from

Tonight
I want to give it all away
Though I know that it'll fade
Into a new day, a new day

Tonight
I want to give it all away
Though I know that it'll fade
Into a new day, a new day
Without you

I regret
My last words said, to you
So benign and lacking thoughts
Reflecting brighter hues

I confess
I called Death, it's true
So I could ask her for a favor
And trade with you

My heart is strong
But it won't beat this drum
My skin will crawl

But can't away from
But can't away from

Tonight
I want to give it all away
Though I know that it'll fade
Into a new day, a new day

Tonight
I want to give it all away
Though I know that it'll fade
Into a new day, a new day
Without you

Every time I think about how it was
It tears out the sutures

All those years with you were just not enough
The past is no future

For months, I tried writing a melody to the lyrics, but it just felt too close. I knew what I wanted, but I couldn't bring myself to do it. Sometimes, I would physically shake whenever I picked up the guitar to try and finish it. A couple of months later, Joe wrote a haunting melody that embodied everything I was trying to do with the song. We recorded an acoustic version of "Sutures" to close out a small collection of songs for our forthcoming EP.

We scrambled in order to finish the record in time for our trip to D.C. We wanted to release it on Martin Luther King Jr. Day, just days before we were due at the Supreme Court. We called it *The Band Who Must Not Be Named*, as a clever homage to Harry Potter. In the Harry Potter series, the Ministry of Magic (the governing body for the magical community) was so afraid of their enemy that they called him "He Who Must Not Be Named." Dumbledore urged the young hero by saying, "Call him Voldemort, Harry. Always use the proper name for things. Fear of a name increases fear of the thing itself." We lovingly dedicated it to the Trademark Office.

* * *

I spotted Ron as soon as we walked into the Supreme Court Institute at Georgetown. He seemed a little frustrated with his iPhone. He told me, "The firm made us all use these things but I'd rather use my normal phone!" I wanted to check in with him since the firm had decided a different lawyer would argue our case before the Supreme Court. I didn't want the moment taken from him. He had believed in me and generously worked pro bono for years. He deserved the opportunity.

"It's easier to teach trademark law to a constitutional guy than constitutional law to someone who does trademarks," he told me. "Besides, I've been busy with my kid's wedding this weekend, so this is a relief. I wouldn't be able to dedicate myself to the arguments as much as I'd like, and you deserve the very best chance to win."

"But we won at the Federal Circuit because of you! You're not secretly wishing you could make the argument?"

"You obviously don't know Jewish weddings!" He chuckled and said, "I'm just looking forward to getting some sleep after all of this is done."

As he sat there in his dark suit and rich red tie, he was glowing. He seemed genuinely happy that the year would begin with his second oldest son's wedding, oral arguments at the Supreme Court, and the inauguration of President Trump. As an unabashed Republican, Ron was tired of leftist politics, "fake news" from mainstream media, and people offended by politically incorrect humor. Most progressives would wince at his Twitter feed. If it weren't for my case, I probably would have never found common ground with him. But as I got to know him better over the years, I learned that he genuinely cared about the plight of marginalized communities. He didn't fit the slightly racist uncle archetype that people liked to pin on conservatives. He was good friends with many attorneys working to cancel the trademark registrations of the Washington football team. He just saw different solutions to many of the same issues I was concerned with. Freedom of speech was one area that we could agree on.

* * *

When I wasn't working on *The Band Who Must Not Be Named*, I was courting organizations to file amicus briefs for our case. It was a quiet term for the Supreme Court; there were only eight justices sitting on the bench after Justice Antonin Scalia passed. The term was only averaging about ten briefs per argued case, which was fairly average.[75] At the Federal Circuit, we had been so focused on technical and evidentiary issues that community perspectives were less of a priority. I felt deeply betrayed by the National Asian Pacific American Bar Association's (NAPABA) amicus brief and didn't want other groups rushing in without understanding the full context of legal issues or pretending to represent a larger group of people without actually consulting them first. Now that we were focusing on larger, constitutional issues, I wanted to make sure that community voices were heard.

Many of the largest and most prominent Asian American social justice organizations agreed to sign onto the ACLU's brief in

---

[75] Franze, Anthony J., and R. Reeves Anderson. "In Quiet Term, Drop in Amicus Curiae at the Supreme Court." The Legal Intelligencer. September 06, 2017. https://www.law.com/supremecourtbrief/sites/supremecourt-brief/2017/09/06/in-quiet-term-drop-in-amicus-curiae-at-the-supreme-court/

support of us: the Asian American Legal Defense and Education Fund (AALDEF), the Asian Pacific American Network of Oregon (APANO), the Chinese American Citizens Alliance—Portland Lodge, the Portland Japanese American Citizens League (JACL), and the Oregon Commission on Asian and Pacific Islander Affairs (OCAPIA). The significance of this was probably lost on the government: every single Asian American organization that the Trademark Office misleadingly quoted to justify the idea that our name was disparaging signed a legal brief in our support.

Over thirty prominent organizations and individuals across the political spectrum came together to sign nineteen briefs in our support. Many of these groups, such as the ACLU and the CATO Institute, would normally find themselves on opposites of sides of other issues but saw a common struggle when it came to the civil liberties at stake in our case. Some of the briefs were filed by groups who were directly impacted by Section 2(a) of the Lanham Act, such as Dykes on Bikes and Erik Brunetti.[76] From radical progressives to strict libertarians, I was extremely proud that we could build such a diverse coalition of different backgrounds and interests.

Not that this was a popularity contest, but the Trademark Office had only four briefs in their support. This included a number

---

[76] Brunetti was the founder of Friends U Can't Trust (FUCT), a clothing company that was denied a registration under the scandalous provision of the Lanham Act. He eventually had a similar experience to mine, making his way through the Federal Circuit and to the Supreme Court as well.

of Native American organizations, including the National Congress of American Indians (NCAI), and of course, NAPABA. This time, NAPABA substantially reduced their rhetoric about our work, though they drew a false equivalency between the Slants and the Washington Redskins, saying that we were "no better. While empowering to a young social justice rock band, that same mark may be debilitating for those who remember life in American internment camps during World War II." Of course, they conveniently failed to recognize that most of the organizations working primarily with incarceration camp survivors, as well as many of the survivors themselves, overwhelmingly were in our support.

Life is full of apparent contradictions, and we often don't fall neatly into the boxes expected of us. For the people who couldn't pick a side, eight briefs were filed in support of neither party. Much to my attorneys' chagrin, whenever I met up with groups who didn't want to sign a brief supporting us, I would encourage them to take a position on the case, even if it meant supporting a different group's interpretation, such as Asian Americans Advancing Justice (AAAJ). While I disagreed with the theory of change in their brief,[77] I understood that they still held similar beliefs and values. That was important to me.

---

[77] AAAJ argued to keep the existing system, saying that applicants who were wrongly accused of being disparaging could "submit evidence of their own reclamation efforts," but I found this idea to be regressive and inequitable in nature. Why would we continue to place additional burdens on marginalized groups for

I didn't always feel this way. For many of the years leading up to this point, I would try to argue down dissenting views. But you can't convince someone who has a different perspective that they are wrong purely through argument. You need to exhibit compassion, allowing the truth to sway hearts and minds. I learned a lot of this from Joseph Santos-Lyons, a mentor and friend from the social justice community (he was also the one who was willing to sign a legal declaration explaining what happened with the AAYLC controversy).

When the Supreme Court first granted cert, I became worried about the potential fallout. I considered dropping everything. The Federal Circuit didn't actually have the power to affect the Washington football team since their case was still pending in a different district court, but the Supreme Court definitely would. I met up with Joseph to get some insight. He was getting ready for a trip to join the Standing Rock Protest. As the executive director of one of the largest grassroots organizations in Oregon, he was used to working with complex issues that often involved conflicting perspectives across community groups. We took a long walk through Laurelhurst Park and spoke candidly about my concerns.

"If we win, then that probably means the Washington football team would benefit from that too. What if this really does open

---

an already expensive and exhaustive process and continue to place decision-making power in the hands of those outside of our communities?

the floodgate for hate speech being registered as trademarks?" I asked.

"Didn't you tell me that people were being denied rights because of their race or their identity in some kind of way? You were denied for being too Asian. Isn't that worse?"

Joseph saw justice in terms of power—who had access to it and how it was used. He understood that people could say racist things whether or not they had a trademark registration. In fact, there were thousands of existing trademark registrations that could be considered scandalous, immoral, or disparaging.[78] The greater concern wasn't trying to punish people for saying hateful things but making sure that marginalized groups could have access to basic rights like freedom of speech. Those lacking power needed more options. It reminded me of John Rawls' Theory of Justice, which essentially argues that the most fair rules are the ones that everyone would agree to if they didn't know what their position in society would be (class, race, intelligence, and ability). This resonated deeply with me.

"I know it's worse. I guess I'm afraid of what could happen."

---

[78] Both the Pro Football and CATO Institute amicus brief lists dozens of pages of them. They include marks such as Baked by a Negro, Anal Ring Toss, Dick Balls, Why Men Love Bitches, and many more. Adult entertainment, alcoholic beverages, and apparel usually received the approval of the Trademark Office.

"The worst thing that could happen is the status quo."

The debate around freedom of speech was almost always entirely focused on those who abuse it. But the price of censorship was often carried on the backs of the underprivileged. I knew that firsthand. As Eric Liu stated, "wit can neuter malice."[79] The government didn't get things like irony and reappropriation. That power shouldn't rest in their hands because it is almost always used to suppress minority views. That's why I made the decision to rally as many perspectives as possible, even if they weren't in my corner. We didn't need tricks to win. We needed the justices to see the issue exactly as it was.

* * *

The moot court wasn't as exciting as I had hoped it would be. It was interesting seeing what different members of the faculty saw as winning arguments and best practices before the court. Everyone had a different idea of how to approach the case.

"Be sure to have an introduction for your argument that can last up to two minutes—they might interrupt you but it's better than not having enough!"

"You should really lean on the idea that Section 2(a) can "chill" speech . . . that's the winning argument!"

---

[79] Author of *A Chinaman's Chance: One Family's Journey and the Chinese American Dream*

John Connell, the lead civil rights attorney at Ron's firm, nervously took notes and was very receptive to all of the feedback. Like my other attorneys, he had no prior experience with the Supreme Court. Each of them saw it for the first time when they took a public tour earlier that morning—I saw the selfie posted shortly after I landed.

As Joe and I walked to NPR's offices from the moot courtroom at Georgetown University, I did multiple interviews by phone. This would be the pattern from about 6 a.m. to 2 a.m. every day for the next week; I was answering questions from journalists in nearly every time zone in the world. Joe thought it was amusing and filmed many of these conversations. There must be over a hundred video clips of me walking with a phone pressed against my face.

Finally, we walked through the glowing corridors of NPR. I tried not to geek out too much. I was a huge fan of public radio and even had their app on my phone. We were taken to a dark, isolated office for a quick photo shoot—probably the worst we ever had. They were insistent on using their own images instead of our press shots even though we were jetlagged and had been wearing the same clothes for two days. Then, we were escorted into a recording studio on the fourth floor for my conversation with Nina Totenberg. We had been trading emails for a couple of weeks, but it still felt surreal and exciting speaking to one of the most well-known voices on air.

When we began recording, I could hear her slip into the soothing "public radio" voice that seems to be a signature of NPR correspondents. She asked numerous questions about our band's history, basic trademark law, and why I was fighting so hard. At one point, she wanted me to provide examples of words that had been successfully reappropriated in our culture. Thanks to my trademark case, I spent years studying etymology. I had plenty of examples ready to give.

"Labels like Christian, guido, and otaku are examples of things that were once considered an insult but have been co-opted and used in a self-referencing way. Those are some of the most common ones."

"Yes, but what else? How about something more recent?"

I felt like she was probing me, trying to get me say more controversial things.

"Well, the term queer is one that I've seen change in my lifetime."

"Queer is NOT an appropriate term used by anybody!" Her sharp response startled me. *Don't tell me that you're that out of touch*, I thought.

"I think that members of the LGBTQ community would disagree with you. That's usually what Q stands for. Plus you have queer studies programs, the Queer Nation, and many organizations. Even my sister uses the term."

"You're wrong. But isn't there another, more common example that you can think of?"

"Plenty of people embrace terms for different reasons, especially in art, and many of them are even registered trademarks." I started rattling off scandalous band names that were also registered trademarks instead of debating her on the nuances of *queer*. "The Dead Kennedys, Joy Division, The Queers—yes, The Queers, and even N.W.A." I left it at that. When she started asking how we felt about our newfound legal fame, Joe chimed in and reminded her "We're musicians first, we want to get back to focusing on our music."

* * *

Before we met up with the rest of the band, Joe and I first staked out the Supreme Court. As we walked through the grand hallways, I saw a large oak door with a golden nameplate that read *Solicitor General*. The Solicitor General is one of the highest-ranking attorneys in the United States Department of Justice. They are responsible for arguing cases before the Supreme Court. This is whom we'd be arguing against in a few days.

"Maybe we should play a prank on him," I whisper to Joe. "You know like when Harry Potter was in the Ministry of Magic when they're doing stuff to Dolores Umbridge? It could be like 'Oh! All of a sudden, his briefs have disappeared!'"

"Nerd."

I drove our rental car a few hours away to the Baltimore airport, where we picked up Ken and Yuya. That weekend, we played an intimate set at an anime convention while a film crew from HBO's *Vice News Tonight* followed us around. I always appreciated it when journalists could see us in our element interacting with kids of color because it gave our story much more context than simply "the band with the offensive name." They could see firsthand the transformation people have when they realize they have the power to seize their own identities.

When we returned to D.C., television crews wanted to film interviews as well as footage of us performing, so we crashed the offices of Gibson Guitars. They graciously let us use their show-room, which coincidentally, was in the heart of Chinatown. It was a beautiful space that had multiple rooms to shoot in. They also let us borrow instruments to perform on throughout the week. Each morning, we'd drive there and film segments back-to-back, while eating at local restaurants during the breaks. Wherever we went, I saw newspapers and magazines that had us on the cover. I often overheard people talking about the case, but they usually didn't re-alize we were sitting right there. It fascinated me to hear the many perspectives on it, especially in the hometown of the notorious foot-ball team.

On Martin Luther King Jr. Day, the release date for *The Band Who Must Not Be Named*, we went right to the steps of the Supreme Court. Originally, we planned to have a rally and concert there, but our attorneys were terrified that it would hurt our case, so I prom-ised to keep a low profile. We just walked up unannounced with an acoustic guitar and began playing a few songs like "From the Heart." We streamed some of the performance and thanked the generous donors who chipped in so we could afford the trip. It was freezing but watching the sun set behind the glowing dome of Capitol Hill provided an unforgettable view. We then spent the rest of the even-ing at the MLK memorial singing with people who gathered around the Stone of Hope statue in honor of the great civil rights leader.

I quietly meditated as I walked around the garden, reflecting on many of Dr. King's famous quotes that were etched in the walls. The lights seemed to magnify the weight of each of the words. One of my favorites was, "Make a career of humanity. Commit yourself to the noble struggle for equal rights. You will make a greater person of yourself, a greater nation of your country, and a finer world to live in." Then, I saw the quote that inspired me the most: "The arc of the moral universe is long, but it bends toward justice." It stirred something deep inside me, and I thought, "*Yes, but that moral arc does not bend on its own. It requires persistence. It requires patience. And it requires people willing to fight for what they believe in.*"

One of our last in-person interviews was inside a Chinese restaurant in Chinatown, around the corner from the Gibson office. It looked like a quintessential Chinese eatery with a gaudy red and gold interior, a large Buddha statue, and live fish tanks in the front. It was one of the more awkward segments that I've done, which is saying something. We did part of the interview in Mandarin and were asked to play some songs in the middle of the eatery. The most memorable part of that session came at the end of the meal we shared: as I opened my fortune cookie, I pulled out a little slip of paper that said "A judgment will soon rule in your favor." *God, I hope so.*

We were so busy that I hardly had time to catch up with Faina, who was house and dog sitting for me while I was in D.C. I encouraged the guys to enjoy the rest of the night off and explore the city, so I could finally have some time to myself. I called her up, but she sounded even more stressed than me! With an abnormally severe winter storm, the water main burst and froze over, so she didn't have running water in the house. The roads were covered in ice, and she couldn't go anywhere either. Her only sources of water were the large gallon containers she got from walking to the store or melting heaps of snow in a pot over the stove.

"I don't know how I can help you from here in D.C. I've sent some messages to plumbers but they're overwhelmed with calls for frozen pipes right now. It might take another few weeks for them to get to the house."

"I've been trapped in YOUR house with YOUR dogs without any water. I can't even take a shower because there's no running water. I can't take it anymore!"

I felt terrible. She didn't ask for any of this. We were supposed to get married in five months. How was I supposed to take care of her from across the country? She was stuck because of me. Oral arguments were scheduled for the next morning, but I wouldn't get home until the evening after that. I took a deep breath and offered a solution.

"I can take the next flight out of D.C., I can probably be home tomorrow . . ."

"NO! You can't do that. This is like the most important thing in your life right now, you're supposed to be going to the Supreme Court tomorrow."

"Honestly, it won't make a difference if I'm there or not. You're now the most important thing to me. I haven't been there. It's my fault."

"This isn't even a discussion. I WILL NOT let you miss this. You've been fighting this for eight years, and I don't want you holding this against me . . ."

"I promise I won't. I'm serious . . ."

"NO. You are staying there and that's final. This is important. I swear, if you do something crazy like come home early, the wedding is OFF!" *Click*. She hung up.

I felt lost and overwhelmed in that moment. I didn't want to lose another person that I loved so deeply, but I didn't want to cause any more suffering either. I needed time to think. I drew a bath and slid in, completely submerging myself. I let out an explosive scream into the hot water, feeling the air and bubbles expel from me. I felt trapped.

Since landing in D.C., I had received over 21,000 messages and phone calls. I handled countless interviews, performances, and appearances while maintaining a calm, confident front. Sometimes it was answering the same, monotonous questions that I had been answering for the past decade. Other times, it was clear that I was speaking with reporters that had no interest in the nuances of our case. They just wanted to seize on the controversy. Some of them even spread weird conspiracy theories about me, accusing me of being secretly funded by Dan Snyder. I had no time to recharge my introverted self. And now, my fiancé was trapped in my house with no access to water while I was selfishly doing my own thing in Washington. It was too much.

I was alone but was suffocating with every breath because I was trying to swallow everything back, as if I were hiding the emotions from myself. I bent forward, hands clutched to my chest as if I were about to vomit, while an unbroken stream of tears forced their way through. *Dramatic much?* I started laughing. *Was I going mad?*

My phone buzzed. It was a text message from Faina. "I'm sorry. I was just stressed out! You got this, you're a fighter. I love you."

I let out a deep breath. Ok, final boss stage. Let's get this damned thing over with.

CHAPTER 13
FINAL BOSS STAGE

~~~

COURTROOM SCENES IN THE MOVIES WOULD HAVE YOU BELIEVE that the most exciting place to be during a trial is in the very front, because that's where all of the action is taking place. If you've seen the iconic moments dramatized in *Inherit the Wind* or *To Kill a Mockingbird*, you'd probably expect there to be long, passionate monologues made by attorneys with Southern accents who are drenched in the sweltering heat. Even the District Attorney in *My Cousin Vinny* was R-dropping like he was from the Arkansas. But none of this was the case on the morning of January 18, 2017, inside the Supreme Court. This was a building filled with cold Roman columns, not Southern charm.

At 10 a.m. precisely, the gavel struck, and the robed justices began walking into the room ceremoniously, sitting by seniority. Even their notes and glasses of water were served by seniority. And so, tradition and decorum dictated that other business be addressed before moving on to the oral arguments in our case.

My eyes darted back and forth between the hanging clock, the justices, and whoever was speaking. Because the court was admitting in attorneys as members of the court, there were a lot of people speaking, taking oaths, and making pledges. Even though my name was being used for one of the biggest agenda items that morning, I would not be able to share any of my thoughts aloud. I will admit: I fantasized about it often. I dreamt that the chief justice would somehow recognize me in the crowd and ask me to speak. I would address everything that the court was ignoring; I would say everything that I wished my attorneys would have the courage to express.

I played the scenario over and over in my head, but I knew it would never happen. I would remain silent and invisible sitting behind an empty row, not even close enough to see my own legal representatives at their desk, let alone be within whispering distance. I imagined that the greatest Supreme Court arguments ever made were delivered in the minds of the people most affected. Whether it was an issue of whom we could marry, what we could say, or how the system failed to deliver *Equal Justice Under Law,* we the people who are affected had more to give than people assumed.

I thought about the ride over earlier that morning. It was chaotic trying to get around the closed streets in D.C. because the inauguration of President Trump was in a few days, so we called for an Uber. The Slants all climbed into the white sedan. The driver was listening to *Morning Edition,* NPR's show on top headlines. The host was talking about President-elect Donald Trump's controversial nominee for Commerce Secretary. Soon, it would be President Trump.

President Trump. The people pushing the hardest against my case wanted to give control over who could decide what was disparaging to the government, a government that would now be led by a man who made dropping the fight against the Redskins a campaign promise. Could we trust the guy who bragged about grabbing women's genitals and regularly insulted minorities to decide what would be considered "scandalous, immoral, or disparaging?" *Maybe the best rules for free speech are the ones that apply no matter who is president or which party is in control of Congress.*

The familiar voice of Steve Inskeep interrupted my thoughts. "What do the McDonald's golden arches, the apple on your iPhone, the NBC peacock, the Nike swoosh, and the MGM lion have in common? They are all registered trademarks, and in the last twenty years, the U.S. Patent and Trademark Office has approved roughly four million of them." *Wait a second, that's our story!* I listened intently and asked the driver to turn up the radio as he pulled up directions on his GPS.

"Supreme Court?" he asked. "Might be tough this morning. It's busy in the area. Why are you all heading down there?"

On the radio, you could hear the hosts talking about the rock band that was challenging a law that day. "Umm . . . that's us," Ken told the driver. "We have to go court today."

"Oh, snap!" He stared intently into the rearview mirror and then looked over at the passenger seat where I was answering email interviews with my phone. I nodded. "Yo, can I take a selfie with y'all?"

"Yeah, but not while we're driving," I chided. "We gotta get there in one piece first."

He smiled from ear to ear, explaining that he had followed the story for years. He then cranked the knob so that Nina Totenberg's voice began rattling the speakers as she said, "The band points to lots of other registered names that are viewed by some as offensive – like N.W.A., the name of a hip-hop group that stands for 'Niggaz Wit Attitudes.'" She heavily emphasized the "z" in *az*. We all looked at each other. Did she just say what we thought she said? On NPR? *Was that what she was trying to get me to say?*

We pulled up to the front of the Supreme Court as the segment was ending, fading out with our song, "From the Heart." *No! We won't remain silent! Know! It's our defining moment! We sing from the heart* . . . We posed for a quick selfie as the driver gave us high fives and fist bumps. Before he pulled away, we could hear the opening notes for "Fight Back" blasting from his car. I wondered what the entrance was like for Luther Campbell (aka Luke Skywalker) when 2 Live Crew was before the Supreme Court thirteen years earlier. As we walked across the street in our matching black suits, it looked like a modern version of the infamous photo from *Abbey Road*.

* * *

My attention snapped forward as Chief Justice Roberts casually announced that arguments would begin for my case, *Lee v. Tam*. Malcolm Stewart, the Deputy Solicitor General, walked up to the lectern centered before the justices. He looked to be in his mid- fif-ties and sported a slight hunch under his dark suit. He coolly delivered the routine opening as if it were just another canned speech. *May it please the court.* He spoke with a closed throat, as if he were doing a tepid impersonation of Ray Romano or Kermit the Frog. Normally, this would be distracting, but I was closely moni-toring every utterance as if I were going to jump up and deliver the rebuttal at any moment.

There was no screaming, no one was out of order. While none of the justices ventured into ASMR territory, I got the impres-sion that they could definitely get into the soothing podcast business if the law thing didn't pan out for them. Maybe things calmed after the passing of Justice Antonin Scalia. The biggest reaction any of them offered came in the form of a snappy comeback delivered in the tone an adult might use to gently correct a child. Would that be considered #Judgesplaining?

The drama wasn't up front. It was in the second row of pub-lic seating, where every palpitation of my heart was felt and deep grooves were being carved into the palms of my hands under clenched fists. There was a completely different set of responses to the questions, except it was all in my head. There would be no long-winded speech about me because I wasn't on trial. No one was. Only one word, *disparagement*, from the 1946 Lanham Trademark Act, was on the stand. Was it guilty of violating the First Amendment or not? The Slants and I had been dragged into this larger clash of ideas; they could care less about how we felt about the matter.

Like the Federal Circuit, the Supreme Court spent a bit of time comparing the trademark registration system with that of copyright. They were concerned that if the government could deny disfavored messages using an inconsistent and vague system in trademarks, there would be little to stop them from adopting a similar provision to exclude other expressive works. Stewart tried articulating the difference by calling the disparagement provision a "reasonable limit on access to a government program rather than a restriction in speech."

The court pushed back. Justice Kennedy asked, "Is copyright a government program? Disparagement clearly wouldn't work with copyright and that's a powerful, government program." Justice Alito followed, "I was somewhat surprised that in your briefs you couldn't bring yourself to say that the government could not deny copyright protection to objectionable material."

Justice Breyer kept trying to bring the conversation back to the rationale for having trademark protections at all. "The ultimate purpose of a trademark is to identify the source of the product . . . what objective of trademark protection does this particular disparagement provision help further?"

"There's always the danger . . . that when a person uses as his work words that have other meanings in common discourse, that it will distract the consumer." Stewart seemed to be constructing a new argument on the spot. "Congress says, as long as you are promoting your own product, saying nice things about people, we'll put up with that level of distraction."

"If that's your answer . . . I can think of perhaps 50,000 examples of instances where the space the trademark provides is used for very distracting messages, probably as much or more so than disparagement. What business does Congress have in picking out this one?"

Part of me was deeply fascinated with how they were picking apart the subtleties of the law and looking at the most extreme scenarios of free speech and trademarks. I leaned forward. My face was scrunched up in deep concentration while some of my band mates were probably spacing out. Then, I noticed Justice Kagan looking over and smiling. *Wait. Is she looking at us? Does she realize it is the band back here or is she just content to see some youth being interested in the law?* I turned toward Joe who was sitting beside me. He had a fixed, forced grin on his face as he stared back at her as if he were afraid of breaking eye contact. *Was this my moment? Was she going to give me the signal to clear up this whole mess?*

"Objection!"

No, this wasn't *Phoenix Wright: Ace Attorney*.[80] I just quietly sat while Stewart threw down another loquacious argument containing a slight condescending dig, "I think it's noteworthy that

---

[80] A popular game on the Gameboy and Nintendo DS. Before I ever applied for trademark registration or stepped into a courtroom, I was playing this during long tour stretches. The most memorable part of the game was the character yelling "Objection!" It was captured in a ridiculous speech bubble accompanied by some dramatic finger pointing. I'm surprised more law students didn't take to it.

everyone recognize that Mr. Tam is not entitled a copyright on the Slants." This guy seemed smart—much better than either of the attorneys who argued at the Federal Circuit—but had the emotional depth of a turnip.

I got that everyone needed to work out the constitutional issues around this outdated law, but I was in a room of people debating the use of the word *slant,* but many of the decision makers didn't care enough to actually speak with Asian Americans about the reappropriated term. They were all comfortable with using my name, speaking about my work as if they knew me, but they had never met me. They weren't there when the only thing stopping me from getting my ass beat on the playground was taking ownership of *chink* from my oppressors. They didn't read the letters we received from children who considered taking their own lives because of how isolated they felt from bullying. Kids who identified with us when we shared our story. Kids who found their own voices. They wanted to be seen, just as I wanted to be seen and simply not smiled at (although that was kind of cool too).

Then, a quiet voice spoke up. "Does it not count at all that everyone knows that the Slants is using this term not at all to disparage, but simply to describe? It takes the sting out of the word." It was Ruth Bader Ginsburg, Notorious RBG! The clouds created by discussions on theoretical applications of constitutional law were temporarily broken by a ray of light. Her simple, but sharp reasoning was music to my ears. There was a flutter of hope. We were seen!

Stewart's response rained all over that. "Well, the examining attorney found a lot of evidence in the form of Internet commentary otherwise."

"*NO!*" I whispered as loud as I could without getting kicked out. *He's talking about Urban Dictionary again. He's referring to false, distorted evidence!* I couldn't call him out for lying or ignorance. No one would listen or care. I believed that facts mattered. How could they expect to have a just result if they needed to use an unjust, dishonest process to uphold the law? I crossed my arms, crestfallen, and watched Stewart burn up the rest of his time justifying the inconsistent decisions made by the Trademark Office.

John Connell was called up to argue on my behalf. Connell looked grandfatherly as he nervously approached the stand, glasses gently resting on the bottom of his nose. He began to deliver his opening speech with measured tones, explaining that if I "had sought to register the mark as The Proud Asians, we would not be here today." He was abruptly cut off by Justice Kennedy, who was eager to push Connell into an absolutist First Amendment position.

"Suppose we had this hypothetical case. The facts are largely parallel to these, other than the band are non-Asians, they use makeup to exaggerate slanted eyes, and they make fun of Asians." The Justice paused for full effect. "Could the government . . . decline to register that as a trademark in your view?"[81]

---

[81] I always felt that this was a trick question for three reasons. First, according to the government's "facts," a substantial composite of Asian Americans largely

"They could not."

Sotomayor and Roberts began trying to whittle away at the First Amendment argument, asking how the law violated my freedom of speech when I could still use our band's name. *It chills speech,* I whispered under my breath, but the debate quickly moved into aspects of commercial speech. Justice Breyer threw different scenarios asking if the government could deny registrations for things like "Joe Jones is a jerk." *Yes, they could deny you if you weren't Joe Jones. You can't use someone's name unless you had consent or substantial evidence of secondary meaning.*

"They could not stop that," Connell firmly stated.

Other justices wanted to talk about government standards on specific time, manner, and place restrictions. But as they danced around the issues, it became clear to me that the court could not decide if registering a trademark counted as government speech or not. "One of the things that troubles me about this case is that it's not as simple as saying it's a government program discriminating on the basis of viewpoint," lamented Justice Kagan. "Because there are aspects of this program that seem like government speech itself,

---

had a problem with our name when they did not. Second, the government had already rejected the idea that someone could be denied registration because of their ethnicity. They allowed the Trademark Office to say I was "too Asian," so that shouldn't matter. And third, the Trademark Office had already registered hundreds of trademarks for *slant, chink, slope, gook, jap,* and other epithets used against Asians by Caucasians. So it wasn't even hypothetical. It was reality.

maybe not quite that, but something approaching it . . . I doubt anyone would ascribe them to the government . . . but doesn't that give the government greater leeway?"

Throughout the hour-long hearing, Justice Thomas remained silent. At one point, he leaned back in his chair and flipped through one of the briefs as if it were a magazine. During one portion of the exchange, he leaned over and whispered something to the chief justice and they began laughing. I was surprised at how snippy the justices could get and how quickly time moved by. By the end, I was exhausted, like I had just finished running a marathon.

Afterwards, we stopped by the lockers and picked up our personal things. Everyone who walked into the courtroom that morning had to rent a small cubby to check in their cell phones, bags, and coats. As we walked out into the crisp morning air, I felt like the weight that I had been carrying for eight years had lifted. One of my attorneys, Joel, said, "Gentlemen! Let's all walk down together at the same time. We have a press conference to get to down there."

I was moving through a fog, reflecting on the sparring that had just taken place a few minutes earlier. I couldn't tell how we did, or if our message was even heard. Correction: My message. The values that we were fighting for, everything that I had been trying to do for the past decade. I had spent almost a quarter of my life struggling against the government because of UrbanDictionary.com! But they didn't get it.

As we descended the steps of the court, I looked out at the plaza and was caught off guard. It was completely filled with people, maybe several hundred, just milling out about. *What are they doing here?* I thought. *Don't they know court is in session? There are no public tours today!*

Then, some of the people below looked up and saw us walking down. The crowd erupted in applause, some shouting and cheering for us. People had their phones out, and I could hear people saying things like, "We're so proud of you!" *What is going on?* I looked at my bandmates and they were all beaming. Many of the journalists whom I had been speaking with over the past week were clapping and smiling as well. *They get it. They see us.*

"Simon! We have to ask you some questions!" Before I could join our attorneys for the press conference, two high school students approached me. They explained that they flew in from California and waited all night in the freezing cold in hopes of catching a glimpse of the oral arguments. By some miracle, their Asian parents let them ditch school as long as they wrote a report about the experience!

"For our whole lives, we heard about you. Ever since elementary school, we learned about the band who was willing to fight for our community, for the dignity of being able choose for ourselves. Thank you for showing us that we can have power. When we graduate, we want to go into public policy development because of you!"

I was floored. The only thing I could think of in response was, "You're freshman in high school and you know what public policy development is?!"

Words matter. I don't think those students knew how much what they said meant to me. It was the defining moment of the day. It was then that I realized it wouldn't matter if we lost in the courts. We had already won in the hearts of these young activists who understood that justice was not an end result, but a process. As Gloria Steinem once said, "Power can be taken, but not given. The process of the taking is empowerment in itself."[82]

With that, I walked over to the media circus in a far corner outside of the court. There was semi-circle of cameras pointed at a small bunch of microphones gathered up like a bouquet. On my left stood Ron, Joel, and John. Behind me, were the members of the band: Ken, Joe, and Yuya. To my right stood Nina Totenberg who seemed to be orchestrating everything. At the very least, she was the most persistent and posed the question on everyone's mind.

"Do you have a statement?"

I looked over at my attorneys, assuming that they prepared for this moment, but they just stared back. They did the hard work in that courtroom; maybe they wanted some screen time for their firm? Ron nodded at me and gestured with his hands as if he were saying, *After you!*

---

[82] Also: "Power's not given to you. You have to take it." – Beyoncé Knowles.

Filled with adrenaline, nerves, and excitement, I could hear my voice shaking as I began to say:

"If the government truly cared about fighting racist messages, they would have cancelled the registrations for numerous white supremacist groups before choosing to wage that battle against an anti-racism band. But they don't care. They wanted to use what they decided was bad language to distract everyone from bad policy. If they really cared about the Asian American community, they would have listened to what we had to say about the matter over these years, but they chose to ignore us instead . . ."

In those couple of minutes, I began addressing everything that I wished they had said in the courtroom. I called out the government for lying, for using bad evidence. I talked about what it meant for someone outside of your community to decide what's best for you. I explained how all of this was so much bigger than our band and that I essentially had to walk away from my career in music to take up this fight. Many of the reporters were fidgeting, uncomfortable with me discussing ideas of institutionalized, systemic racism when they were all just trying to catch a sound bite before their deadlines.

"We want to hear from your lawyers!" The interruption put an end to my frazzled stump speech. It wasn't the Trademark Office or the court, but it kind of felt like it.

The rest of the day, like many of the months that followed, was crammed with a series of interviews, debates, and appearances. That night, I shared my story in an intimate but jam-packed community arts center for an event billed as "An Evening with the Slants." The audience shared in laughter and tears as I candidly described moments from the journey. We played some of our songs using borrowed instruments, and the crowd sang with us. *No! We Won't Remain Silent! Know! It's our defining moment . . .*

CHAPTER 14
TRICKLE UP THEORY

WHEN I GOT BACK TO PORTLAND, everyone was asking me how things went. They all asked if I won or not. But the Supreme Court doesn't announce a decision that day. Or that week. Or month. Unless it is an emergency,[83] the justices will take their time to carefully consider the issues and debate among themselves before releasing the decision. No one knows when the court opinion will be published until the moment they begin reading it aloud in the courtroom, so the involved parties are never even there. Unless the people in attendance that day have been following the case directly, most won't have any idea what the justices are talking about.

---

[83] The opinion for *Bush v. Gore* was delivered one day after oral arguments since the nation was waiting for an answer on who would become the next U.S. president. *New York Times v. United States*, known as the "Pentagon Papers Case," was decided after four days during an emergency out-of-term session. It was great for the First Amendment, bad for Nixon.

One of things I learned from the mini-boss stages I had to overcome before getting to the Supreme Court was how slowly justice actually moves. Each appeal before the Trademark Office, the Trademark Trial and Appeal Board (TTAB), and the Federal Circuit took at least two months before there would be any kind of answer. Supreme Court cases could take even longer, especially the high profile cases.[84] The bigger the case, the longer the wait; they saved the most prominent decisions for the month of June. Using every measurement available (news coverage, number of amicus briefs filed), everyone expected ours to be June. Knowing this, I decided to make one last ditch effort to influence the decision: I went on tour.

I had an idea. I thought of it as a "trickle up theory." If the law clerks and Supreme Court justices were as considerate about the political winds around a case as everyone assumed, maybe they would continue to listen for stories even after the case was heard. Why not find ways to further influence the decision? While I was in the courtroom, I felt unheard. Now I wanted to make as much noise as possible, so I planned a massive cross-country trip consisting of over eighty appearances in sixty days, hitting as many law schools, intellectual property law associations, and organizations as possible. No petitioner or respondent at the Supreme Court had ever done anything like that, not even 2 Live Crew. What could we lose?

---

[84] For a fascinating read on this subject, check out Duke Law Journal article *The Best for Last: The Timing of U.S. Supreme Court Decisions* (Epstein, et al)

The plan was to get our story out to as many legal influencers and policy wonks as possible. I would be on the road from March to most of May and get back a couple of weeks before my wedding. I hatched this plan on the way back home from D.C. But an unexpected wrench was thrown into the works: Emily, Yuya's partner, was pregnant. How could he continue to tour with us when they already had to watch over five kids? He had only been our drummer for a few months; now he had no choice but to plan his exit. It reminded me of a scene from one of my favorite films, *That Thing You Do.*

Del Paxton: Ain't no way to keep a band together . . . Sooner or later, something makes you crazy . . . Money, women, the road. Hell, man, just time.

Guy Patterson: Well we've only been together a few months

Del Paxton: Some bands I been with, that's months too long.

No matter, the show must go on.

* * *

We prepared for the spring tour in a space borrowed from an old furniture store that had been converted into a community center in Southeast Portland. We would go in at night to rehearse all of our material, both as a full production as well as a stripped-down acoustic show. It was a huge room with floor-to-ceiling windows that faced one of the city's busiest intersections, SE 82nd and Division. I knew it well since I did quite a bit of community organizing work in the area. Sometimes, we'd broadcast live stream videos and ask our fans to help with fundraising efforts for a new building. Today, it is a gorgeous space known as The Orchards, a mixed-use center that includes offices for a number of social justice organizations and forty-eight affordable housing units developed to support the needs of the surrounding community.

One of my favorite memories from this time was filming for a segment on *The Daily Show with Trevor Noah*. We spent fourteen hours with the crew and filmed in locations throughout the city, using our lackluster acting skills to improvise something based on their concept. The original story had correspondent Ronny Chieng obsessed with the stereotypical rock star lifestyle of sex, drugs, and rock n' roll. Having heard about a badass band causing so much trouble that the government sued them, he flew to Oregon to get the inside scoop. He was filled with frustration and disappointment when he learned I spent most of my time with community activism work instead. But eventually, he comes around when he realizes that taking on the government was the most rock star thing a band could do—especially when Ruth Bader Ginsburg was in our corner. Even though they cut down most of the story for the final piece, it was fun to help them produce it. They even gave us a gigantic pastry with our logo on it from Voodoo Doughnut! I kind of felt bad for Ronny because the producer had him wearing uncomfortable, super tight leather pants all day long as part of the original premise.

In the few months before leaving for tour, I worked with Faina to plan our wedding. We had a small budget that we wanted to stick to so that meant we did nearly everything on our own, including designing invitations, coordinating all of the different vendors, and even buying flowers in bulk for making centerpieces and arrangements. I approached the logistics of the wedding with the same mindset as booking a tour, which meant creating spreadsheets and signing a lot of agreements. Meanwhile, Faina could focus on all of the visuals, which included hand painting our own signs. It definitely helped that she was an illustrator and oil painter.

We met during one of the most tumultuous times of my life. At first, she had a hard time keeping track of all of my "jobs" or understanding why I had so many. When we first started dating, I was a marketing director for a nonprofit, worked as an adjunct at a few local colleges, was a touring musician, wrote books, traveled as a keynote speaker, had a side-hustle of renting out my car, and owned a couple of businesses (booking agency, consulting firm), in addition to serving on the board of directors for nearly a dozen organizations. I also helped my sister open a restaurant at one point. Mind you, this was all at the same time. She couldn't figure out why I had so many legal bills and debt accrued just for trying to get a trademark. I later found out that she did some research on me before our first date and felt intimidated—there were a lot more search results than the typical date. But as we got to know one another, she learned that I was a total geek who loved dinosaurs, art, and people.

I loved that Faina came from a similar, yet entirely different world. She was born in St. Petersburg, Russia and moved to the Pacific Northwest when she was six. I was born in San Diego and moved to Portland in my twenties. She worked with oil paints. I had music. She grew up with pelmeni, I with wontons. She wasn't squeamish when it came to eating offal—in fact, she approached different food cultures with the same genuine curiosity that she wished others would have for her own.

We would often get lost in bookstores and art museums for hours at a time, enraptured by the worlds around us. As an artist, I didn't have to explain myself if I got caught up working on my craft. She would often paint for over fifteen hours at a time, completely absorbed in what she was creating. Case in point: she was fine with me touring for months right before the wedding date.

I've found that relationships are just like books: they grow with us, they provide insight when we need it most. We like how they smell. We want to take them with us when we travel, at home we want to curl up with them in bed (especially on rainy days). Sometimes, we're introduced through a friend. And other times we use the Internet to find them. Most importantly, they help us find ourselves. With Faina, I found parts of myself that couldn't be captured by a résumé or media profile. Without saying a word, she made me want to become the best version of myself. It was like a form of self-care.

* * *

The Band Who Must Not Be Named tour kicked off during my birthday weekend. We climbed into our humble tour vehicle, a converted Metro twenty-passenger short bus filled with equipment, a few seats, and a couple of makeshift beds piled on top of our merchandise boxes. I never used either of the beds. I was almost always driving or helping the driver, rehearsing my next presentation, or working on the upcoming wedding. A few times, I was caught nodding off while sitting upright and still working on my computer. When I was too exhausted to work, I preferred to roll up a couple of t-shirts or a towel and curl up in the neck of a fitted guitar case. It provided better support than any contoured pillow, and when combined with the gentle rocking of the bus, would put me to sleep better than any coin-operated massage bed in a motel (cleaner too).

The first few days of the trip consisted mostly of playing venues and a college as we traveled down the West Coast. Once we got to Los Angeles, some heavy traffic put us behind schedule—not a good thing when you have speaking engagements and other appearances stacked on the same day. We were putting pressure on Yuya, who happened to be driving, to get us to UCLA in time. He took the wrong exit, which forced us onto the long squiggly Beverly Glen Boulevard. The bus wasn't meant for aggressive driving, so it was swaying and squeaking. At one point, I looked up as the road started to curve, but Yuya was distracted and wasn't turning with it.

"HEY! LOOK OUT . . ." I started to yell, but he was making the turn too late and too fast. The front wheel missed the tall concrete curb, but it caught one of our rear wheels, popping us into the air slightly with a loud noise resembling a shotgun firing. *Are we OK? Just keep going. We'll deal with it later, it's only two miles away.* He kept driving, though a little more slowly now. A new, strange rattling sound could be heard.

We all stepped out to survey the damage. The tire was torn open, and the wheel looked dented. *OK, let's split up. We've just got a few acoustic songs, and I'm speaking after. Ken, Joe—you're with me. Grab*

*some merch and let's run. Yuya, go with Peter and get this thing fixed ASAP,
then pick us up. Our next thing is in three hours.* I was frustrated but there
wasn't even time to be upset. It wasn't the first time that we had
some kind of mechanical issue; it wasn't even the fiftieth. The most
important thing to me was to keep the ship afloat and sailing without
missing any of our obligations. Good thing we had Peter Cho, our
sound engineer, on this tour.

The first time Peter did sound for the band was at an anime
convention in Canada. The event didn't have any idea of how to put
on a concert, and they only had some DJ equipment for the show.
Peter happened to be attending and found out what was happening,
so he helped out, creating an improvised solution. This happened at
a couple of our anime convention shows in the Northwest. I appreciated that he was someone who knew how to get things done. He
never complained; he just had a whatever-it-takes attitude, and I
knew he would be an asset on tour. I put him in charge of getting
the bus fixed while I kept the shows going.

Unfortunately, the damage was much more extensive than
replacing the tire. When our bus kissed the curb, it jarred a critical
belt loose, which got shredded up, tearing up components around
it in the process. A repair shop told us it would be a full day. When
one day turned into two, I knew we had to keep going. Ken, Joe,
and I took a last minute flight to our next gig in Tucson; Yuya and
Peter remained in Los Angeles with the bus filled with all of our
equipment and merchandise. A few days later, they picked us up,
and we double-timed it to get caught up with our remaining schedule. But then the bus broke down again. And again. And again.

Bus problems on that trip were so frequent that we started getting into a natural rhythm of making temporary repairs while figuring out how to get to the next show. Every shop swore it was an easy fix, but the same belt would often snap after a few days. Commercial diesel bus repair shops were no better. We even started carrying spare parts. And though we made it to almost every show, we'd be filled with dread every time the familiar sound of the belt being shredded could be heard. We knew that once the belt was gone, we'd be dead in the water. We were sitting on a powder keg of five adults confined to a small space with immense pressure and frequent, but unpredictable problems popping up. Soon, the bus wasn't the only thing breaking down.

By the time we got to Boston, half of the band wasn't speaking to me. Those members didn't budget for problems that we encountered on the road and were upset that they weren't getting paid as much as they hoped. But I wasn't getting paid at all. I used all of the extra money I earned from speaking engagements to make sure that they had food, a hotel room every night, and extra cash to send home. The band deserved to be compensated, but I felt like my sacrifices and extra work weren't being appreciated. So when people started making passive-aggressive comments or complaining, I began to shut down. I thought, *"It was never that bad when Aron, Jonathan, and Tyler were in the band. Most of the time, we didn't get paid! We were just happy to have some food and make it back safely."* Thankfully, the other half of the group was doing everything they could to help me. They'd remind me of my upcoming wedding and even do a little extra to make sure I got some rest myself.

It was tough playing shows while feeling frustrated and defeated but speaking engagements were worse. I didn't have loud music, other musicians, or flashing lights on stage to distract the audience if I needed a moment to breathe. Most of the time, I was totally alone up there. These events were all over the map. Often, organizations wanted me to speak so attorneys could earn credits for continuing legal education (CLE),[85] but sometimes they could take an extreme approach. Either they didn't believe in my expertise at all and would require an intellectual property lawyer to provide an overview of my case (I usually had to end up correcting the bits they got wrong), or they would ask me to debate one of their local law professors, which seemed to be an unfair setup. I accepted anyway. I was on a mission to share my truth, even if it meant taking on people with fancy law degrees and many published works.

At first, I would prepare by studying all of our legal briefs and trying to argue just as an attorney would, supporting my positions with case law, legal jurisprudence, and well-reasoned fact patterns. It seemed like the most logical approach. But things rarely worked out that way because the audience assumed that I, a non-lawyer, couldn't possibly know very much about the law. I quickly changed tack.

---

[85] In most states, attorneys need to teach or enroll in classes totaling about 15 hours of CLE credit per year. These days, I teach an average of 40 CLE hours or more per year even though I haven't been to law school.

"I started the Slants to change assumptions about Asian Americans. I wanted to shift the conversation about identity, reappropriation, and the people that get to make decisions about what's right for my community."

When I began sharing my story, the dynamic in the room quickly changed. Instead of debating ideas of where the limits of free speech should be, I talked about how the existing lines were often used against marginalized groups, including me personally. I elaborated on what it felt like to have the voices of your community drowned out because a single bureaucrat determined that an anonymous, wiki-joke website had more credibility than our experts, surveys, and organizations. I talked about the kids we worked with and how we performed for prisoners, mental health patients, and families of incarceration camp survivors. This made all the difference. I realized that people can always argue about legal ideas, and even use them to justify the disparate impact of bad policies, but they cannot argue our stories. Our stories matter.

I started telling our story, the Slants story, everywhere I could that tour: at shows, law schools, anime conventions, and at these legal debates. I could feel the tide moving. We even played a "Tiny Desk" style concert at the headquarters of the ACLU where we unleashed our cover of Bruce Springsteen's "Born in the USA." It provided a powerful new twist to the words *Sent me off to a foreign land to go and kill the yellow man*. This experience reminded me that fighting for change always requires us to be rooted in love and compassion so that we don't lose ourselves in the process. Those attorneys and law students didn't need to hear from another legal expert—there were plenty of those in the world—they needed to listen to the perspective of someone most deeply affected by our system. We don't win by arguing with others, we win by changing hearts. *I hope you're listening, Supreme Court!*

We wrapped up *The Band Who Must Not Be Named* Tour with a final show at TEDxBend in Oregon. During the course of our tour, I wrote talk called "Yes, Read the Comments Section." It was about learning how to connect with people we disagree with. I suggested that instead of arguing to win, we should focus on listening instead. I argued, *Apathy is not compatible with love.* When we arrived in town, I was surprised to see our band was on the front page of the local paper with the headline "Bridging Divides." I liked that.

Finally, after two very long months on the road and overcoming unimaginable difficulties, I made it home. And on May, 31, 2017, I married Faina in the beautiful Lan Su Chinese Garden.

CHAPTER 15
DECISION DAY

~

JUNE 19, 2017.

Monday morning. After working fifteen-hour days every day for almost a month straight, I am bleary with exhaustion. It is one of the few remaining days that the Supreme Court could possibly publish their decision on my case. Fifty-fifty chance it happens this morning. I stumble to the restroom and catch a glimpse of the notifications light on my phone furiously blinking like a lighthouse through my foggy state of mind. I grab it.

753 notifications.

Oregon Public Broadcasting's tweet is before my eyes: *SCOTUS Rules in Favor of the Slants*. I open my email and see my attorney's one word note with the decision attached. "Congratulations."

I'm shaking as I open the file, trying to work my way through the dense legal opinion written by Justice Alito. I want to know how the court is divided, what they actually say, how my life's work is judged by the nation's highest court. I'm only a few pages in when a ring erupts in the silence. It's a reporter trying to get the scoop. It is only minutes after the high court's decision. They ask me the obvious question:

"How do you feel?"

* * *

The question was one that I had anticipated. It's a routine, run-of-the-mill probe designed to elicit quick emotion, not articulate thoughts. The scenario was one that I had been imagining over the past few months.

But in this moment, I'm stumped.

I stammer out something that sounds like a canned speech, including being "humbled and thrilled," though I'm not feeling anything at all. I hang up and text Alex, my publicist. *Supreme court ruled in our favor.* I publish a statement on the Slants' website and social media.

Another call. Then another. The email count is doubling every few seconds as the screen refreshes, messages on Facebook begin pouring in.

Alex texts me back. *Fuck yeah. I'll get press release out. Will be a busy day!!! Congrats!!!* It's been about thirty minutes since the decision was released, and I'm already at about 2,000 messages.

We begin setting up interviews every ten minutes for the next ten hours, but most of my calls are interrupted by other reporters who are "breaking" the story. And it does feel broken: I quickly scan the news and see how every major media outlet begins reporting on the issue: "Washington Redskins Win Supreme Court Decision," "Redskins Score Major Victory in Supreme Court Case," "Offensive Speech Now OK Says Supreme Court." I click on the only headline that mentions the band name, and a photo of the Redskins' football helmet appears on my screen.

* * *

For years, I dreamed of this moment of vindication. I imagined how it would feel to be a part of the legacy of social justice jurisprudence, even if it was only through an obscure part of the law. Just a few months earlier, I had a dream where the Supreme Court ruled in our favor. In that scenario, the curiosity about our David vs. Goliath case led people to look at how the law was being applied: inconsistently, subjectively, and improperly. People weren't talking about football teams; instead, they were finally paying attention to the narrative of the marginalized. Of course, it was only a dream.

The euphoria that I had been expecting was replaced with dread and disgust. The press had reframed our struggle into a narrative around a racist football team. I didn't feel vindication for our victory; I felt a deep sense of injustice. And I knew what the inevitable follow up would be: some of the fermenting anger against the most hated man in football was about to come my way.

* * *

Throughout that day, I received hundreds if not thousands of congratulations from friends, colleagues, attorneys, and fans. My phone rang constantly as I answered call after call and ran from location to location for local and national news interviews. It took adrenaline and hot tea to keep my energy up. And while it became tiresome to be asked the same limited question from reporters about the Washington football team, my answer turned reflexive. I felt far more responsibility to provide an answer to the flurry of tweets from a number of Native American activists.

There's no doubt that my critics were dismayed by the Supreme Court ruling because it appeared to deliver victory on a silver platter to Dan Snyder, owner of the Washington Redskins. On social media, I was accused of being a native-born person of color perpetuating the work of colonizers. They characterized this decision on trademark registration law as the opening floodgate for hate speech. They intimated that I single-handedly doomed all efforts to remove racist mascots from pro sports.

I tried to address some of their concerns by offering clarity around our process and how trademark laws work. I tried to express how the law I'd been fighting had allowed the government to deny rights based on people's race, gender, and sexual orientation. I even explained that I'd met with over 140 social justice groups, including numerous confederated tribal leaders. I sincerely wanted to engage with empathy. But my engagement on Twitter only seemed to create greater fury, more harsh personal accusations of bad will and selfish motivations. It was like when we won at the Federal Circuit but even more intense. How can one convince someone that placing all of their hopes on a flawed legal strategy was doomed?

Frustration, confusion, and sadness began seeping their way into my heart.

* * *

I was driving home later that afternoon when I remembered to return my mother's call.

"Congratulations! I saw the news. *Gongxi, Gongxi*! I tried calling you, but it kept saying your voicemail was full."

"*Xie Xie*, I'm sorry I wasn't able to call you back earlier. I had about 40,000 messages."

"Waah, 40,000! Will you be in the Chinese newspaper?"

To my parents, the measuring stick for success is if one makes it into the Chinese newspaper. It's how they understand the importance of news in the world. I remember the first time I told my father that I was featured in TIME Magazine.

"So? I don't read that magazine."

He didn't mean to be dismissive; he just didn't understand the significance of it. Or perhaps he had insight into what I had been missing all along: in the big picture, it didn't really matter.

As my mom and I talked about the family and my recent nuptials, she caught me off guard.

"Now that it's over, I hope you can smile again," she says.

"What do you mean?"

"You used to smile and be happy and joke around. For a long time, I haven't seen you smile. *Ni meiyou xiao*."

I started getting defensive. "I smiled a lot at my wedding," I tried to assure her. "I'm happy."

It was almost as if her frown could be heard over the phone. "I just worry about you."

I felt my lips quiver as the moisture in my eyes welled up.

"I have to go." Then hang up.

* * *

When I got home, Faina gave me a warm embrace that I just wanted to sink into forever. We'd only been married nineteen days. What a start. Our dog nuzzled up to my leg before flopping onto his back to not so subtly ask for belly scratches. She asked me how I was feeling, the very same question that kicked off the strange, desultory day. I absurdly asked for clarification. She saw my condition, sat me down, and began making me something to eat, the first I'd had all day.

"I have an interview in seven minutes."

"That's OK, darling. You eat fast anyway . . . but don't forget to mow the lawn. You said you'd do it."

"I just helped expand the First Amendment and won a Supreme Court case. Don't I get a pass or something?"

* * *

The interview was with a persistent TV news station in Southern Oregon that wanted to use Skype. I agreed to take the interview after they emailed and called my publicist at least a dozen times each earlier that day. Despite their enthusiasm, they didn't do any research on the band or our case. They asked questions about who I was, what I did in the band, and the origin of the Slants' name.

"You can Google that, all of the info is on the website," I said with great annoyance. "But sure, I first thought of the band's name in 2004 . . ." I launched into the same genesis of the band that I've told hundreds of times before. Finally, the interview ended. Faina looked a little surprised. She had seen me deftly handle interview after interview over the past couple of years. She had never seen the veneer crack, at least not in public.

The phone continued to buzz with alerts, including low-battery warnings. Then, it rang a few minutes earlier than my next scheduled call. It was Spencer, my friend and attorney who kicked off this grand adventure by recommending I apply for a trademark registration many years ago.

"Hey Spencer."

"The man of the hour! Congratulations! I wanted to wait all day to call because I knew you'd be busy and probably overwhelmed. I hope you're celebrating."

"Oh. I just have interviews. I have another one in a few minutes."

He asked me if everything was OK. He told me that I sounded like something terrible happened. In ten years, he'd never heard me like this.

"No, I'm just really, really tired. I haven't had time to process even. But I think I'm happy, I'm probably excited. I snapped at the last reporter though because I'm sick of the misunderstanding about this case and our band."

"Listen," he gently said, "I have been thinking about this all day. There were so many times where you could have given up. But you didn't. You had every opportunity to just stop and no one would have blamed you. You kept fighting because you saw an injustice. Everyone else in history just gave up fighting this law because it was too tough. You stuck with your principles. And you won. You made the country better. There will always be people who will misunderstand, but you stood up when no one else was willing to do it. And what you did will benefit them, too, though they may never know it. Even if people blame you for the actions of others who abuse this case, you helped bring freedom to people who needed it. People don't understand how important individual liberties are and what others had to go through to pave the way. But you are truly a hero."

The next interview went much, much better.

* * *

Who cares what other people think?

We often ask ourselves this question as if it's easy to live unaffected by the opinions and words of others. In fact, we graciously share this rhetorical question in the form of advice to our friends who are tormented by emotional struggles, usually around some aspect of their identity: how they look, if what they're doing is socially acceptable, how things may bring honor or shame to their family.

While I wasn't directly taught the ideas of *Guanxi* or *Mian zi*, the Chinese concept for "Saving Face," it was reinforced through my family upbringing in terms of how we interacted with others. We were told not to contradict others, especially in public, and even more so if they were our elders or strangers.

As children, it was heartbreaking to see my mom smile and nod to store clerks who would make fun of her accent, as if she couldn't understand what they were doing. The worst was when these were customers in our family's restaurant. My mom would be extra kind to them, even when it was extremely degrading.

"I want some flied lice! Chicken flied liiiice," they'd say with a chuckle.

"Chicken Fah-ride rice" would be her response. She'd speak more slowly, trying to carefully articulate each syllable. "Anything else?"

"Egg Frow-wah soup." More stifled laughter.

"No problem," she'd say with a smile.

In the back, I would tell her that the customers were being rude. But she would scold me instead! She never wanted to upset them, to cause a scene. She believed in killing people with kindness: always be respectful and things would work out sooner or later. She didn't want to let others get a rise out of her; it was her method of being subversive. While many people around her continued this kind of mistreatment, some would eventually come around and treat her with extra respect. Even her former mother-in-law, whose emotional abuse drove my mom to a divorce, would later apologize for her racist, tormenting behavior. That's some serious badass *guanxi*.

My father was a bit different. Though he had a short temper, he was also good-humored and thought many of the micro-aggressions he dealt with in his life were harmless jokes. He'd often joke back, trading tit-for-tat. When I asked him how he would deal with people who were mistreating him, he'd respond, "Fight back!" But when it came to family members, especially those who were being misogynistic or homophobic, he'd cautiously admonish them in private so it wouldn't lower their Face in front of others.

Pairing my parents' respective approaches with the modern American bravado of being unaffected by the opinion of others programmed me with a conflicting set of responses. As a timid, introverted child, my version of "fighting back" usually only happened when my anger or humiliation boiled over. It often resulted in passive-aggressive behavior in the form of harmless pranks but even then, I'd feel some pangs of guilt.

My older brother usually liked to bully me in the way that siblings often do: making fun of me . . . sometimes with tickles, sometimes with punches. One day, I saw an episode of Punky Brewster where a fed-up sibling dumped a bucket of ice in the bed of their tormentor, then covered it with a blanket so they wouldn't find out until they slipped into bed.

I got excited about the idea and filled a five-gallon pail with ice. But when I looked at my brother's bed, I felt both guilt and fear of retaliation, so I ended up pouring it into my bed instead! I thought the prank was a good idea; I didn't want to see it wasted. When I told him about it, he roared in laughter and called me an idiot. But he also felt bad about it, so he left me alone for the next few weeks, opting to play Nintendo with me instead of beating me up. It was like an advanced Jedi-mind trick or something.

As I got older and developed my own sense of justice, my approach to fighting back changed. Instead of allowing offenses to fester, I would call them out. To me, it was important to keep others accountable: hopefully, this would reduce suffering or indignity for others. But I'd usually do so privately or with gentleness (when at my best, at least . . . we all falter) in hopes that they'd be willing to self-correct. It was very much like how my father navigated the world. But because I'd often do this without an apparent rise in emotions and instead lean on very literal uses of language to articulate my points, I'd be accused of being an emotionless robot.

Instead of worrying what others thought, I began to look at things through a lens of compassion. I focused on how they felt. I developed a habit of profusely apologizing for things, even minor offenses, hoping to kill others with kindness. In that regard, I became like my mother. But unlike her, I didn't feel embarrassment on the whole.

It was that American idea of being unaffected: what others thought of me wasn't of the least importance. I believed in doing what was right, even if it was controversial, misinterpreted, or cost me some pride. After all, my perspective was that people should deal in the currency of empathy, not ego. Negative criticism rarely bothered me. But if it seemed that people were upset because of suffering, that would weigh heavily on me. Likewise, I wasn't motivated by praise. But if that praise stemmed from deep, overflowing joy in another person, I would be deeply moved.

Thus, the day of my so-called "First Amendment victory" was a cataclysmic mix of trepidation and sorrow for those who felt that an important protection against offensive speech was lost. Those negative emotions co-existed with the exhilaration from knowing that our case liberated marginalized groups from government overreach and inequitable processes.

I felt as if my heart were on a pendulum, wildly swinging from one end to another, but without the ability to stop and process the experience. When reporters and angry activists pulled me back-and-forth, comments like those from Spencer brought me back to my center. I cared about how people were feeling. The problem was I just didn't know how I felt.

Almost eight years of my life—about 2,800 days—were poured into this battle for self-identity. But I didn't even have 28 minutes to pause in solitude and reflect . . . until I mowed the lawn.

* * *

After the final scheduled interview of the day, I go out to dinner with Faina for a low-key celebration . . . at least it's supposed to be a celebration. Like the rest of my day, my mental and emotional state is a graded blend of bittersweet contradictions. I am weary, as if all eight years of my journey were being experienced in one day.

She says I look depressed. I muster up all of the positivity in me, and we talk of happier things instead: what life would be like moving away, starting over, and living without the expectations of others pressing down on us. I spent so much of my life focusing on the idea of expanding liberty for others; now I just wanted a little freedom for myself. Throughout the dinner, my phone screams at me like a petulant child. When the waiter gives us the check, she says I don't have to work on the lawn if I don't want to.

* * *

It's 8:00 p.m. and still sunny.

I open the back door of the house but it feels more like opening the door to a blazing oven. It is so hot that I swear I could cook an egg on my skin. I start up the electric mower and begin crisscrossing my way across the lawn, avoiding the cord at all costs, since I already ruined one earlier in the month. A moment of panic sets in: I can't hear my phone or feel its incessant vibrating notifications over the sound and bumps of the mower. But I think about Faina's words from earlier: You don't have to answer if you don't want to. It rings some more.

I don't answer.

I turn the phone off.

All of a sudden, the heat doesn't feel so bad.

I finally have some peace and time to consider everything that has taken place: the trip to the Supreme Court in January, the weeks I spent on the road talking to law students and experts about our story, the wedding . . .and today, decision day. Words and emotions swirl, kicking up memories like the blades of grass flying around me and sticking to my skin.

Some of the messages of pain and anger replay in my mind. Comments about me being self-absorbed and apathetic to the plight of others sear through me, cutting me into pieces. It doesn't matter if they know me or truly understand the nuances of obscure trademark laws or not: my heart aches at their suffering. Perhaps they're right, even.

On the other side, I think about Spencer's words and all of the people I've met over the years who sent their personal congratulations. People who understand the pain of having the agency over their own self-identity stripped away. Now they have the ability to empower themselves without the full weight of the government used against them. Maybe they're right, too.

My vision begins to blur and I can't tell if the saltiness I taste is from pouring sweat or tears inching down my face. I continue working my way around the yard, going over the contours over and over again like it is a soothing mantra for meditation. My heart's palpitations slow, and calm starts to settle in. This isn't so bad. I can help those who are hurting; I can find peace in this process, too. Instead of feeling oppressive, the ninety degree weather coats me like a warm bath.

CRACK.

I accidentally run over a solar-powered pathway light at the edge of the grass. At first I'm angry. Then, I feel guilty for knocking it over. For a second, I'm tempted to ask the light how it feels. But its decapitated structure tells me everything—it's how I've been feeling all day long.

CHAPTER 16
PAINT IT BLACK

IT DIDN'T TAKE LONG for the media to focus on something other than our Supreme Court decision. Within a few days, headlines were already focused on other controversies from the new president: Trump blamed hacking by Russians on President Obama, he was leading the charge to undo the Affordable Care Act, and he was attacking journalists. After a short spike of interest following the airing of our segment on *The Daily Show with Trevor Noah*, our case was more or less considered old news.

Despite the mainstream media moving on, a number of groups were still talking about the long-term impact of our case and trying to guess what it meant for trademark law, pending cases (such as the Washington football team's case and other marks rejected for being *scandalous* or *immoral*), and what freedom of speech means for a democratic society. The most vocal group, at least on social media, was represented by Native American activists who still wanted answers. We traded hundreds of messages, but I think very few of our exchanges left anyone feeling good. We agreed on so many other things, including the need for people to stop using racist mascots, but differing ideas about my case drove some to believe I was motivated by only the most selfish reasons.

During this time, Jacqueline Keeler reached out to me. We had traded only the occasional message since we met after the Federal Circuit ruling two years prior. Most were polite, but there wasn't anything substantial. She was largely absent from the online conversations about our case, but many of the people criticizing me would tag her in their tweets. I wasn't sure how she felt about everything, but I assumed that she wasn't thrilled. Still, we met up at the Red Robe Tea House in Old Town Chinatown, something of a remote office for me.[86]

I got there an hour early and waited anxiously, drinking cup after cup of hot tea. As I waited, I reflected on the long path to victory and the price paid in order to get there. My small mountain of debt seemed paltry compared to the larger spiritual, emotional, and mental toll. What would my life have looked like if I were able to fully throw myself into my art (or literally anything else) instead? Would I have been able to spend more time with the people I cared

---

[86] If you've ever seen footage of me in an Asian looking Portland place, it was probably at Red Robe. I was there so often, they would begin fixing my usual order when they saw me walking in. The owners kindly let me set up media interviews in their teahouse when they weren't busy. I always asked the reporters to buy something in return.

about? Could I have done more to protect against unintended consequences?

After I wrote *Sutures*, I never had another dream about meeting Perla in that old diner. I thought about her often and her last words to me: *You're a fighter!* She told me that even though she knew that I would often avoid conflict. Whenever I got into fights as a kid, whether with bullies or with my brother, I'd lose. But I think she meant that I would always fight for the people I loved. It's true: I'd do anything for them, sometimes to a fault. But a lifetime of fighting can change a person. Inside and out, we carry scars and sensitivities that may be invisible or misunderstood by others.

Perhaps I felt so nervous because I felt hurt. Maybe misunderstood.

When Jacqueline walked in, I was caught off guard when she gave me a warm embrace. Before I could say anything, she said "Congratulations! I'm genuinely happy for you." *Huh?* I was obviously confused. She began to tell me that after we last met, she had a lot of time to reflect on the conversation we shared and what I was actually fighting for. She realized how big of a problem it was to have a law governing offensive content when the main administrators tended to be privileged whites who didn't receive training on cultural competency issues. And she realized that the pain she was feeling was derived from being so attached to a legal strategy that might have been flawed.

We talked candidly about some of the tribal leaders and experts with whom I had spoken over the years, including lawyers who worked on the case to get Pro Football's trademarks cancelled. Many of them felt conflicted. They wanted to support me but were afraid of the backlash they might receive and how it might affect the appearance of solidarity in the larger campaign to get mascots changed. They preferred the Slants to be the ones to challenge the law, since we had a set of facts dealing with ideas about reappropriation and social justice.

"Everyone was afraid that if Dan Snyder won, he'd rub it in the faces of the Native community. He might make things a lot worse. My case would be less of a direct impact."

"For me as a Native person, when I first heard about this strategy to take on Pro Football using an obscure law to get their trademarks cancelled, I thought it was quite clever. After speaking with you, I started looking at the bigger picture of the First Amendment. I realized that it would only be a short-term win at best. I think we have an obligation to take to heart the rights of all Americans, especially other marginalized groups."

"I think other groups could do a better job supporting each other's communities. I don't see nearly enough Asian Americans showing up for Native issues. I need to be better about that myself. So despite the heat I'm receiving, I welcome others holding me accountable, even if there are some misunderstandings along the way."

"That's putting it lightly!" She smiled. "I know some of the people putting you through the ringer. There are Native-created parody accounts of you that exist just to criticize you. It doesn't help that all of the headlines seem to only be about the football team. How does that make you feel?"

"It's killing me." I explained, "I don't want to be forever associated with Dan Snyder, but it seems to be unavoidable. Part of the cost of fighting for our name was the risk that that would happen." I thought about it for a moment. "This is what white supremacy does. It reframes issues around itself and pins marginalized groups against each other, fighting for the scraps. But if us winning helps a people find their voice, then I think was worth it."

We were doing what the government never bothered doing: speaking. No one at the Trademark Office asked what Native Americans thought about the *Redskins'* mascot; it didn't even cross their minds that so many considered it offensive until someone brought a lawsuit to cancel their registrations. In fact, they even defended the team! Similarly, the government didn't believe it was worth asking Asian Americans how they felt about *the Slants*; they just assumed that they knew best. They didn't recognize how degrading it was to strip people of their voices until a lawsuit was filed. If they took the effort to listen, things might have turned out differently. But then again, racism is so institutionalized in our legal system that the results would likely be exactly the same.

Over the years, my attorneys would often sit on panels or give presentations about the case for legal audiences. They told me that the room was almost always divided, with about half in support and half against. I usually didn't have that issue; whenever I spoke, the room would swing my way. I have piles of notes from attorneys saying *"I was deeply against your side until I heard you speak, until I heard your story and what you went through.*" That's because when we're talking about disparaging speech, we're really talking about dignity. It's very hard to argue that you care about the dignity of the marginalized when you see what the Trademark Office's policies were actually doing to groups like the Slants and Dykes on Bikes.

The challenge of creating policies around speech is that it rests on assumptions. You assume the intention and the possible impact of what certain phrases might mean and do. But language and symbols are much more complex than that. I once delivered a presentation on our case to policymakers in Australia. The audience gave me a standing ovation, and a government representative told the room, "This would never of happened if *the Slants* was applied for in our country. We have protections against hate speech, but we also understand how important reappropriation is for the people. Bravo!" Sadly, I had to tell him that when we applied for the Slants in Australia, we were rejected for being "scandalous."[87]

Jacqueline and I sat quietly for a few moments while sipping tea and thinking about the deep issues being faced by our country before switching to lighter topics. We spoke about mutual friends in the community that we shared. She told me about the book she

---

[87] A law review article was written on this experience in the European Intellectual Property Review: *Comparative Analysis of US and Australian Trade Mark Applications for The Slants* by Vicki Huang. She explains that the Examiner's Manual there discourages examiners away from social activism.

was working on. I shared my secret wish of going on a vacation one day.

Before leaving, she told me that she was going to be on a progressive radio talk show called *Edge of Sports*. "They're bringing me on to talk about your case. I don't know how much it will help, but I'll try and bring a different perspective. And keep your chin up . . . I know many of the people saying hurtful things about you mean well. Hopefully it will be better soon."

The next day, Jacqueline went on air and defended me. She spoke frankly, saying that the legal strategy of cancelling the trademark registration was flawed because it would go up against the First Amendment. She reminded people of the many other tactics they had at their disposal, from protesting Nike to putting pressure at the school district level. "We should celebrate what Suzan Harjo and Amanda Blackhorse did, all of the awareness that their cases brought to Native issues, but it's time for a new strategy." She provided context and explained many of the things that I had been through.

When asked about my case, she said, "In the end, we're going to see it as a good thing."

* * *

Over the years, I came across many interesting articles and stories about intellectual property law. One of my favorite moments was learning about the history of Agloe, New York. Agloe was originally a "copyright trap," or a "paper town," that was created by the mapmakers Otto Lindberg and Ernest Aplers of the General

Drafting Company in order to thwart plagiarism.[88] The name was essentially a scrambled anagram of their two names.

In 1937, Lindberg and Alpers published a map with the fake town of Agloe located at the intersection of two dirt roads near the foothills of the Catskill Mountains. Agloe was a copyright trap: if anyone else published a map with Agloe, they could use it as definitive proof that their work was stolen. A few years after their map was published, their rivals Rand McNally produced a map with Agloe on it. *We're going to sue them,* thought Lindberg. *They stole our work!* When the two companies met at this remote intersection, they found a surprise: an actual town.

It turned out that people kept driving to this intersection expecting to find a town. So one day, a man built it. He named it Agloe, since that was what was on his map. He began with the Agloe General Store, and during its peak, it also had a gas station and two homes. Eventually, Agloe and the General Drafting Company disappeared, though the town did make a brief appearance on Google Maps.

The story is about assumptions. Lindberg and Alpers assumed that Agloe would only ever be a paper town that could secure their intellectual property. Visitors assumed that it was a real place (so did Rand McNally). But assumptions have power. They can change the world. Recall that it only took arbitrary red lines on a few

---

[88] *Paper Towns* was a book, and later a film, written by John Green that was based on the history of Agloe.

city maps to displace and disadvantage tens of thousands of people for generations (they continue to do so, even decades after legal segregation was banned). As John Green once said, "It's easy enough to say that the world shapes our maps of the world . . . but what I find a lot more interesting is the way that the manner in which we map the world changes the world."

Every so often, a student or someone working in law will ask me, "How do you win a Supreme Court case?" "*It's easy,*" I tell them. "*Just stop thinking like an attorney and start thinking like an artist instead. Don't just see things—or people—for what they are. See them for what they can be.*"

It's amazing what kind of change can take place when we begin to change our assumptions of what is possible. When I think back on the Asian Americans that have gone to the Supreme Court over the past two centuries, I realize that all of those cases were about assumptions. Takao Ozawa and Bhagat Singh Thind challenged the country's notion of who could be considered white. Chae Chan Ping tested the limits of the government's ability to limit immigration, even overriding treaties if they wanted to. Fred Korematsu and Minoru Yasui pushed back against the United States when it assumed that its own citizens posed a threat if they happened to be of Japanese descent. Yick Wo proved that a law which was race-neutral on its face could still be unconstitutional if it was administered in a prejudicial manner. So where does my case land?

* * *

In the Summer of 2011, I was invited to bring the Slants to the Oregon State Penitentiary. The Johnny Cash fan inside me was so excited, I immediately started planning an outfit that would be all black. That excitement overshadowed everything else. As such, I didn't think much of the waivers we were required to sign in order to perform. They were filled with "hostage disclaimers" and ensured that we wouldn't sue if we got shanked, killed, or maimed while there. It didn't cross my mind that the idea of sending an all-Asian American band into a prison with one of the largest populations of white supremacists could be a dangerous one. I mean, I signed similar forms just to perform at high schools.

Things changed when we showed up and were handed bright orange vests to wear over our clothes. Aron asked if we could take them off mid-concert since our own suits could get quite warm and it was a very hot day.

"Sure," the guard said, "but if something happens out there, those vests let us know who not to shoot."

"Yo, can I get two of them vests?" I asked, "I want a backup in case I lose mine."

We continued through security with significant precautions at every step. There were bars and armed guards everywhere. The clanging of the doors would echo loudly every time one would open or shut. Obviously, the place was designed for containment, not comfort. The only thing I knew about prisons was what I learned from books, TV, and movies (and this was before *Orange is the New Black* was around, so at the time I didn't see the prison industrial complex as a way to perpetuate white supremacy). I thought about the kinds of people that were sent to a maximum-security prison: drug dealers, murderers, rapists. *Was this a good idea?*

Eventually, we stepped onto a large field surrounded by tall concrete walls. They called it "The Big Yard." I looked up at the sentry towers, placed strategically every so often with searchlights and mounts for weapons. There was a large running track with a grassy field in the center. At the end was a small stage with a thin line of plastic police tape stretched across the front. I read the words, *POLICE LINE DO NOT CROSS.* It was the only thing that was going to separate us from nearly two thousand convicted criminals.

"Um . . . I don't know if they follow those kinds of instructions," I told the guard, "I mean, that's kind of why they're in here, right? They can't follow instructions."

He told me not to worry. They had a plan. He told us that if anything happened, we should drop everything and run through the chain link fence behind the stage. "Our guys will be stationed there so once you're through, we can secure the fence."

"Ok, let me get this straight," I said. "If something happens, *run.* You'll be on the safe side and *if* we make it through, you'll lock the fence behind us." *Did they get this plan from the Walking Dead?*

While we played, a small crowd assembled in the front while a larger one walked around, getting the only hour of outdoor time they'd have for the day. As we launched into our cover of "Paint it

Black," hundreds of the prisoners jumped and cheered. It was incredible, watching a sea of orange and blue ripple in front of us.

At the end of the concert, I was standing near the edge of the police tape (on the safe side, of course), when a group of shirtless white men started walking towards me. As they got closer, I could see the words emblazoned across the chest of the man in front: WHITE POWER. He and his companions were completely covered in swastikas and white pride tattoos. The man in front walked up to me, blocking out the sun in the process. He seemed nervous as he handed me a piece of a paper with a small, sharp pencil.

He asked me for an autograph.

I didn't know what to do. The only thing going through my mind at the time was the scene in Jurassic Park where they explained to the children, *If you don't move, the T-Rex won't see you.* I thought maybe it would work here. It didn't. But then he said four words that cut right through me.

"It's for my daughter."

I turned over the paper. It was a makeshift flyer for our show in the prison. He wanted to tell her that he had met the band. *My* band.

"I know what you must be thinking. I've made a lot of mistakes in my life, and they're ones that I don't want my little girl to make." He said he wanted to show her that he could learn, that he could change his heart and mind even if he couldn't change what was stained into his skin.

That was one of the most powerful moments in my life. I went in with all kinds of assumptions, but those changed when we began to have that conversation. For the rest of the day, I walked around, on the other side of the police tape, and listened to the stories of the men behind bars.

I started the Slants because I wanted to change people's assumptions about Asian Americans. Assumptions can be powerful. This deliberate act of claiming an identity was something that the government considered to be disparaging. Laws are designed to maintain the status quo. The legal system on trademark law felt like a prison created to keep disruptive ideas from coming into the mainstream.

The government thought that they were protecting the public from harm, but they were actually erecting walls designed to discourage people from mobilizing for social justice by using language to reappropriate ideas. They used walls to divide us, both within our own communities as well as outside of them so that we would be pitted against other marginalized groups. They weren't protecting us, they were trying to keep us complacent.

Against all odds, that wall came down. It all began with a name worth fighting for.

EPILOGUE
#BADASIAN

FIVE MONTHS AFTER THE SUPREME COURT published their decision, Faina and I moved to Nashville, Tennessee. The Trademark Office didn't receive a floodgate of applications to register hate speech as some feared; instead, they saw a wave of applications from people using terms in a reappropriated, self-empowering manner. Under the previous law, they would have been denied for being "too Asian," "too black," or "too gay."

In 2018, a year after we won our landmark decision, I still didn't have the paper registration for our trademark. When I inquired, they told me that my case required "special handling," so I just went online, paid the fee, and ordered copies for myself. It arrived nine years—nearly 3,000 days—after Spencer first encouraged me to apply.

I also started a nonprofit organization with members of the band to provide support for Asian American artists looking to incorporate activism into their work. To this day, I continue to travel around the world sharing the Slants' story, playing music, and making trouble.

I've received many touching notes from people over the years who have been inspired by our band's work. It overshadows the occasional hate mail and death threats.

One of the most special things I've seen is from Katerina Jeng and Krystie Mak, co-founders of an independent media company that celebrates Asian American identity through storytelling. They started the group one month after the Supreme Court issued its decision. They named it Slant'd. On October 13, 2017, they received their federal trademark registration without any troubles. Ten months later, I received a thank you note from them with an embossed keychain that says "BADASIAN."

ACKNOWLEDGEMENTS

FOR THEIR GENEROSITY, WISDOM, AND COM-PASSION, I thank the many people who have made this journey through activism and the arts possible. This includes the many people involved with the work of The Slants (band members past and present), our publicist Alex Steininger, the attorneys who carried this over the finish line (Ron Coleman, Joel MacMull, and John Connell), and the attorney who started all of this trouble to begin with: Spencer Trowbridge. Deep gratitude to Natasha Dwyer for editing and emotional support throughout this process, my family members, and the countless organizations and people who lifted their voices in support of The Slants' work.

Most of all, I would like to express appreciation for the love of my life, Faina, for encouraging me to write this book.

QUESTIONS AND TOPICS
FOR DISCUSSION

1. Conflicting ideas about freedom of expression are at the heart of Simon's story. How important is the right of self-identification for human rights? Do the benefits of free speech outweigh the negatives? How can laws against hate speech be used against marginalized groups?

2. For most of Simon's journey, he tries to separate his art from his activism. Do artists have a social responsibility to incorporate activism into their work? How is art similar to activism? How does the personal life or activist beliefs of an artist affect our appreciation for their work?

3. Simon's first lessons on reappropriation begin at an early age. When he confronts his bullies with an epithet, he says, "Confused, they stopped. And they walked away." Later, he suggests "Taking control of a term allows one to take

greater control for self-conception and limits the abilities of others to categorize them in a totalizing way." What are some examples of people reappropriating negative stereotypes, images, or words that you've seen? Why do people embrace these ideas? How does it change how others interact with them?

4. A reoccurring paint point for Simon is the government relying on articles from UrbanDictionary.com and the misleading report that The Slants' concert was cancelled over outrage for the name. Why would the government continue to use information that was reported as untrue? How do we avoid using inaccurate information or fallacies when dealing with disagreements?

5. When it comes to our actions or how we use language, do intentions matter or is it only about the impact? How could our legal system better address this gap?

6. A large portion of The Slants' audience seemed to consist of non-Asian Americans who interacted with Asian culture through anime conventions. What are some examples in the book of fans crossing the line between appreciation and cultural appropriation or fetishization? How can people develop a sincere curiosity of other cultures without exploiting them? Does it matter? Why or why not?

7. For many years of the story, Simon is haunted with Perla's death. How does grief change him? How has it change you or your loved ones? What does her death take from him and what does it give him?

8. Both the Federal Circuit and the Supreme Court are fascinated with comparing trademarks and copyrights. In what ways are they similar? How are they different? Do you believe that trademarks can be expressive, and if so, should they be protected like other forms of speech?

9. One of the largest concerns for groups opposing Simon's case is that eliminating the law would empower hateful content to be registered trademarks. If people can still use "scandalous, immoral, or disparaging" trademarks without a registration, why does it matter? Could the law be written in a way that respects applicants with good intentions but still prevent hate speech from being registered? What can affected community groups do to reduce hateful ideas other than cancelling a trademark registration?

10. Throughout the last few years of Simon's case, The Slants is often compared to the Washington football team. In what ways do you believe they are similar? In what ways are they different? Does having the First Amendment require us to protect speech that we have odious and

offensive?

11. At the Supreme Court, Simon encouraged community groups who disagreed with him to file or sign onto amicus briefs that opposed him. Why was this important for him to do this? Do you agree or disagree with this idea? How do you think this affected the outcome of his case? How did it affect Simon as an activist?

12. Simon provides a deeply personal account about his legal journey that spanned nearly eight years. Have do you think litigants of high profile cases are changed by the process and attention? How does learning about his experience affect your view of others who might be going through a legal process themselves? Who are our laws and legal processes developed for? What can legal experts do to better accommodate those affected by our legal system?

13. After winning his case at the Supreme Court, Simon spends quite a bit of time grappling with responses by those affected by the case. Some have argued that he didn't need to because it was up to the court. What responsibility should those who are advocating have when it comes to unintended consequences of their actions?

14. Simon ends the book with three stories about assumptions: meeting with Jacqueline, paper towns, and meeting a white supremacist. What were some of your assumptions before reading this book? How have they changed? How can assumptions and expectations about large groups of people affect public policy? How can assumptions about policy and law affect people? What are some ways we can be held more accountable to our preconceived views?

For additional content and to see photos and videos from

Simon's journey, visit: www.slantedbook.com

ABOUT THE AUTHOR

Photo: Kristal Passy

Simon Tam is an author, musician and activist. He is best known as the founder and bassist of The Slants, the world's first and only all-Asian American dance rock band.

In 2018, he founded The Slants Foundation, an organization dedicated to providing scholarships and mentorship to artists combining activism and community engagement into their work.

simontam.org

@SimonTheTam

Printed in the USA
CPSIA information can be obtained
at www.ICGtesting.com
LVHW092026100923
757717LV00002B/3